Ivan the Terrible

IVAN
THE TERRIBLE

Francis Carr

David & Charles
Newton Abbot   London

Barnes & Noble Books
Totowa, New Jersey

British Library Cataloguing in Publication Data

Carr, Francis
 Ivan the Terrible
 1. Russia–History–Ivan IV, 1533–1584
 2. Ivan IV, *The Terrible, Czar of Russia,*
 b.1530
 947'.04'0924

 ISBN 0-7153-7958-5
 ISBN 0-389-20150-2 (United States)

Typeset by ABM Typographics Limited, Hull
and printed in Great Britain
by Redwood Burn Limited, Trowbridge and Esher
for David & Charles (Publishers) Limited
Brunel House Newton Abbot Devon

First published in the USA 1981 by
Barnes & Noble Books
81 Adams Drive
Totowa, New Jersey, 07512

Contents

Introduction

Russian and western historians have often pointed out that Russia has always been part of the European family. Paul Dukes, in his recent *History of Russia*, says 'there can be little doubt that a white race with a Slavonic language and folklore, and a considerable involvement in the Orthodox variation of the Christian world-view, must be considered fundamentally as an outpost of the west.' Russia is obviously part of Europe if skin colour and language are considered the chief criteria. Her religion is surely a secondary factor, since conversion to Christianity would not make the Chinese European. In the world of music, literature and art, Russia can certainly be considered as part of Europe. Taking into account her political hostility towards Europe, her rejection of European concepts of individual freedom and human rights, Russia can with equal validity be considered as an outpost of Asia. Poles, and others who have lived near Russia's borders, have no doubts as to which concept is the more apt.

Peter the Great is reputed to have said: 'Europe is necessary to us for a few decades—and then we can turn our backs on her.' Ivan the Terrible, and Joseph Stalin, who learnt much from him, made it quite clear where their sympathies lay.

I have not forgotten the terrible pre-war years. That is what all my symphonies, beginning with the Fourth, are about. The 'Leningrad' Symphony is not about Leningrad under siege; it is about the Leningrad that Stalin destroyed and Hitler merely finished off. The majority of my symphonies are tombstones. Too many of our people died and were buried in places unknown to anyone, not even their relatives. It is impossible to write a composition for each one of the victims—which is why I dedicate my music to them all.

Dmitri Shostakovich
Testimony

If progress is the end, for whom are we working? Who is this Moloch who, as the toilers approach him, instead of rewarding them, only recedes, and as a consolation to the exhausted, doomed multitudes, can give back only the mocking answer that after their death all will be beautiful on earth. Do you truly wish to condemn people alive today to the sad role of caryatids supporting a floor for others some day to dance on?

Alexander Herzen
From the Other Shore

1
Ivan's Inheritance:
The Eastern Slavs on an Endless Plain

The Russians spare their tyrants; they kill only those monarchs that lack barbarity. Alexander II was assassinated in spite of his liberal reforms; Nicholas II and his family were slaughtered when he no longer ruled. Ivan the Terrible, Peter the Great, Catherine II and Stalin, Russia's most tyrannical despots, died in their beds.

Here we see the basic weakness of the Russian people—their frightening passivity, their acceptance of their roles as members of a giant community, not as individuals with definite human rights. The border between Europe and Russia is not just a man-made line running north and south; it is also the line that divides those who believe in human rights and those who passively accept the constant danger of the labour camp and death in spite of innocence.

In 1967, Laurens van der Post, the South African anthropologist, wrote *A Portrait of All the Russias* after a journey into many parts of that country. This is how he begins the book:

> For years I had been troubled by the image Russia presented to us in the outside world. My trouble with the Russian image was precisely that I could not discover a Russian individual in it. No matter how much I read, or how closely I scrutinized my newspapers, the Russians remained a vast, uniform, undifferentiated and forbiddingly ideological mass. Worse, the characters I met in contemporary Russian literature seemed to insist on performing pre-determined official roles, wearing always the same fixed masks, like characters in an ancient Greek play . . . The Russians have an overwhelming instinct to conform, a tendency to be incapable of doing openly what others are not doing, or of challenging authority on a specific issue . . . What we value as expressions of individual taste can easily be suspect in the Soviet Union as forms of dangerous self-indulgence, bourgeois deviationism and lack of solidarity.[1]

The fathers and mothers of today's Russians, and their ancestors, are the men and women who lived and died under Stalin, Lenin, Peter and Ivan the Terrible, dictators who deprived them of security, while

9

insisting that their oppression was a necessary means of guarding their security.

While the political map of the western world after the fall of Rome, in 410 AD, underwent many changes during the next one thousand years, the economic map, showing the main trade routes, remained basically the same. The main commodities that were produced and transported across the continent and the middle east were corn, wine, iron, timber, amber, sugar, gold and wool. Throughout this long and turbulent period, the main export from the steppes of Russia was slaves. Our word for slave comes from the medieval Latin word *sclavus*, a Slav captive. The original meaning of the word 'Slav' may have been a man who worships.[2]

Slaves were Russia's most important commodity throughout the first four hundred years of its existence as an organised community, from the late ninth century, and also for the four hundred preceding years, when the Slavs had no administrative system. The early Russian princes themselves conducted this trade, exporting their subjects to Constantinople and the lucrative markets of Baghdad. Conflicting claims to ownership of these slaves led sometimes to war between the princes.

The Slavs first made their appearance in the fifth century, covering a broad sweep of land between the Baltic and the Black Sea. This is also the land of the Vandals and the Goths, who crushed the Roman Empire and set up their brief kingdoms in Spain, north Africa and Italy. In the fourth century, from barren Mongolia came the Huns, prevented from invading China by the Great Wall. They reached France but soon fell back to eastern Europe and the Russian plain. One simple device gave them superiority over their western enemies—the stirrup, an invention unknown in Europe. Their short-lived empire included many Goths and Iranians, forbears of the Slavs.[3] The next invaders from Asia were the Bulgars and the Avars from western Mongolia. The Avars harnessed the Slav women to their chariots and used the men as front line soldiers in their attacks against Byzantium. The Slavs were absorbed by these invaders; unlike the Vandals and the Goths, they made no concerted effort to move westwards away from the Huns. In the seventh century came the Turkish Khazars, sweeping over the southern Slavs, and in the ninth century, from the north came the Vikings. All these tempests brought varying degrees of havoc, slavery and the constant payment of tribute. The Russians have had a long schooling in the discipline of subjugation.

It was the Vikings who gave the Slavs their first ruling dynasty and who taught them the arts of war and trade. The year 862 is given as the date when the Viking chief Rurik first established himself as Prince in Novgorod. But two years *before* this, the Vikings were attacking the greatest city of the western world, Constantinople, ancient Byzantium, once an outpost, now the inheritor of the Roman Empire. On 18 June 860, 200 Viking ships sailed through the Bosphorus and attacked Byzantium, taking the defenders completely by surprise. We have a graphic account of this onslaught, given by the Patriarch Photius in a sermon to the frightened Greeks in his cathedral of St Sophia:

> What is this? What is this grievous and heavy blow, this anger? Why has this dreadful bolt fallen on us? A race has crept down from the north, as if it were attacking another Jerusalem. These people are fierce and have no mercy. Their voice is as the roaring sea. I see a fierce and savage tribe fearlessly pouring round the city, ravaging the suburbs, destroying everything, ruining everything, fields, houses, beasts of burden, women, children, old men, youths, thrusting their swords through everything, taking pity on nothing, sparing nothing. This city, which reigns over nearly the whole universe—what an uncaptained army, equipped in servile fashion, is sneering at thee as at a slave![4]

The Viking-led Russians would not have had such an easy time if the Emperor, Michael III, and his army had not been fighting on his eastern border in Asia Minor. On his return the Russians withdrew. This nightmare was not forgotten by the Greeks: five centuries later, in 1422 when Constantinople was again besieged, this time by the Turks, the sermon of Photius was once more read out in the cathedral.

Like the Huns, the Vikings came from a land that was too poor and barren to support them. The Huns hurtled through Asia and Europe on the backs of their small but rapid horses; the Vikings sailed and rowed their way round the coasts of the western world in small ships which could navigate the roughest seas. Both Huns and Vikings were driven by the love of conquest, of movement and of speed. From the early ninth century the Vikings spread to England, Normandy, Sicily and the Slav homesteads along the rivers from the Baltic down to Kiev. They even completed the circle by establishing themselves as a corps of bodyguards of the Byzantine Emperor.

The compilers of the first Russian chronicle, *The Chronicle of Past Years*, composed in the eleventh and twelfth centuries, give a remarkably candid account of the arrival of the Vikings as overlords. It was not just a simple matter of conquest. The early Viking freebooters had already ventured down to Novgorod, but had returned to their homeland:

> The people [the Slavs] then began to govern themselves. But it went badly. Clan rose against clan, and there was internal strife amongst them. Then they said to each other: 'Let us seek a prince, who can reign over us and judge what is right.' And they went over the sea to the Varangians [the Vikings], to the Rus, for so were these Varangians called. These particular Varangians were known as Rus, for some Varangians are called Swedes, and others Norsemen, Angles and Goths. They said to these Varangians: 'Our land is large and fertile, but there is no order in it. Come therefore and reign, and rule over us.'[5]

In 862, perhaps a little earlier, three Viking chiefs came south to rule, Rurik, Oskold and Dir, and the House of Rurik continued to rule for the next seven hundred years—until the death of Feodor, the second son of Ivan the Terrible. Rurik hesitated before accepting the Slavs' invitation 'because of the savage habits of the people'.[6] The Arab geographer, Ibn Rusteh, in the early tenth century, described a Viking-Russian settlement in the Novgorod area around this time:

> Concerning the Rus, they live on an island (or peninsula) which lies in a lake. It is very unhealthy, and so marshy that the ground quivers when one treads on it. They fight with the Slavs and use ships to attack them; they take them captive and carry them to the Khazars and there sell them as slaves. They have no villages, no estates or fields. Their only occupation is trading in sable and squirrel and other kinds of skins. They have many towns.[7]

These towns were fortified trading centres, sited on the rivers.

The early Slavs extended westwards as far as the River Elbe. Hamburg, at the mouth of the Elbe, was built by the Saxons to prevent Slav expansion further westward. The eastern Slavs, those living in what is now western Russia, occupied the network of rivers which could carry the Viking ships down to Byzantium. The Vikings and Slavs strove to conquer this city, waging three more attacks, in 907, 941 and 944. Byzantium was too strong for the Russians to capture, but this ambition has survived to this day. It has never been renounced. By trade and efficient organisation, the Vikings gave the Slavs a basis for the prosperity of Kiev and Novgorod. And by the trade links with Byzantium, forged at the point of the sword, the Slavs gained their first benefits from the more advanced western world. They sold themselves as slaves, and also grain, timber, beeswax (for candles), leather and furs. In return they received weapons and salt, that most important preservative of meat.

In 324 AD, the Roman Emperor Constantine chose Byzantium as his new capital, renaming it Constantinople. It was better sited for the defence of the empire against the Persians, but there was another reason for the move, which was to have long-lasting and tragic consequences. Constantine wished to create a Christian centre for his empire, a city which was untarnished by Rome's persistent paganism. This grand, Utopian scheme hastened Rome's destruction. The imperial city and two-thirds of the vast Roman Empire, including England, Gaul, Spain, north Africa and the whole of Italy fell to the barbarians only ninety years later. To quote Professor F. W. Walbank, in his study of the decline of the Roman Empire in the West, *The Awful Revolution*, 'It was a rump of the original which survived within the eastern provinces, and a rump it remained. The survival of the eastern Empire really represents the saving of one part at the expense of the other; indeed the very strength of Constantinople diverted barbarian attacks to the west.' Moving the capital of a small country is a painful, costly operation; shifting the capital of a vast imperial power nearly a thousand miles to the east is like a heart transplant, an operation which involves the death of the donor—and an uncertain future for the recipient. In the war between Christianity and the older gods of Rome, both sides suffered. Europe had to wait for a thousand years to recover its pride and prosperity when the Italian Renaissance reforged its links with ancient Rome. And at the same time Constantine's holy city fell to the more powerful forces of the new religion of Islam. One can easily imagine some of the possible consequences of a decision of Henry II of England to move his capital from London to Bordeaux in Aquitaine, to defend his possessions against the French, and to dissociate himself from the pagan elements in the English character.

There were, of course, other reasons for the fall of Rome. It was certainly not ruined by sexual immorality; this myth can be believed only by the ignorant. The disastrous plague in the middle of the third century, the smallness of the army (650,000 in a total population of 70 million at the time of Constantine), the Hunnish and Gothic invasions, reliance on slave labour, and the confusion in the minds of the Romans themselves, caused by the conflicting beliefs in Christianity and the old Gods—all these contributed to Rome's collapse. As late as the reign of Theodosius (379–95), the Senate maintained their faith in the old religion. According to Zosimus, the members

> could not be induced to subscribe to blasphemy against the Gods. No one
> was converted by the Emperor's speech, exhorting them to abandon what

13

he called their errors. No one was willing to leave the traditions which had been handed down since the foundation of Rome. They said that by upholding the traditional religion, they had kept Rome safe from conquest for twelve hundred years. If they changed the old beliefs for the new ones, they could not tell what would happen . . . All the ancient customs of Rome fell into disregard. And so the Roman Empire was mutilated and became the home of the barbarians.[8]

The Vandals had been converted to Christianity, and Alaric the Goth had been made a Roman general. He also had been converted to the new faith. But the Vandals and the Goths saw no reason why they should not sack Rome, Alaric ravaging Greece and finally Rome in 410, and the Vandals sacking it again in 455.

For Ivan the Terrible and all Russian rulers, the fall of Rome and the fall of Byzantium, a thousand years later, were object lessons of the greatest importance. Here was supreme power attacked and finally smashed by its enemies. How did it happen? How could it have been prevented? How could Moscow be made even more powerful than Rome and Byzantium? How could Moscow make all potential enemies powerless to defeat, even to attack, her?

It was not only Rome and the western empire which suffered from Constantine's move to the east. The transfer of power from Italy to Greece, from Romans to Greeks and Asiatics, from Roman to Greek Christianity was a move from the world of change to the world of immobility. Rome's decline was not so catastrophic that she could not be reborn. After five centuries the Greek Church was superseded as a cultural force by Roman Catholicism. But long before that happened, it was backward, primitive Russia's misfortune to be stamped and moulded by the religion and political ideas of Byzantium, the less creative, more despotic branch of the old empire. Nearly all the authors of the empire wrote their works in Latin; after Constantine, the fountain of secular poetry and drama dried up.

In Russia, Latin remained an unknown tongue. This ignorance was indeed encouraged by the state, as it was the language of heresy, the most dangerous sin. For centuries Russia remained in ignorance of the great gifts of Roman civilisation, of Roman law and administration. Culturally far behind the rest of Europe at the time of the Renaissance, Byzantine Russia fell still further behind when this new age began. Everything Roman, pre-Christian and secular in art and literature was held to be subversive, coming from an alien and contaminated source. Not until the end of the seventeenth century could Latin be taught in

Moscow. Russia's first university, in Moscow, was not built until 1755, more than five centuries after the University of Oxford received its first charter in 1214. (University College was probably founded by King Alfred in the ninth century.) Greek literature too was completely unknown in early Russia, as it was pre-Christian, secular and sexually uninhibited. To the simple-minded priests of Kievan Russia, much of Greek literature and art would have struck them as works of the devil.[9] Russian literature did not begin to flourish until the nineteenth century, five hundred years after Dante, Petrarch, Boccaccio and Chaucer.

The two main elements in the first centuries of Russia's emergence from isolation and obscurity are cruelty and Christianity, and in both the Russians indulged passionately. Rurik's successor, his kinsman Oleg, overcame his chief rivals who were the leaders of the first attack on Constantinople, by inviting them onto his ship, which had brought him down from Novgorod, and murdering them. He followed his victims' example by mounting another destructive raid on Constantinople in 907 to improve trade relations, using, the Chronicle tells us, two thousand boats. This number may be an exaggeration.

The next attack on Russia's most beneficial neighbour came only three decades later, when Oleg's successor, Igor, attacked the northern provinces of the Byzantine Empire, Thrace and Bithynia. Various forms of extreme cruelty were perpetrated, including crucifixion, burying alive and driving nails into the head. The most powerful weapon in the Byzantine armoury was their gun which used the element known as Greek fire. This secret weapon repulsed the Russian attacks on the empire, but only after much pain and savagery. It certainly acted as a deterrent against more frequent incursions. Greek fire was a compound containing a distilled fraction of petroleum thickened with various plant or tree resins. The liquid shot from the Greek flame thrower could continue to burn for a long period. It could be aimed above an enemy craft and the flaming liquid would pour down upon the crew. The best description of this effective fire power comes from the *Alexiad* of Princess Anna Comnena, the daughter of the Emperor Alexius I, in her account of a successful engagement near Rhodes in 1103:

> The barbarians now became thoroughly alarmed . . . because of the fire directed upon them; for they were not accustomed to that kind of machine, nor to a fire which naturally flames upwards, but in this case was directed in whatever direction the sender desired, often downwards or laterally.[10]

The liquid would continue to burn when lying on the water.

Igor was killed by a Slav tribe which resented his demands for an extra tribute. His widow Olga succeeded him, as his son, Svyatoslav, was still a boy. The twin achievements of her reign are her conversion to Christianity and her savage reprisal attack on the rebellious tribe which killed her greedy husband. She certainly knew how to punish and command.

Fear of the Russians and their readiness to obey are two important features mentioned by their neighbours. Sharaf al-Zaman Tahir Marvazi, writing in Iran in the eleventh century, considered that one Russian soldier was equal in strength to a number of men in any other army; if they had horses 'they would be a great scourge to mankind.'[11] Ibn Fadlan, in the tenth century, commented on the bravery of the King of the Rus (the Prince of Kiev), and his followers: 'These are the men who die with him and let themselves be killed for him.'[12] Sudden attacks were mounted against settlements which were heavily outnumbered by the Russians. Ibn Hauqal gives an account of the destruction of the Khazar capital of Atil, at the mouth of the Volga, in 968. In and around the town there were forty thousand vineyards; after the onslaught not a grape remained. Such was the gorging of fruit and vegetables in the town by the invaders, that they gave themselves a severe form of dysentry. So many olives and cucumbers were consumed that many Russians died, and the army withdrew. As summed up by Hilda Ellis Davidson in her study of *The Viking Road to Byzantium*, the Russians 'descended like locusts on the fertile fields, orchards and gardens' of their southern neighbours.[13]

While holding the reins of power for her son, Olga tricked the Drevliane, the rebellious Slavs mentioned above, into a similar orgy of over-indulgence. She first lured one deputation into a stone chamber inside a burial mound, and then buried them alive. A second group of tribesmen arrived, still trusting Olga. Enjoying the comforts of a heated bath-house, they were all burned to death. Still not satisfied, Olga then told the tribe that she would come to them to mourn at her husband's grave in their territory, and invited them to a great funeral feast. Again they trusted her, became drunk and were easily butchered. Their town was then burnt, the terrible woman having sent pigeons and sparrows with flaming torches tied to their bodies, which flew back to the wooden houses from where they had come. They had been requested by Olga as a tribute; in return she promised them peace and goodwill.

With equal passion Olga embraced the new religion of Byzantium. She journeyed to the great capital and was given a lavish and hos-

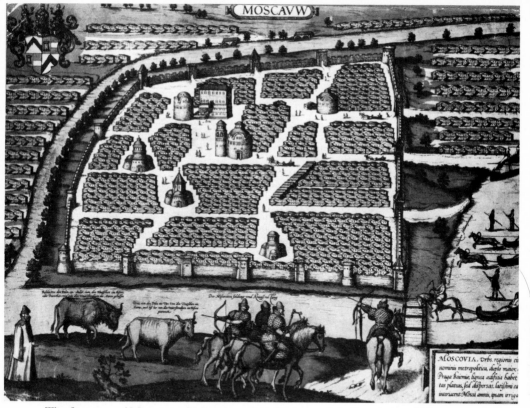

The first map of Moscow, which appeared in Herbertstein's *Description of Muscovy* in 1556 (*Novosti Press Agency*)

Dinner for the *Oprichniks* in the monastery of Alexandrovskaya from a contemporary drawing (*Novosti Press Agency*)

Russian baths from a lithograph by D. Dermatie in 1780 (*Novosti Press Agency*)

Troitsko-Sergiyevskaya Monastery in Zagorsk, Moscow Region, from a nineteenth-century painting (*Novosti Press Agency*)

pitable reception by the Emperor Constantine VII in 957. He saw Olga as the representative of a large and increasingly powerful neighbour, whose adoption of Christianity could bring about friendly and peaceful co-existence, if not dependence. Olga saw Christianity as a most effective buttress to the state. Greek Orthodoxy had long ago made its peace with the state, a subservient peace which Jesus himself would have passionately condemned. In the west the conflict between Church and state was promoting, and would continue to promote, the growth of liberalism and the rights of the individual. In the Byzantine Empire the Church and state were locked in a static alliance, which effectively prevented the growth of political and spiritual freedom.

Olga built the first Christian church in Kiev, Saint Sophia. It was pulled down in 1017, but by that time her grandson, Vladimir I, in 988, had also become a Christian and had taken vigorous steps to graft the Christian system firmly onto the young Russian state. There were obvious immediate benefits in giving his subjects a direct cultural link with the most civilised city in Europe. Foreign influence soon made its mark. Greek architects in 1037 began a large cathedral of Saint Sophia, built in imitation of the great cathedral of Saint Sophia in Constantinople. Eight years later another cathedral, also named after Saint Sophia, was begun in Novgorod. These magnificent buildings are the finest examples of the culture of Kievan Russia. They are rich in beautiful mosaics, murals and icons. As in other Russian churches, there are no statues, the making of which was seen as a continuation of pagan practice. This tabu placed on sculpture was reinforced by the Russians' deference to a decision taken by the Church in Constantinople after a fierce debate, that, while graven images were blasphemous, two-dimensional representation was not. Such was the level of theological discussion in the Christian Church at this time.

The cathedral in Novgorod was embellished with impressive bronze gates, designed by Ruffin of Magdeburg, and the doors were painted by artists from Sweden. Only the wooden churches in Russia owe nothing to the Byzantine model, having evolved from peasants' huts. In fact, with this exception, all architecture in Russia is based on Byzantine or western models.[14] But the absence of sculpture, and the Church's condemnation of it, inflicted a serious stultifying blockage in the developing Russian character. The Russians were not free to cultivate this art form until the eighteenth century, three hundred years after the Italian Renaissance. A similar break was placed upon the development of early Russian Church music by its insistence on unison for all choirs. Departure from the authorised melodic line was unthinkable; singing in harmony did not begin until the second half of the fifteenth century.[9]

But Russia was now part of the European community. The priests, the only literate men available, were Vladimir's civil servants and legal advisers. They advised him that death was not the Christian, Byzantine punishment for robbery, arson and horse-stealing. Slavery from now on was recommended. In Kiev, as in Constantinople, the Church was the state. With what was already typical Russian impulsiveness, Vladimir insisted on the instant conversion of all his subjects. In some areas, especially in the north around Novgorod preachers of the new faith were only listened to after the soldiers had moved in with fire and the sword. Around Kiev they were more docile, though many fled into the woods, and there were martyrdoms—how many was not recorded. Vladimir himself had a harem of eight hundred women; in the opinion of a visiting German chronicler, he was a *fornicator immensus et crudelis* —cruel and immeasurable in his excesses.[15]

His vast harem did not discourage him in procuring a wife from Byzantium, the sister of the Emperor Constantine VIII. He succeeded in this arrogant demand only after he had seized the Greek town of Chersun (now Sevastopol) in the Crimea. If the order was not complied with, Constantine was told, 'it will be the same with your town as with Chersun'. Vladimir knew that it was the custom in Byzantium for the bridegroom to present the bride's family with a gift of great value. Princess Anna, who was most reluctant to leave her home, finally arrived in Chersun and was married to Vladimir; whereupon Chersun was handed back to Constantine. While these negotiations were going on, the newly baptised suitor raped the daughter of the governor of Chersun, and then married her to a Viking Quisling, Sigbiorn, who had betrayed the town by shooting a message from inside the walls advising Vladimir of the best way to cut off the town's supplies from merchant ships.[16]

Vladimir's choice of the new Church language had disastrous results for his subjects. He allowed two Greek brothers, Cyril and Methodius, known as the 'apostles of the Slavs', to write and preach in a Bulgarian dialect, not used by the Slavs of Kiev and Novgorod. This 'Church Slavonic' tongue made them feel remote and subordinate, and entirely dependent on the Greek and newly converted Russian priesthood. They still had no knowledge of the Greek language itself, which would have given them a direct link with the literature of the ancient world.[17] The enormous importance of language, as a help or a hindrance to every form of progress, and the consequences of adopting a language of limited usefulness, have been neatly indicated by G. P. Fedotov in his study of Kievan Christianity:

> Russian cultural aspirations found a drawback in their Slavonic language, narrowly limiting the circle of available translated literature. This fact explains a tragic lack in ancient Russian culture, a complete absence of rational scientific thought, even in the theological field.[18]

One feature of life in Constantinople, which has not been often mentioned, was the attitude to death and destruction. This left a lasting imprint on Russian minds. Even in times of their greatest prosperity, rumours were passed around of the citizens' approaching doom. In the centre of the capital the holy cross at Milion was surrounded by an iron chain. Under the cross, it was believed, was buried a key which would unlock this chain. As long as no one took this key, the city would be impregnable. Some strange inscriptions in foreign languages on certain monuments were rumoured to foretell the sack of Constantinople by the Russians. In the tenth century a visiting Arab, Harun ben Yahya, described a long procession from the Emperor's palace to the cathedral of Saint Sophia. The buildings were hung with silk; the members of the Court were arrayed in robes of red, white and green silk; and finally the Emperor himself, wearing his crown and magnificent attire, appeared holding a golden box. It contained just a handful of earth. Behind him walked his chief minister, admonishing him frequently to 'Think upon death'. At each injunction, the Emperor would open the box and kiss the earth. While doing this, he wept.[19]

The Greeks today fear the God of Death—it is one of the strands which unites them as a nation and with their ancient Christian past and their even older pagan heritage. The old pagan gods, the gods of Homer and Sophocles live on, and they have always feared their gods, lovingly and respectfully. They passed on this fear to their Slav neighbours. The Russians have always regarded their rulers with fear, as they are the agents of death. The Russians absorbed this fatalistic attitude to life, the belief that we are weak, passive creatures, always at the mercy of implacable gods, or God, and that the monarch is the divinely appointed god on earth, an implacable judge and executioner. No Russian believed this more passionately than Ivan the Terrible:

> Russian political thought in the Middle Ages had been influenced by a treatise written in the sixth century by the Byzantine deacon Agapetus.

The Russians showed a special fondness for the following passage of this treatise: 'In the substance of his body, the Emperor is like any man, but in the power of his office he is like God, the Master of all men; for there is on earth no higher than he.'[20]

When the Russians were converted to Christianity, they learnt of the virtues of love, hope and forgiveness. But they could not find much comfort in the Church's attitude to slavery. They learnt that slaves are mentioned in both the Old and the New Testament. In the third book of Moses, called Leviticus (ch 25, vs 44–6), God himself tells Moses that 'thy bondmen and thy bondmaids shall be of the heathen that are round about you; of them shall ye buy bondmen and bondmaids. Moreover of the children of the strangers that do sojourn among you, of them shall ye buy, and of their families that are with you, which they begat in your land; and they shall be your possession. And ye shall take them as an inheritance for your children after you, to inherit them for a possession. They shall be your bondmen for ever.' And in the New Testament Saint Paul, in his Letter to the Colossians, instructs servants to 'obey in all things your masters, not with eye-service, as men-pleasers, but in singleness of heart, fearing God.' The original Greek word used is *doulos*, slave, which has been wrongly translated in English editions as 'servant'.

It is in this same chapter of Saint Paul's commandments (v 12) that Christians are told to 'put on bowels of mercies, kindness, humbleness of mind, meekness, long-suffering.' The Princes of Kievan and later of Muscovite Russia derived great benefit by their subjects' cultivation of these qualities.

Vladimir's father, Svyatoslav, as Grand Prince of Kiev, gave the Russians great prestige as conquerors by his distant campaigns against the Bulgarians and the Greeks. At one time he even made plans to move his capital to the banks of the Danube. Having overcome Bulgarian resistance (in 970) with an army of 60,000 men, he then invaded the Byzantine province of Thrace and captured Philippopolis, only 200 miles west of Constantinople. In this town he massacred 20,000 of the inhabitants.[21] The effect throughout the Empire and the Balkans of this catastrophe can easily be imagined.

Vladimir himself celebrated his assumption of power as Grand Prince of Kiev in 980 by killing nearly a thousand of his subjects as a sacrifice to the old Slav gods—Svarog, the supreme God, the god of cattle, the wind god, and the god of thunder. Nine years later Vladimir was baptised and became a member of the Greek Orthodox Church. The main consequences of his membership of this particular form of worship have been mentioned. There was yet another factor which made its mark. When Vladimir turned to Byzantium for guidance, its Church had already passed its peak as a creative force. Its former strength and enthusiasm had been seriously weakened by academic arguments over details of ritual and also in a debasing struggle of prestige with the growing secular power of Rome. In 1054 this struggle was to bring about a final break with the Papacy, which increased Byzantium's isolation. Increasing Roman influence in the Balkans was affecting the Patriarch in Constantinople; he allied himself and his Church to the Emperor in a subservient position, in a combined effort to assert their supremacy. Also, in the speed with which Vladimir converted his subjects, the finer aspects of Byzantine doctrine, those relating to the status of the individual, were overlooked. What was absorbed by the Russians were the three ideals of uniformity, immobility and inflexibility.

The early chroniclers have left an account of the reasons given by Vladimir for his choice of Christianity. It may not be factually true, but it is symbolically instructive. Missionaries of various kinds came to Kiev, we are told, to impress the Grand Prince. First came Muslims from the Volga Bulgars. All went well until he was told that the followers of Muhammed do not drink wine. 'Drinking', said Vladimir, 'is the joy of Russians; we cannot exist without it.' The Bulgars left and Catholics arrived; their beliefs were unacceptable, for reasons not made clear. Then came Jews from the Khazars, Russia's southern neighbours. Vladimir asked them why they had no homeland. The reason for this, according to the Christian monks who wrote the first chronicles, was that they were scattered 'because of their sins'. The Slav prince, making his message to his own subjects quite clear, asked the Jews: 'Do you want us to share the same fate?' The debate was ended by the envoy from Byzantium, who delivered a speech of some five thousand words. As a final test of the various faiths of his more powerful neighbours, Vladimir sent observers abroad to report on the services in the Roman, Greek, Jewish and Muslim churches. What made the envoys recommend the Greek faith was the beauty of its ritual. From now on in Russia, emphasis was laid on the form rather than the spirit of the doctrine.

Two important arts were brought to Kievan Russia from Byzantium, the icon and church music. From now on the icon, the Greek word for image, plays a central role in moulding the Russian mind. The princes and the priests used icons as instant propaganda, the ideal medium for a large population mostly illiterate until the twentieth century. Not only was the subject portrayed divine—God, Jesus, Mary and the saints —the image also was divine, an object that was holy and had magic powers in times of danger. It also gave the prince greater prestige as God's representative on earth. When God was declared officially dead in 1917, the need for icons still remained. The plethora of images of Lenin, and his successors while they are alive, shows that the State still finds this form of mass production effective and necessary. The constant pilgrimage to Lenin's tomb, the amazing patience shown by the long queues of silent Slavs waiting for an opportunity to see the Leader with their own eyes, this devotion can only be explained in terms of religious faith. If there is no God in heaven, then surely Lenin can be presented and accepted as God on earth.

Music was Byzantium's second gift. Once heard, a Russian church choir is never forgotten. Here indeed is a form of beauty and truth, one that leaves words behind. The Russian language by itself is musical; when sung it takes on an element of instant elation, even when the music is sad. And it is one of the great virtues of the music of the Greek Orthodox Church that it gives its congregations instant consolation and warmth. Loneliness and isolation are forgotten; a sense of comradeship and hope is restored. After many centuries this love of music gave rise to that great outburst of inspired composition in the nineteenth century, the age of Borodin, Mussorgsky, Rimsky-Korsakov, and Tchaikovsky.[22] Every nation gains from a sense of individuality, of uniqueness, of some quality that can be regarded as a proof of that uniqueness. What Turgenev said about the Russian language can be said with equal validity of Russia's music: 'In the days of doubts, in the days of oppressive reflections, concerning the destinies of my native land, you alone are my stay and my staff, my great, mighty, true and free Russian language. It is past all belief that such a tongue has been given to any but a great people.'

This belief in greatness, in racial superiority, was given its first official blessing by the Greek Orthodox Church. All three monotheistic religions, Judaism, Christianity and Islam, present a picture of historical progress which places the countries of their adherents in a central and superior position, as followers of the only true, orthodox faith. In other countries, this conviction has been weakened by the distractions of material progress, the growth of agnosticism, which is sceptical about such concepts as destiny, and by close contact with their neighbours who often proved superior in one form or another, in spite of their different religion. In Russia, isolation, lack of physical comforts, and the apparent meaninglessness of internal and external wars, all contributed to Russia's willingness to believe implicitly in the Greek Orthodox message, preached by the Kievan monks, that Russia was chosen by God to teach the world how to live. The Jews, the first chosen race, had been driven from their homeland because of their sins, it was maintained; Rome had fallen because of her sins; Byzantium was now the holy city, which was passing on God's message to the new and growing territories of the eastern Slavs. If Byzantium should fall— her lands were, unlike Russia's, diminishing—Kiev, Novgorod, Vladimir and the other Russian towns would then become God's chief messengers of His gospel.

Even before Olga's and Vladimir's conversion to Christianity, even before the arrival of the Vikings, the Slavs were showing a national characteristic which separates them from all other peoples in Europe. In all the countries of western Europe agriculture provided the basis of their economy, with the feudal manor as its focal point. In Kievan Russia, a barter, or money economy prevailed, with the fortified trading post as its centre. These trading centres attracted the majority of the population, for security and for trade. The importance of the trading centres, or towns as they became, was to dwindle during the next few centuries. Not until the late nineteenth century was such a large proportion of the total population concentrated in the towns. There was a pronounced contrast between the loneliness of existence as hunters, trappers and farmers in a flat and empty land, and the companionship of others in a primitive but friendly community in the fortified trading centre. Both forms of life had their perils and discomforts; given a choice, it was natural that so many chose to be townsmen with restricted horizons and freedoms, rather than individuals with too much insecurity. Those town communities organised their own councils and assemblies, as one would expect. The *veche*, the popular assembly, was run by a council, or *soviet*, which in some towns could demand the redress of grievances, and the prince was pledged to preserve this institution and carry out its demands. The *veche* was an assembly which any male citizen could attend; its powers varied at different periods. In times of crisis, the assembly could choose a new ruling prince and decide whether or not to declare war. The *soviets* of Novgorod and Pskov were the most developed and independent.

When Vladimir died, Kiev witnessed scenes of bloodshed and confusion that would be repeated there, and later in Moscow and St Petersburg, when the throne was fought for by determined men. Just before his death, the ruthless Vladimir was planning an offensive against Novgorod, which one of his sons was holding; his son had had the temerity to refuse his father's exorbitant demands for tribute. Bloodshed was avoided thanks to Vladimir's death, but in Kiev itself his eldest son, Svyatopolk, murdered two of his brothers whom he feared would usurp him. One of the brothers, Boris, was stabbed while on his knees at prayer; both he and the other brother, Gleb, were canonised by the Church which was appalled by this double crime. The situation rapidly deteriorated, as war broke out between Vladimir's sons. Svyatopolk fled from Kiev but returned with Polish troops; an army marched south from Novgorod and once more the Grand Prince was driven out. He was killed while appealing for help from Turkish tribes on his southern border.

Civil war broke out again after the twenty-five year reign of Yaroslav (1019–54), the first Russian ruler to formulate a detailed code of law, the *Russkaya Pravda* (or Russian Justice). It is an unfortunate shortcoming in the Russian language that 'justice' and 'truth' share the same word, *pravda*. What the state decrees as justice is therefore given the additional force of truth, or correctness. A similar double meaning is contained in the word *mir*. This means 'peace' and 'world'. Thus reasonable demands in speeches, articles and on banners for peace with Russia's neighbours are given a simultaneous overtone implying a desire for global supremacy. Yaroslav based his code on those of two Byzantine Emperors, Leo III and Basil I. No single date is given for it. Regrettably, it did little to lessen personal insecurity in Kievan Russia, as private acts of revenge could be considered legal, and the Church acknowledged itself to be equally responsible with the state for enforcing the laws. In one particular detail, the change from the death sentence for certain crimes in the Byzantine codes to imprisonment or slavery, the Russians could consider themselves fortunate.

The foundation of Kievan society, the ownership of slaves, continued unchanged by the new legal code and Vladimir's conversion to Christianity. Under Yaroslav any slave who struck a free man could be killed[23] and prison cells were added to the churches. Here the prisoners could be beaten. Those who did not accept the new Christian order could be classified as sorcerers, and as such could be exorcised. The Metropolitan Ivan (1080–9) decreed that these men and women could be 'violently punished—but not beaten to death'.[24]

We are all moulded by the land in which we live—and by the climate. History, in essence, is the story of that moulding, tracing the development of people in different surroundings. The anvil on which the Russians have been hammered has produced a people with traits that are perfectly understandable but also decidedly uncomfortable for the rest of the world. The eastern Slavs, the peasants, traders and princes of past and present Russia stand on an endless plain, stretching from Poland to eastern Siberia, with only one low range of mountains, the Urals, to break the monotonous landscape. With no natural barriers, their neighbours, at all levels, personal, village, provincial and foreign, are potential enemies—and potential victims. Their lives are dominated by extremes, by the long, freezing winter and the short but pleasant summer; by the boring inactivity indoors in winter, and the day-long work on the land to make the most of the inadequate summer; by the loneliness and silence of isolated farms and small villages in an under-populated expanse, and the inadequate housing in the large towns. The Russian peasant over the centuries has developed the ability to work and fight in the most uncomfortable conditions, enduring extreme cold and hunger. In World War I they could fight for four days without food, and for four days without sleep. They have learnt the dangers of physical and political individualism, of departing from the official line. Even the roads through the marshes and the forests have taught them the perils awaiting anyone who makes his own way. They are under-standably mistrustful of all strangers, and understandably quick to adopt a defensive-offensive attitude when strangers or foreigners show indifference. Their attitude is best summed up in the words of Jesus Christ: 'He who is not with me is against me' (St Matthew ch 12, v 30).

But in the early days of Russia, when the principal town was Kiev, life for the average peasant and citizen was not all hardship. The prince of each province provided some security, and there was an element of freedom and adventure that was to decline in subsequent centuries. The brightest hour of Kievan Russia was the reign of Vladimir Monomakh, who has been compared to England's King Alfred. He ruled for twelve years, from 1113 to 1125, and in that time he raised the prestige of all the principalities to their highest level. Peace had been imposed on Kiev's most dangerous enemy, the Polovtsy, on her southern border; there had been five major campaigns against them in the twenty years before Vladimir began his reign, and in each he had taken a leading part. In 1111 he inflicted such a crushing defeat that the Kievans were spared their destructive raids for the next twenty-five years.

In these early centuries of Russian history, the combination of Viking aggressiveness, Byzantine Christianity and Slav energy, obedience and communal town existence produced a state, or rather a loose confederation of states, which impressed all visitors. The urban population may have been about one million, in and around three hundred towns and trading posts. Of these towns Kiev, Novgorod and Smolensk were the largest. In the eleventh, twelfth and early thirteenth centuries, four Kings of Hungary, three Kings of Poland, three Kings of Denmark, two Kings of Norway and four German nobles married Russian princesses. Vladimir Monomakh's aunt, Anna, Yaroslav's daughter, was Queen of France, the wife of Henri I; by this marriage she is one of the ancestors of Elizabeth II, Queen of England. (Isabella, daughter of Philip IV of France (1285–1314) married Edward II of England (1307–27).) Monomakh's father, Vsevolod, married the daughter of the Greek Emperor, Constantine Monomachus; his sister married the German Emperor, Henry IV; and his son, Mstislav, married Christina, daughter of Inge, King of Sweden.

Vladimir himself married an English princess. This was Gyda, the daughter of King Harold II. After the Battle of Hastings, Harold's two sons and Gyda fled to Denmark. There they were sheltered and entertained by Sweyn II (1047–74), the nephew of Canute, and the king whose defeat by Duncan is mentioned in the first act of Shakespeare's *Macbeth*. Vladimir was then Prince of Novgorod. News of the English exiles soon reached him; he had probably heard of England from Danish and Norwegian traders as under Canute it had been part of the Scandinavian Empire. With little delay, he took this opportunity offered to him of being able to marry an English princess. Through the good offices of the King of Denmark this marriage was celebrated in 1067.

Gyda gave birth to a son, Mstislav, who ruled in Kiev for seven years. Around 1200, the Danish historian Saxo Grammaticus referred to the marriage of his parents, saying that 'the English blood on the one side and the Russian on the other side, concurring to the joyful birth of our prince, caused that mutual kindred to be an ornament unto both nations.' (As translated by Richard Hakluyt in his *Principal Navigations, Voyages, Traffics, and Discoveries of the English Nation*, 1589.)

The Anglo-Russian partnership of Monomakh and Gyda and the reign of their son, Mstislav, saw the last great period of Kievan Russia. Monomakh's sister, Ianka, founded the first school in Russia for girls— in most countries at this time an unheard-of institution. At this school in Kiev reading, writing, sewing and singing were taught. Sons of the princes and nobles went to Constantinople to complete their education. After Mstislav's death in 1132, Kiev's supremacy ended, and the princely families in the other provinces reduced the promising confederation to a collection of disorganised rival and sometimes warring tribes. Russia failed to solve the problem of succession; her continued failure has meant that she has been plunged into confusion and disarray time after time. The deaths of princes, Tsars and communist dictators have been followed by arrests, imprisonment, killing or civil war in every century.

One document of literary merit from Kievan Russia that has survived is a long letter written by Vladimir Monomakh, entitled *Instructions to My Children*. He gives us an insight into the many hazards that everyone, princes and peasants, had to face at that time. Monomakh was tougher and luckier than most of his subjects. And he was kind. If only more princes had been like him, Russian history might have been transformed:

Fear God by doing unstinted charity. Thou art great, O Lord, and thy works are wonderful. Human understanding cannot grasp all thy miracles. Who would not praise and glorify thy Power and thy great miracles and goodness that are evident in this world. My children, listen to me, and, if you cannot accept all, heed at least half! Fail not to kneel to the ground three times, if you cannot do it more often. Above all, forget not the destitute, but feed them according to your means. Give to the orphan and protect the widow, and allow not the strong to oppress the people. Give alms generously, for such liberality is the root of all good.

Honour the elders as your father, and the younger ones as your brother. Be not slack in your houses, and watch everything. Do not rely upon your squire, nor your servant. If you go to war, be not idle; depend not upon your generals, nor abandon yourself to drinking and eating and sleeping. Put out the guards yourselves, and lie down to sleep only after you have placed the guards all round the army; and rise early . . .

Whatever good you know, do not forget it; and what you do not know, learn it, just as my father had learnt, staying at home, five languages— for this makes one honoured in other lands. Indolence is the mother of all vices. I concluded nineteen peace treaties with the Polovtsians. I have undergone many hardships in the chase. Near Chernigov I have with my own hand caught ten or twenty wild horses in the forests. A stag once gored me; an elk stamped on me, while another gored me; and a bear bit my knee-cap. A wolf leapt at my thigh and threw me with my horse. Yet God has preserved me. I have often fallen from my horse; I twice injured my head, and frequently hurt my hands and feet in my youth. The protection of God is fairer than the protection of man.

Fear neither death, my children, nor war, nor beast, but do what men have to do, whatever God may ordain. Just as I have come out hale from war, from encounters with animals, from water, and from my falls, even so none of you can be injured or killed, if it be not so ordained by God. And if death come from the Lord, neither father, nor mother, nor brothers can save you.[25]

This letter was written shortly before Monomakh's death in 1125. In the early days of Kiev, in the tenth century, the ruling house of Rurik was small in number, and the seniority of each principality was easily assessed. But now there were more than eighty princes, and the different branches of the family had developed decided views on their own importance. All manifestations of culture and civility, however long-lived, are patently fragile; Russia had only just emerged from centuries of danger and tribal backwardness. The winter was not yet over.

2

Ivan's Inheritance:
The Mongol Hammer

Led by Vladimir, Yaroslav and Vladimir Monomakh, the early Russians laid the foundations of a country, a loose confederation of principalities with a recognisable degree of unity and prosperity. The difficulties in their way—the open terrain, the cold climate, and family hostility among the princes and their supporters—were kept at bay for two centuries. But before Monomakh became Grand Prince of Kiev, the confederation was torn by half a century of sporadic civil wars. After his eldest son's reign, these bloody conflicts began again and Kiev itself was sacked in 1169 by Andrei Bogoliubsky, Prince of Suzdal, Monomakh's grandson. The Russian capital had become the richest, nearest source of plunder, a magnet for vandalism and rape. Andrei's soldiers slaughtered men, women and children in large numbers. Everything of value in Kiev's palaces, churches and monasteries was smashed or carted off to Andrei's northern capital, Vladimir. Andrei was named after his estate and wooden palace of Bogoliubovo, Love of God.

The town of Vladimir was not far from the little settlement of Moscow, which was first mentioned in 1147. Other towns, such as Rostov and Suzdal, complained that Vladimir was a city 'built by our slaves and masons'. Andrei was a keen builder; his cathedrals of St Sophia and of the Assumption served as models for the Italian architect Fioraventi, when he came to Moscow to build another cathedral of the Assumption for Ivan III, Ivan the Terrible's grandfather, three hundred years later. Andrei welcomed settlers, especially builders, from the Bulgar tribes on the Volga and Slavs from Poland. But he infuriated the other Russian princes and town leaders, especially those of Novgorod and in southern Russia, by his assumption of dictatorial powers. In 1174, only five years after his ruthless destruction in Kiev, he himself was stabbed to death by a gang who supported his brothers. The palace of Vladimir and the town itself were sacked, and for the next two years the towns of Rostov, Suzdal and Vladimir were torn by civil war. Order was restored by Andrei's successor, Vsevolod III, who claimed that he was 'father and master' of all the other Russian princes. He insisted on punishment without trial, even in Novgorod, which had already developed the basic elements of an independent state. But after Vsevolod's death, disunity reasserted itself among the princes, whose armies enjoyed dismantling the fragile beginnings of Russian civilisation.

Their mutual destruction made resistance doubly futile when, from the Gobi Desert of Mongolia, came eastern Asia's last invasion of Europe—the terrible onslaught of the Tartars. For the next two hundred years Russia was but one small part of a vast Asiatic empire, stretching from China to Iran. The Tartars reached Poland, the Adriatic and the outskirts of Vienna. Europe was saved only by the death of the Great Khan Ogedei back in his capital of Karakorum, half the world away in Mongolia. His generals withdrew to the capital for the election of a new leader, but kept their western armies in the land of the eastern Slavs. The Mongol explosion in the first half of the thirteenth century had begun with the invasion of northern China and Samarkand by Ghengiz Khan; then Iran and the Crimea fell to the hordes led by Subotei and Jebei; Hulagu crushed Iran and Damascus; Kublai Khan swept through Korea, Hangchow and Canton; the Russians were killed, captured and raped by the Golden Horde of Batu, commander of the Mongols' western army.

The Iranian poet, Amir Khuzru, has given us a close-up view of Russia's new masters:

> Their eyes were so narrow and piercing that they might have bored a hole in a brazen vessel. Their stench was more horrible than their colour. Their heads were set on their bodies as if they had no necks, and their cheeks resembled leather bottles, full of wrinkles and knots. Their noses extended from cheekbone to cheekbone. Their nostrils resembled rotting graves, and from them the hair descended as far as the lips. Their chests were covered with lice, which looked like sesame growing in bad soil.[1]

These thick-set horsemen wore their clothes on their bodies till they fell off in rags. The smell was offensive but washing, they believed, would offend the all-important water spirits. Towns were rapidly surrounded and then subjected to a hellish blitzkrieg. A contemporary Russian account describes the Tartar bombardment of Kiev with painful detail:

> The Mongols were like dense clouds. The rattling of wagons, the bellowing of camels and cattle, the sound of trumpets, the neighing of horses and the

32

cries of a vast multitude made it impossible for people to hear one another inside the city. Many battering rams hammered the walls ceaselessly, day and night; the people were frightened and many were killed, the blood flowing like water. There was darkness because of the Tartar arrows, and there were dead everywhere. The arrows obscured the light, so that it became impossible to see the sky. The Tartars took the city of Kiev on the Day of Saint Nicholas, 6th December (1240) ... They approached the city of Vladimir from all sides and began to hit the city walls with rams and to pour great stones into the centre from far away, as if by God's will, so that it seemed like rain within the city. They took the city, which they set on fire. Death followed, by metal and flame. Then the Mongol columns swept on.[2]

Five years later a fearless envoy from the Vatican, Giovanni Pian de Carpini, travelled to the city of the Great Khan at Karakorum. One of the staging posts along the way was Kiev. Only two hundred houses, he reported, were left standing. The bleak plain around the battered city was still littered by the white bones and skulls of the slaughtered Russians. Those not killed were taken away as slaves and whores. Novgorod was the only large Russian town to escape destruction, saved by a thaw of its swamps and marshes, but it had to pay a heavy tribute. One of the contemporary descriptions of Mongol ferocity gives this frightening picture:

The prince, with his mother, wife, sons, the boyars and inhabitants, without regard to age or sex, were slaughtered with the savage cruelty of Mongol revenge. Some were impaled, or had nails or splinters of wood driven under their finger-nails. Priests were roasted alive, and nuns and maidens raped in the churches before their relatives. No eye remained open to weep for the dead.[3]

Living for two hundred years in this new world, the Russians could not survive without lasting signs of Mongolian influence. The Norman conquerors of England introduced an element of toughness and discipline into the Anglo-Saxon character; but their rule was temperate and a model of restraint, as compared with the ruthless Mongol way of life, with their indifference to the suffering of others and their casual attitude to death. Years of servile submission leave their mark; prostration before the absolute ruler becomes an accepted habit; rule by fear of the death penalty and hideous torture is seen to work, and its grim advantages become apparent: it quickly eliminates rivals and assists promotion. Conscription into the all-powerful army is accepted as a preferable alternative to enslavement; the army is seen as the obvious instrument for conquering the world, an intoxicating Mongolian,

Messianic dream, an effective compensation for a life of pain and danger. All large armies need large doses of drugs, preferably those which leave the body intact and fill the mind with dreams of conquest.

Other Mongolian influences include army tactics and organisation, government administration, especially in the control of tax collection and punishment. The position of women deteriorated under the Tartars; their role as second-class citizens was made even more servile by the Mongol custom of the harem and general separation of the sexes. The Tartars also left their mark in language and clothing. Kreml (Kremlin, fortress) and terem (the women's quarters in a house, now the garret) are both Mongol terms.

Russia was now a land of constant disaster. Murder and enslavement, carried out by Mongolian soldiers, men from neighbouring Russian provinces, or by gangs of wandering brigands, both Russian and Mongol, made life for every Russian hazardous in the extreme. What the Russians soon learnt was the Mongols' double standard. This consisted of the acceptance of a code of behaviour by which you argued that what was yours you preserved jealously, what was your neighbour's you took if it increased your security. This was the attitude of the princes of Vladimir and Moscow; this is the attitude of Russia today. All the principalities of old Russia were forced to surrender their independence to safeguard the state of Muscovy; the countries of eastern Europe have had to surrender to Russia, since their very existence as sovereign states is held to be a real threat to Russia's security.

The courageous ambassador from the Vatican, Giovanni Pian de Carpini, noticed this double standard of the Mongols, when he visited their vast realm and the capital of Karakorum in 1245:

> Although they possess no book of religious law which obliges them to do right and avoid doing wrong, they nevertheless have certain traditions that either they or their forefathers have devised, and, according to these traditions, certain actions are considered sinful. It is, for instance, a sin to poke one's dagger into the fire, or to touch the fire with it, or to take meat from the pot with it, or even to hack meat with a hatchet near the fire, for they think that this would take the force from the fire. It is sinful to lean upon the whip with which they beat their horses, to pour milk or other drinks on the ground, or to urinate inside a tent. Anybody who does so intentionally pays for it with his life.
>
> If he does so unintentionally, he has to pay a large sum of money to purify the people. Furthermore, if anybody is given a morsel of meat, and cannot swallow it, but has to spit it out again from his mouth, they dig a

St Basil's Cathedral, begun in 1555, on Red Square, Moscow, seen from the east. In the foreground is the *Lobnoye Myesto* where public executions took place. Taken from an engraving by A. Olearius which was published in the Netherlands in 1627 (*Novosti Press Agency*)

St Basil's Cathedral (*Novosti Press Agency*)

hole underneath the tent, drag the person in question through this opening, and then kill him without pardon. Anybody stepping on the threshold of the tent of a duke is equally punished with death. They have many similar customs, but it would be impossible to list them all.

On the other hand, killing people, invading other countries, seizing other people's property against all rules of law, whoring, committing wrongs against other people, all this is not considered sinful.

They are extremely arrogant toward other people, and look down on all others with disdain. In fact, they regard them, both noble and humble people alike, as little better than nothing. Toward other people the Tartars tend to anger and are easily roused. They are the greatest liars in the world in dealing with other people, and hardly a true word escapes from their mouths. Initially they flatter, but in the end they sting like scorpions. They are crafty and sly, and wherever possible they try to get the better of everybody else by false pretences. If they intend some mischief against others, they have an admirable ability to keep their intentions secret, so that others cannot take any precautions or countermeasures against their clever plans.

Drunkenness is honourable among them; when anyone has drunk too much, he will be sick on the spot, but even so will carry on drinking again. If they want something, they will not stop asking for it, until they have got it. They cling fiercely to what they have, and in making gifts they are extremely miserly.

They have no conscience about killing other people.

Good characteristics of the Tartars: in the whole world there are to be found no more obedient subjects than the Tartars, neither among lay people nor among the monks; they pay their lords more respect than any other people, and would hardly dare lie to them. They are accustomed to deprivation. If therefore they have fasted for a day or two, and have not eaten anything at all, they do not easily lose their tempers. When riding they can endure extreme cold and at times also fierce heat.

The men do nothing but occupy themselves with their arrows, and to a small extent look after their herds; for the rest they go hunting and practice archery. They are all, men and boys, good shots. They are very agile and courageous. All work rests on the shoulders of the women; they make fur coats, clothes, shoes, boots and everything else made from leather. They also drive the carts and mend them, load the camels, and are very quick and efficient in their work. All women wear trousers.

All property is in the hands of the Great Khan, so that nobody dares to say: 'This belongs to me.' Everything, household chattels, cattle and people, is the property of the Khan. The Khans and the dukes take from the property of the subjects whatever and however much they like, and also have unlimited rights to dispose of their persons as they wish.

Chingiz Khan promulgated orders to which the Tartars strictly adhere. Only two shall be mentioned here. The first order says: Anybody who on his own authority aspires to Imperial dignity, shall be executed without grace or pardon. The other order says they must subjugate the whole world, and must not live in peace with any people who has not first surrendered to them. According to some prophecy made to them, they are to be conquered by another nation; but they do not know which nation that will be. Those who are able to escape will, so they say, have to observe that law which their future conquerors will also observe. That means that both the victors and the defeated will have to observe the commandments of Chingiz Khan.[4]

For two hundred and fifty years the Russians and the Mongolians interbred, as unnumbered thousands of Russians became slaves and soldiers in the Mongol army. Russian conscripts played an important part in the campaigns of the Mongols, and a Russian division was stationed in Peking. Craftsmen and other labourers were despatched in droves to Mongolia. The Russian and Mongolian upper class inter-married; when Mongol power declined in the fifteenth and sixteenth centuries, a large number of the richer Mongols worked with the Russian nobility, and at least 130 families became Christian and served the Russian state. Among them were the Godunovs, Turgenevs, Glinskys, Naryshkins and Yusupovs, all names which would one day become famous. (Natalia Naryshkina was the mother of Peter the Great.)

The Russian princes were allowed to remain in their provinces, but only if they acted as the agents and tax-collectors of the Golden Horde. The only cultural link with Europe was the Greek Orthodox Church; this also was permitted to exist by the new overlords. It was indeed promoted by them, as the priests were given total exemption from tax. If the Church had encouraged the slightest resistance to the Mongols, it would have been crushed without pity. Thus, the Christian religion, while giving comfort and consolation and hope for a better life after death, was clearly seen by the Russians as the inseparable ally of the state—not only at the provincial Russian level, but also at the highest, Asiatic level, with Russia forming just one part of the vast Mongol empire. The early Church was undoubtedly a civilising force in a world of coarseness and cruelty; but its influence was limited by the language of its ritual, which few understood, by the rich, theatrical robes of the clergy, which contrasted strongly with the dress of the faithful, and by the clearly stated message that eternal damnation could be the fate in store for all those who sinned.

Total submission was the only means of survival. The Church sub-mitted to the prince; the prince obeyed the Khan of the Golden Horde; the Khan prostrated himself before the Great Khan of all the Mongols. It is not surprising that the Russians admired their masters. The system worked. The Mongols numbered about one million; with an army of less than 150,000, they were the masters of around 100 million people. Their victories, their superior military and government administration, their impressive postal service, their obedience—all these contributed to an attitude of respect, although it was extremely painful for countless men and women. The richer Russians learnt Turkish, the Mongols' language; in the fifteenth century the court of the Princes of Moscow was still speaking Turkish. Byzantium had already preached the gospel of the monolithic state; now the Golden Horde was demonstrating how the state could be made yet more powerful and implacable. Slavery was an old terror for the Russians; the Mongols merely brought a far greater proportion of the population down to that level.

An essential element of Mongol rule by fear and terror was torture. The Russians were subjected to frequent flogging and mutilation. Noses, ears, hands and legs were hacked off; melted lead was poured down the throat. Men and women were impaled, racked and whipped to death. Being burnt alive was a common punishment for dissidents denounced by the Church or the Mongols as heretics or magicians—a fate shared by countless victims of the Christian Church in western Europe. Death was made not only as painful as possible; it was made even more hideous by turning it into a public spectacle.

Giovanni Pian de Carpini, the envoy from the Vatican, remarked on two aspects of life in the Mongol empire which sum up concisely the position of the individual. The basic right to choose where you want to live did not exist; and, even in war, you were not allowed, if you were a soldier, to preserve your life by fleeing or being taken prisoner. Life under all Russian dictators has followed this pattern.

The Great Khan of the Tartars has extraordinary power over all his subjects. Nobody dares to settle in any part of his empire without his express direction. In fact he determines the places of residence for the dukes, the dukes in their turn those of the commanders of a thousand, they in turn those of the commanders of a hundred, and the last those of the commanders of ten. If at any time or place he gives them an order, be it for war or for peace, be it for life or for death, they obey without question. Even when he demands somebody's daughter or sister for a wife, she is given to him instantly without argument. Actually, every year, or every few years, he orders maidens to be assembled, so that he may choose and keep those he likes; the others he gives to those around him as he sees fit . . .

In the event of war, those who flee are all punished by death. If soldiers are taken prisoner, then unless their comrades free them, they equally must pay with their lives.[5]

In spite of the appalling difficulties confronting them, two Russian princes achieved victories which gave the Russians a reassuring measure of self-respect and patriotism, Alexander Nevski and Dmitri Donskoi. Their success served as an invigorating reminder of Russia's former independence, and as proof that tyrannies, however powerful, can be overthrown.

No one in the thirteenth or fourteenth century could have been certain what would happen to the Russians. They might have disappeared as a nation like the Naimans or the Merkits of western Mongolia, defeated and absorbed by the armies of Ghengiz Khan; or they could have joined the western Slavs, the Poles, and become Catholics. No one knew how long the Mongols would remain strong and united. No one knew if the most attractive virtue of the Mongols, their tolerance of other religions, would weaken the Russians' devotion to the Christian faith, or if the Russians would adopt the faith that the Mongols adopted in the fourteenth century, that of Islam. What then kept the Russians together? What kept their sense of nationality alive?

Christians would like to think that it was the Christian religion. But other nations, such as the Goths, the Vandals and the Lithuanians, became Christian and this did not save the first two from disappearing as nations from the map, and the Lithuanians from becoming a small state on the edge of the Baltic, finally disappearing as a tiny province in the vast Soviet empire. The answer must surely lie in the way in which the Russians reacted to oppression. Other peoples, subjected to the miseries that the Russians had to undergo in the reigns of Ivan the Terrible, Peter the Great, Catherine and Stalin, or during the Mongol period, would have fought back or fled. Many Russians did fight back, many fled, but not in sufficient numbers to bring about the destruction of their oppressors. To soften their existence, many Russians joined and worked for their oppressor. And this is the pattern today. The easiest way to secure some comforts in a police state is to join the ranks of the vast police force. But the majority of Russians over the centuries have been conditioned *not* to react, simply to suffer passively.

In his *Letter to the Soviet Leaders*, Alexander Solzhenitsyn outlines some of 'the incomparable sufferings of our people'. And it is this great capacity for suffering without breaking, without the reactions of revolt or change of character, that the Russian Church fostered and encouraged. No nation has been more influenced by the story of Christ's passivity and passion. In the nineteenth and twentieth centuries, Russians who were sickened by their own history, became atheists because, in the words of N. A. Berdyaev, they could not 'accept a Creator who makes a cruel world full of suffering. They want to form a better world themselves.'

Compounding the miseries of this suffering, perhaps a result of it generation after generation, there is that 'succession of convulsive self-denial and self-destruction, which is so fatal for us, and which is so characteristic of the Russian mentality', as Dostoyevsky has so accurately described.

The way the Russians suffered the long period of Mongol supremacy showed Ivan the Terrible and all subsequent rulers in Russia how the eastern Slavs would behave when they were driven hard and punished even when they were innocent. Alexander Nevski and Dmitri Donskoi have inspired all those Russians who *have* reacted, who *have* fought back against the oppressor. But the Mongols had only these two heroes to contend with. They were finally defeated by their own internal rivalries and decline in military strength. Nevertheless both Alexander and Dmitri are important because they tell us clearly what the Russians *can* achieve when passivity is thrown aside, when the other cheek is not offered, when action is taken to challenge the established might of the overlord.

In 1236, only a year before the Mongol invasion, Alexander Nevski successfully repelled a Swedish attack on Novgorod, led by Jarl (or Earl) Birger, who had been encouraged by the Pope, Gregory IX, to lead a crusade against the non-Catholic Russians. Without waiting for the Swedes to begin their assault on Novgorod, Alexander dashed ahead of his army with only a small detachment to the River Neva. Here he caught the Swedes by surprise, routed them and sunk several of their ships.

In spite of the prestige he thus gained for Russian arms, and in spite of the perilous situation in which Novgorod was placed in the following year when the rest of Russia was overrun by the Mongols, the citizens of this town forced him to abdicate. The nobles, when not at war, liked to have a more easily controllable man at their head. But once again Novgorod was attacked, this time by the Germans, in 1241. Alexander was asked to resume leadership and once again he saved the city.

The invaders, the Knights of the Sword, had installed themselves as the ruling caste over the Letts and the Estonians, and were now taking advantage of the Mongol invasion of Russia. They built a small fort a few miles to the south of Novgorod, blocking its vital supplies of wheat. Alexander led his men against this fort, captured it and went to relieve

Pskov, which the Germans had besieged. The final battle was fought on the ice of Lake Peipus, to the north-west of Pskov. With their heavy armoured cavalry in the centre, the Germans advanced in a wedge-shaped formation. They burst through the Russian line and would have won the day had not Alexander kept part of his cavalry well to the flank. When the Russian line was broached, these horsemen charged, and completely routed the Germans, pursuing them across the ice for five miles.

Only three years later, Novgorod was threatened again, this time by the Lithuanians. They seized the town of Torzhok, through which came the city's main supply of wheat. This serious threat to Novgorod's existence was rapidly crushed by Alexander, who won two battles against the invaders. A man of less restraint and wisdom might have involved the whole of the large province of Novgorod in a suicidal battle against the Mongols. In 1247 Tartar envoys came to Novgorod demanding a heavy tribute. Never having tasted defeat and destruction by the Tartars, and having just repulsed the German and Lithuanian attacks, the men of Novgorod actively resented this humiliating order. Riots broke out and the lives of the envoys were endangered. Alexander restored order and made it clear to the inhabitants that resistance would be useless. The crippling tax was paid.

His advice was ignored sixteen years later when several towns on the Volga refused to pay the tribute. A large Mongol army gathered to pulverise the offenders. Undaunted, Alexander journeyed to Kara-korum to intercede with the Grand Khan for his people. In this he was once more successful but for the last time. On his return to his own capital of Vladimir he fell ill and died. The Metropolitan Archbishop Cyril announced the grim news in the Cathedral of St Sophia, saying: 'My dear children, know that the sun of Russia is set.'

This could well have been the end of the Russians as a nation. The Kievan Russians had been scattered; their towns smashed. The Mongols had brought havoc to one of the three areas to which the Kievans had fled, Galicia, and had impoverished another, Novgorod, by cutting it off from the trade of the Water Road, the rivers linking the Baltic and Byzantium. The third region, the great forest area of Vladimir and Moscow, the Mongols were now squeezing dry by heavy taxation and slavery. Those who fled went east or south, as slaves, craftsmen or soldiers, to the Muslim Mongols, or west to Catholic Poland or Lith-uania. Both these two countries now extended their borders at Russia's expense, as far as the Ugra River, only 100 miles from Moscow. Thus during this period the seeds were sown of wars which the Russian grand princes and tsars would feel encouraged to wage when the Mongols no longer controlled them.

The Russian Church canonised Alexander Nevski for his courageous battles and wise counsels; in 1942, the Russian government, realising the importance of this saint as a patriotic hero, issued a new medal for bravery, the Star of the Order of Alexander Nevski.

It is not difficult to understand why the Russians admired the Mongols. In some ways Mongol civilisation was superior to that achieved by the Russians; and they admired their impressive air of authority. After their whirlwind conquest of the Russian principalities, Batu, the leader of the Golden Horde, began his report to his superior, the Great Khan Ogedei:

> Through the power of eternal Heaven, and the grace of the Imperial Uncles, we have destroyed the city of Mtskheti, in Georgia, and made the Russian people slaves. We have subjected eleven states and peoples to our rule, and have tightened the golden rein . . .

Ogedei himself made this statement:

> The empire founded by my father, Chingiz Khan, in the midst of troubles, I wish to free from its troubles. I want to give it happiness by letting it set its foot on the ground and its hand to the soil . . . We shall introduce the following rule: the individual units of a thousand soldiers in the various regions, shall provide postmasters and stableboys, and at each stage, a post station shall be established, so that couriers shall ride via the mail stages . . . I have seen to it that wells were found and dug out . . . For those people in cities, I set up a garrison and appointed baillifs, and thus made life secure for the people of the empire.[6]

Some of the other aspects of Mongol life recorded by Carpini in 1247 shed a revealing light on Russia's new masters, showing features which the Russians found attractive, even if they offended the Church:

> Everybody can take as many wives as he can support. Some have a hundred, some fifty, some ten, some fewer. As a general rule they are allowed to marry all their relatives, except their mother, daughter, and their sisters by the same mother. They may marry their sisters on their father's side, and even their father's other wives after his death.[7]

The importance of this lies in its implied attitude to women: sex was permitted for all married couples, including relatives, and, by implication, it was not tabu outside marriage. The Mongols were obedient and poor but none were encouraged to be chaste. To act as a brake on general promiscuity, there was 'a law or custom by which they kill any man and woman *they have found* committing adultery', but death was a common punishment for a wide variety of acts. In the Russian provinces of the Mongol empire, the Church would not permit marriage between relatives, so the Mongol disregard for this sexual tabu was not unattractive for some Russians. The family is an institution which frequently makes one or more of its members prone to the attractions of a more permissive society. If a man could marry his father's other wives, a father could marry his son's wives. Ivan the Terrible often rode out of Moscow with his son on raping expeditions, and often used his son's mistresses. According to one contemporary, he also maintained a harem of fifty concubines. This can be regarded as a continuation of the promiscuous way of life of Vladimir and other Kievan princes, but, as many aspects of Ivan's life reveal a Mongol influence, his promiscuity can be seen in a general context of debased Asiatic morality. [8]

Carpini commented on the Mongols' attitude to religion, their belief in God and their basic concepts of pictorial representation, which also had a distinct appeal:

> The Mongols believe in one God, the creator of all the visible and invisible world; they also believe that all the good and all the chastisements in this world originate from him, but they worship him neither with prayers, nor with hymns of praise, nor with any other religious ceremonies.
>
> Nevertheless, they still have certain idols made out of felt in the shape of human figures, which they set up on both sides of the entrance to the tents. Beneath these idols, they put up figures which look like an udder, and which, they believe, protect their herds and provide them with an abundance of milk. Other idols are made from silk, and they are highly honoured . . . Beside the entry on the women's side of their dwellings is another image, with a cow's tit for the women, who milk the cows; on the other side of the entry, toward the men, is another statue with a mare's tit for the men, who milk the mares . . . The dukes and commanders always have a stuffed he-goat as an idol in the middle of their camp. They also make an idol in honour of their first Emperor, Chingiz-Khan. Some Mongols put these idols on a beautiful covered cart, and anybody who steals anything from this cart is put to death without pardon. [9]

Marco Polo came to Mongolia from Venice twenty-four years after Carpini returned to Rome. For seventeen years he lived and travelled there as the honoured guest of Kublai Khan. From Polo came the information about this monarch's love of beauty and culture, the artists, philosophers, scholars and craftsmen drawn to Pekin from the widely differing regions of his vast realm, his tolerance of other religions, the domes and pavilions of Pekin, his winter capital, and Xanadu, his summer palace of Shang-tu, 225 miles north-west of the capital. In the second half of the thirteenth century, this Mongolian despot created in Pekin and Shang-tu a heaven on earth, with white and golden buildings with tent-shaped roofs, with parks and man-made lakes, rolling lawns, arcades and avenues, a paradise which delighted Polo and those who read his book *The Description of the World*. In the seventeenth century this was read in England by Richard Hakluyt and Samuel Purchas, who passed this vision on to the poets and painters of the Regency, to Coleridge and every romantic. Coleridge read Purchas' description of Shang-tu, where 'Khan Kubla commanded a palace to be built, and a stately garden thereunto. And thus ten miles of fertile ground were enclosed with a wall.' The poet fell asleep for three hours, and on waking wrote the world's most famous tribute to Mongolian civilisation.

Marco Polo also inspired Christopher Columbus. He sailed westwards in 1492 hoping to find the rich, romantic land once ruled by 'the great and wonderful magnificence of Cublay Kaan. When I came to Juana (in the Bahamas), I followed its coast and found it to be so extensive, that I thought it must be the mainland, the province of Cathay.' The Mongols failed in their dream of conquering the world, but they succeeded in inspiring it.

Polo explained the intimate partnership of man and horse which built and maintained the 5,000 miles of their empire, a partnership which inspired the Russians and their other subjects with their powers of endurance:

> The Mongols live at most times on mare's milk, and of horses and mares there are about eighteen for each man, and when any horse is tired by the road, another is taken in exchange. For they carry no food but one or two bags of leather in which they put their milk . . . When there is need they ride quite ten days' marches without eating any cooked food and without lighting fire. Often they live on the blood of their horses; for each pricks the vein of his horse and puts his mouth to the vein and drinks of the blood till he is satisfied. And they carry dried blood with them, and when they wish to eat they take some water and put some of it in the water and leave it to dissolve, and then they drink it. And they have their dried mare's milk too which is solid like paste. When they go to war, they carry about ten pounds of this milk.[10]

It was this quality of great mobility that led both to lightning conquest and great vulnerability, as the Mongols had to rely on native, Russian co-operation in administering, and taxing, their western regions. They may well have been surprised to find such willing co-operation from the princes of Moscow.

Daniel, Alexander Nevski's son, became in 1276 the first Prince of Moscow, a town whose history begins with treachery. In 1147, one of the sons of Vladimir Monomakh, Yury, nicknamed Dolgoruky or Long-armed, tricked the owner of the fortress, Stephen Kuchka, out of his bed one night, placing a tame bear near the building. Hearing its cries, he was persuaded to go out and kill it. He was immediately set upon by Yury's henchmen, stabbed and strangled. Daniel more than doubled his province by buying or seizing his neighbours' lands. The chronicles make a special mention of his treachery in his grabbing of the province of Kolomna. He and his successors could not have carried out this policy of aggrandisement without the support of the Mongols. Every Russian prince had to travel to Sarai, the capital of the Golden Horde, on the lower Volga, to be confirmed as governor of their territory. This rank would not be given if they did not placate, or bribe, the Khan with expensive presents, and they would not continue as governor if they did not ruthlessly extract the Mongol tribute money from their subjects. The early princes of Moscow showed a remarkable disregard for their fellow Slavs in the other principalities, and a steady determination to satisfy their masters. When in 1319 Prince Michael of Tver was summoned to Sarai to explain his opposition to the claims of Prince Yury to the office of Grand Prince of Vladimir, he was decapitated and impaled, having been denounced by Yury, his own cousin—an act which must have disgusted his hardly fastidious overlords. Michael's sons appealed to the archbishop. He could not deny that the Princes of Moscow was indeed 'the base and treacherous servant of the Tartars'. But the Church made no protest. Yury himself was killed by the sons, who poured a rain of arrows into him when he was making another visit to Sarai. One of the sons was then killed by the Moscow faction.

Hoping to put an end to this display of family hatred, the Mongols made Alexander of Tver Grand Prince. Only a year later, in 1327, the inhabitants of Tver refused to pay the Mongol tribute and killed the Mongol envoy and his bodyguard. Ivan I, brother of Yury and now Prince of Moscow, rose—or descended—to the occasion. He immediately offered his services to Khan Uzbek in Sarai and undertook to lead an army of 50,000 Tartars to punish Tver. The town was ravaged, his fellow Slavs butchered. Receiving this lavish present, the Mongols made Ivan Grand Prince. Even this did not satisfy him. He made the Church, in the name of the senior cleric, the Metropolitan, excommunicate both Alexander and the whole town of Pskov, for giving him shelter. There could not have been a clearer demonstration of the Church's impotence.

When Alexander risked his life ten years later, going once more to Sarai, he was given back his old province of Tver. But such magnanimity was not to Ivan's liking. He persuaded the Khan to reverse this decision and was only satisfied by having Alexander murdered.

An essential element in Ivan's aggressive policy was his use of the Church. He needed it for prestige and the aura of respectability that it still retains today; it needed him for sheer reasons of survival. The Metropolitan Cyril left the battered, deserted city of Kiev in 1299, and made Vladimir his home. This too proved insecure, as rival princes struggled for possession of the town. In 1325, when Daniel was Prince of Moscow, the Metropolitan Peter moved to this town; it was surrounded by forests; it was safer from attack from envious Russian princes and their armies. This inaccessibility attracted settlers from other parts of the Russian lands. The Metropolitans continued to stay in Moscow in spite of the increasing severity of the sovereign's rule. The state certainly flouted many Christian principles, those of love, compassion, humility and peace, but the system worked. Honesty was not the best policy, in the view of each successive prince of Moscow, but they stayed in power. Each prince handed on to his successor a larger estate; each prince had the support of the Christian Church. Ivan I, with his Mongol army, made it quite clear that no Russian province could consider itself safe from a Muscovite attack. So it was safer for the Church to remain in Moscow, in spite of the unchristian, and anti-Christian, activities of its prince. The Church in Byzantium and Kiev had been just an adjunct of the state, a supporter of strong-arm methods. The Church in staying in Moscow was merely considering its own safety and continuing an old tradition.

The Church's doctrine that the Grand Prince, and later the Tsar, was God on earth was in fact potentially suicidal. If the Grand Prince could crush the liberties of his subjects and seize the territory of his neighbours, if he could ally himself with the Mongols by not only inviting an army of 50,000 to punish the citizens of Tver, but also leading it, then it was obvious that he could obstruct, imprison or kill a Metropolitan or close a church if he, or God, in his infinite wisdom, ordained it. This total support of the sovereign was also suicidal in that the authority of the Church was only credible as long as the sovereign remained invincible. The collapse of its image in 1917 was therefore inevitable. It sank or swam with the monarchy. Since then persecution has recharged it.

The two centuries before the reign of Ivan the Terrible are dominated by the single-minded policies of his ancestors. The most consistent feature of their reigns was war: wars against their fellow Russians, wars against their neighbours, wars against the Mongols. Ivan I and his successors could not have carried out this determined programme of expansion if the Mongols had wished to prevent it, by heavier taxation or by direct military intervention. The princes of Moscow kept themselves in favour with the Golden Horde by seeing to it that the Russians paid the heavy Mongol tribute money. Ivan I earned the nickname of Kalita, or Money Bag. His poorer neighbours were either bought out or pushed out. During the twelve years of his reign Moscow more than doubled in size. His son, Simeon, was nicknamed Gordi, or Proud, for, as the Chronicle reported, 'the Khan put all the other Princes in his hands'. He preferred to be regarded by them as their 'father', no longer their 'elder brother', asking for obedience 'without contradiction'. He was killed by the Black Death, which struck his realm in 1352. (Death totals are not known. This plague in 1348–9 killed a third, perhaps half of the population in Italy, France and England. Its last appearance in England was in 1665. In 1390, 80,000 people, according to the chroniclers, died of the plague in Novgorod.) His brother, Ivan II, reigned for only six years, but during that time he eliminated those princes who asserted their independence by reporting them to the Khan. Ivan, arriving at the Khan's tent, had to walk on the stripped and mangled corpses of his cousins, murdered at his request. On his return to Moscow, he built the Church of Thanksgiving in the Kremlin. He then invited the sons of the murdered princes to the Kremlin and put them in prison, where they soon died. Ivan secured from Sarai the right to preside as judge over all the other Russian princes.

Of the nine princes of Moscow before Ivan the Terrible, only one challenged the power of the Mongols. This was Dmitri, the son of Ivan II, nicknamed Donskoi, for his great victory in the Battle of Kulikovo, on the River Don, in 1380.

Dmitri fitted well into the family pattern, showing two qualities which favoured the growth of Moscow, long life and having few sons, thereby avoiding family hatreds in arguments over succession. Two qualities he did not share with the other princes of Moscow. He did not believe in ingratiating himself with the Mongols and he did not make a point of saving his life by deserting his army on the eve of battle.[11] Ivan the Terrible followed this family tradition at the gates of Kazan, when thousands of his army lost their lives in capturing it.

Dmitri Donskoi stands out as a hero in this period of egoistic aggrandisement; but even he, in the early days of his reign when still a youth, imposed his will over the citizens of Nizhny-Novgorod, who did not want his nominee as their prince. He sent his Metropolitan to the town and closed all their churches until they submitted, demonstrating clearly the fate in store for the Church if it ever had the temerity to oppose the monarch.

It is not surprising that the Mongols could not maintain their initial force and fury. As their ferocity, discipline and unity diminished, the spirit of resistance among the Russians grew. After forty years of peace with the Tartars, the war against them began in 1365 when the men of Ryazan refused to pay their taxes and defeated the Mongol force sent up from Sarai to punish them. Six years later came retribution. A large army descended on Ryazan and spread destruction over the whole province. In 1378 Nizhny-Novgorod was attacked and set on fire by the Mongols to punish the town for having killed a small force of 1,500 soldiers. They were still experts in overkill.

Dmitri decided that the time had come to assume the offensive. The Golden Horde, and the other armies of the Mongols, no longer maintained their standards of inflexible, unquestioning obedience, and the office of Khan could now be won by assassination. In his first battle, on the River Vozha, a hundred miles south-east of Moscow, he was nearly defeated. After three vigorous counter-attacks he staved off disaster and finally won the day. He then boldly decided to march south to meet the powerful army that Khan Mamai was assembling for an all-out assault on the rebellious Russians.

Dmitri assembled, from all parts of the Russian lands, the largest army the eastern Slavs had ever mounted: estimates of the numbers of this holy crusade, blessed by the Metropolitan, Sergei, vary between 150,000 and 400,000. Some of the princes advised Dmitri to wait on the northern side of the Don, but he chose to deploy his forces on some low hills on the southern bank, to the west of the village of Kulikovo. It was a good offensive position as it commanded the open, low-lying ground that now separated the two armies. But defensively it was weak, as the Don barred the Russian line of withdrawal.

As the mists cleared on the morning of 8 September 1380, the two armies moved forward and joined battle. After several hours of continuous slaughter, the superior numbers of the Mongols began to gain the upper hand. They had advanced in a simple formation of five parallel lines of infantry with heavy cavalry support. Dmitri was using a more open formation with a strong cavalry force well to the left flank, in the cover of a wood overlooking the battlefield. Only when most of the

Tartars had passed this position did this hidden cavalry emerge. Seeing fresh troops to their rear, the Mongols were thrown into confusion. The main body of the Russian army then pushed forward and gained the Mongol camp.

It was a great victory, but some two-thirds of the Russian soldiers were killed or captured. The survivors returned to Moscow, while the Mongols assembled a new army and set out for a war of revenge. They appeared before the walls of Moscow in 1382, and a three-day battle ensued, at the end of which the Mongols agreed to discuss terms for a peaceful settlement. Had Dmitri been there he might have refused to talk, sensibly mistrusting the Mongols, but he was still away to the north of Moscow, assembling new forces. In the event, the Mongols followed the tactics of Princess Olga, back in the tenth century, and killed the Russian delegation. They then stormed the capital and put the defenders to the sword. It was recorded that 20,000 Russians were killed or captured. The Mongols then returned to their own territory.

In spite of this appalling reverse, Kulikovo remains as a great landmark in Russian history, comparable to the victories of King Henry V of England, but of far deeper significance as France was never the destroyer and oppressor of England as the Mongols were of Russia. For the first time the massed forces of the Tartars had been defeated; Moscow had shown itself as the rallying point of the Russian people; the need for an efficient, centralised state with a powerful standing army had been brought home to everyone; and Dmitri himself became an inspiration to subsequent generations for his courage in battle and his resistance to the oppressor. He died in 1389, seven years after the terrible sack of his capital. This was the last time the citizens of Moscow were attacked by the Mongols, until 1571, when the Crimean Tartars took advantage of Ivan the Terrible's disastrous wars against Poland and Lithuania, when he left his capital with inadequate defences. After Kulikovo, the long night of foreign domination began slowly but surely to give way to a new dawn of national independence.

This was not the end of Mongol domination; it continued with diminishing effect for another century. But it left marks in the Russian way of life that have remained to this day. The early princes of Moscow and Ivan the Terrible himself were quick to learn from the masters, and they used Mongolian methods to strengthen their own ideas of how their people and those of the other Russian principalities should be controlled and exploited. The ideas of kingship and statecraft which existed in Russia up to this time were those of Byzantium; but only a hazy and at times undecided view as to the correct interpretation of Byzantine theory was shown by the Kievan Russian princes. It was from the Mongols that their descendants learnt at first hand the principle of centralised and ruthless control. From them also they learnt the habit of obeisance and the practice of corruption, for power came to the grand princes of Moscow by successful bribery of the Tartar officials, not by force of arms. These three features of Russian life, disregard of human rights, servility and bribery, became predominant and have remained so to this day.

The *prikazi*, the Muscovite government departments, were similar to the Khan's *divans*; and it seems likely that the fusion of civil and military functions, still a characteristic feature of Russian administration, is also a legacy from the Mongols. From them the Russians learnt much in military organisation and tactics, principally those of encirclement and the use of gunpowder, battering rams and catapults. Devices which led to easier administration from the capital were adopted wholesale, such as the system whereby peasants living along the main roads were compelled to provide horses for transport and messengers. The Mongol system of taxation by households was also copied, as was their system of customs dues. They learnt from them too the importance of a more general use of coinage. Another Tartar institution that became permanent was the supply and sale of drink as a nationalised, government activity. The Roman Emperors promoted the production of bread and circuses to keep their subjects happy; the Russian tsars and communists have promoted the drinking of vodka to keep their people from being too unhappy. The greatest legacy of the Mongols to the Russians and the rest of the world was their concept of unlimited power. The Vandals hacked for themselves a permanent place in history, leaving their name as bywords for wilful, ignorant destruction; the Mongols gave the Indians and the world at large a one-word description of a man whose word is law, a mogul.

In spite of the fact that the Mongols remained as a threat on the Russians' southern border, this did not prevent the princes of Moscow waging war on their fellow Slavs; in fact the mere existence of the Mongols provided the Muscovites with an ideal excuse for threatening to attack, and actually attacking if there was any resistance. In the first 150 years of Moscow's existence—just five generations—the 500 square miles of Prince Daniel, the first prince of Moscow, had swollen to 15,000. After Dmitri Donskoi's death in 1389, his son Basil I seized Nizhni-Novgorod; his successor, Basil II, took Mozhaisk, Serpukhov and part of Ryazan; his son, Ivan III, undermined and seized the large and powerful province of Novgorod, as well as Chernigov, Perm, Vyatka, Yaroslav and Tver. Ivan III has been called by some Russian historians Ivan the Great; his conquests were certainly extensive. He expanded his territory fourfold, by purchase, intimidation, and where that failed, conquest. Even before his reign, Moscow's appetite and methods have been compared to those of a boa-constrictor.[12]

Ivan's son, Basil III, crushed all resistance in Pskov and Smolensk, and then occupied the still independent part of Ryazan. In the words of Bernard Pares, in his excellent *History of Russia*, the other Russian princes provided each prince of Moscow 'with a number of separate preys which he could easily absorb piecemeal'.[13] A grim feature of Ivan III's destruction of Novgorod's independence was his wholesale expulsion of families. Over 150 families of the nobility and merchant class were transported to Vladimir and the Volga; 7,000 individuals were uprooted and sent to live near Moscow; to replace them, Muscovite families were shifted to Novgorod. Like slaves, innocent men, women and children were carted off to new areas, deprived of security to bolster the security of the state by a more dangerous enemy than any foreign country. Ivan extracted from Novgorod three times the tribute money paid to the Mongols. For this he was boldly denounced by the Metropolitan: 'You are worse than the Tartars! Fear God, for he will not spare you on the Judgement Day.' Ivan signed a promise that he would 'bind himself to refrain from spilling the blood of members of the faith'. This oath was soon broken, and the Metropolitan threatened to pronounce a curse of God upon him. Only one person in Russia could issue threats and get away with it; a few days later, the Metropolitan's food was poisoned with rapid results. Novgorod had escaped destruction by the Mongols when they invaded Russia two hundred years earlier; now the inhabitants were starved, tortured and executed by one of their own race, the Grand Prince of Muscovy. He invaded Novgorod and took 10,000 prisoners. They were beaten like cattle and decapitated, then the corpses were hacked to bits and thrown into the many ponds and lakes around Moscow to feed the crayfish. The women were sold to the harems of the Crimean Tartars.

No understanding of Russian history is possible without taking into account the constant maltreatment of the peasant, as a slave, serf or cannon-fodder. The general name for a *free* peasant, as written in the early chronicles, was *smerd*, a man who stinks. A slave was a *rob*, a shorter term for a worker, *robotnik*, or *kholop*. As Herman Andreyev has

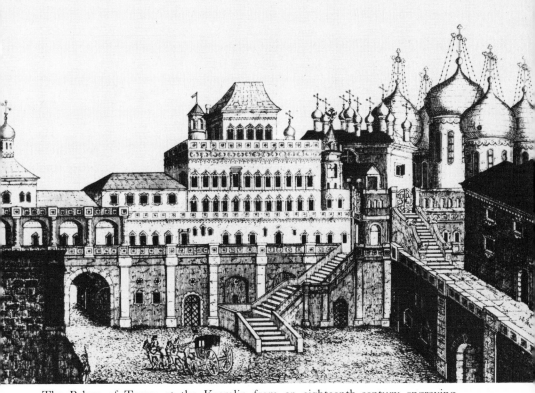

The Palace of Terem at the Kremlin from an eighteenth-century engraving. 'Terem' is a Tartar word for women's quarters (*Novosti Press Agency*)

Red Square on Palm Sunday in the early sixteenth century, taken from Olearius' *Travels in Moscow*. On the right is the Spasky Tower of the Kremlin (*Novosti Press Agency*)

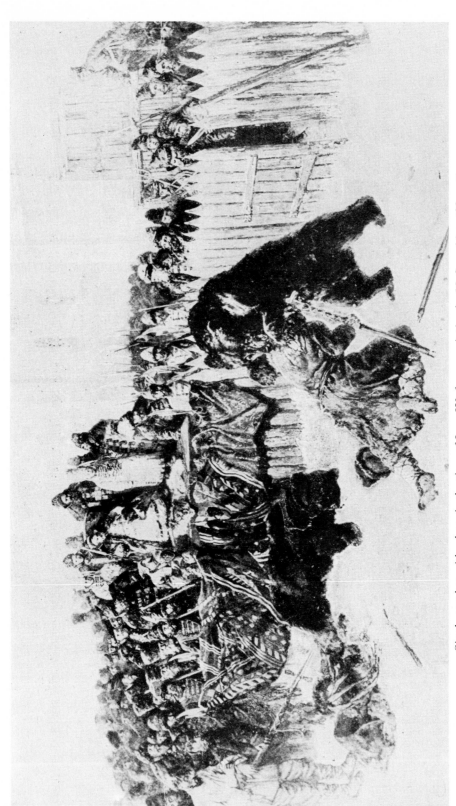

Single combat with a bear in the time of Ivan IV, from a painting by N. Sverchkov (*Novosti Press Agency*)

stated in a recent collection of essays, 'slavery for the people has always existed in Russia'.*[14] After the *Russkaya Pravda* of Prince Yaroslav (c 1040), no real improvement in Russian justice was made in the opinion of another Russian historian, Lev Kopelev, until the reigns of Tsar Alexei and Peter, some six hundred years later.[15] Under the terms of Yaroslav's law code, the fine to be paid for killing a free peasant was merely 5 *grivennik* (5 farthings). In 1169, during a war between Novgorod and Suzdal, the defeated men of Suzdal were sold within the province of Novgorod for 2 *nogata*, a third of the price of a goat.[16]

We have already seen how Ivan I smashed all resistance in Tver by bringing in a large Tartar army, and, in the words of the Russian historian Sergei Elagin, 'drowning the Christian city in blood'. Ivan III and his clergy punished heretics by burning them to death in wooden cages. It was intolerable that anyone, whether noble or peasant, should dare to disagree with official religious doctrine. In this respect, Russia certainly showed European, not Mongolian, characteristics. Christians, not Muslims, tortured each other with long trials and death by fire for heresy. As Herman Andreyev has written:

> There is no such thing as a homogeneous history of a united Russia. If there is anything that has endured through the whole of Russian history, it is the constant suppression by the State and the Church of ignorant, tormented people, fleeced by all possible methods . . . Up to 1861 [the official emancipation of the serfs], almost without any opposition on the part of the Orthodox Church, peasants were robbed, beaten, exchanged for dogs, driven into communes like animals into herds, decked out in military uniforms and compelled to kill other people.[17]

This reference to conscription is of crucial importance. War was regarded as the central feature of state policy by the princes of Moscow. While most of them avoided armed conflict with the Mongols, they felt free to embark on frequent campaigns against their fellow princes and their western neighbours. Ivan III, Ivan the Terrible's grandfather, stated this policy quite plainly: 'The land of Russia is from our ancestors of old our patrimony.' This was historically inaccurate, as the land of Russia had never been one country, merely a loose, shifting confederation of principalities. It was also morally indefensible. If all princes went to war to reconquer land which their ancestors had owned hundreds

*'The power, liberty and progress that we associate with modern England and America required as a precondition the emancipation of the serfs. Emancipation formed the necessary prelude to the growth of trade, manufacture and colonisation, as well as to the intellectual and political developments of Tudor and Stuart England.' *History of England*, G. M. Trevelyan, 243.

of years earlier, there would never be any peace in any land. Armed with this doctrine of intervention, the descendants of every defeated prince, duke, knight or landowner could take up arms against their neighbour. Europe, following this principle, would have become a welter of angry Gascons, Burgundians, Tuscans, Lombards, Nea-politans, Bohemians and Pomeranians, all permanently at war. Parallels can be drawn with the houses of Hapsburg, Hohenzollern and Savoy, but their unification programmes were, in comparison, models of reason and friendly persuasion.

During the fifty years preceding the reign of Ivan the Terrible, Moscow was frequently at war with Lithuania and Poland. To his ally, the Tartar Khan of Crimea, Ivan III stated clearly that the war would go on until every place once owned by a Russian prince was captured; truces would only be made 'in order to draw breath'. From 1492 until 1532, Moscow was fighting her western neighbours almost continuously. Ivan also intervened in the affairs of the Tartars, sending in his soldiers to fight for rival Khans, defeating Shah Ahmed and Khan Alegam of Kazan. The forcible seizure of the other Russian towns by Moscow was a form of civil war among the Russians. Ivan III's father, Basil II, was named the Blind. Supporters of a rival claimant to the position of Grand Prince seized him in a church where he was giving thanks for his release by the Tartars after a skirmish, and both his eyes were burnt out with a bar of hot iron. This was an act of revenge. After the funeral of Basil's father, his uncle, Prince Yury of Galich, had tried to throw Basil over the Kremlin wall. A fight broke out; Yury's right hand was crushed and his teeth knocked out; and his son was blinded in one eye. Yury was held down and beaten by some deacons, and the Metropolitan himself had both eyes blackened. Dozens of Russians from Galich were thrown into the river Moskva. When the Metropolitan saw the sightless young Prince of Moscow, he died of heart failure. The new Metropolitan, who tried to mediate between the two factions, was seized and flogged by two princes who had been dispossessed by Basil's father. Not sur-prisingly during this early period of Moscow's history, cultural activ-ities, outside the monasteries, were non-existent. Some of the princes were illiterate; Dmitri Donskoi, for example, could not read according to the Chronicle.

As can be seen in the chart on page 57, civil wars have broken out frequently in Russia when control at the centre has collapsed, when one principality was fighting another, and when large parts of the country have risen in revolt. To discourage these outbreaks, the princes of

Moscow and the tsars have always maintained large standing armies. The larger the territory under their control, the greater the danger and the larger the standing army.

Civil Wars and Revolts in Russia

10th Century	972–980	
11th Century	1015–1019	
	1054–1113	
12th Century	1139–1146	
	1157–1167	
13th and 14th Centuries	Mongol Rule—frequent civil wars	
15th Century	1425–1431	
16th Century	1510	
17th Century	1604–1613	
	1670–1671	Razin
18th Century	1773–1775	Pugachov
19th Century	1825	Decembrist Revolt
	1830	Polish Revolt
	1863	Polish Revolt
20th Century	1905	
	1918–1921	

Some historians have described the wars of the early princes of Moscow simply as stern, but short-term measures taken to forge the nation. But all wars are waged as temporary measures. Those who instigate the wars and those who have to fight in them sincerely believe that life somehow will improve once the conflict is over. Historians also fall into this mood of wishful thinking when justifying the wars of young nations. They talk of the need for security, the forging of the nation, the heroism of the warriors who defeated the enemy. In painting this noble picture, no mention is made of the security of the neighbouring states whose people often shared the same blood and faith. No regrets are expressed for the deaths, the suffering and the ruined lives amongst the victorious nation which has lain so painfully under the hammer of that forge. No mention is made of the heroism of those who lost their independent existence. No one believes any more in the Divine Right of Kings, but some people still cling to a belief in the Divine Right of national success: if a nation is successful, God must have favoured it whatever was done to achieve that success.

After the Russian nation had been forged, whenever that stage is supposed to have been reached, the wars continued unabated. From the early days until the twentieth century, wars have dominated Russian history in every century. In the ninth and tenth centuries the Russians fought five wars against Byzantium; in the eleventh and twelfth centuries Kievan Russia was torn by intermittent civil wars for seventy years; civil wars broke out again once the burden of Mongol control had begun to lighten. During the thirteenth and fourteenth centuries the Russians fought 41 wars against Lithuania, 30 wars against the German Baltic states, and 44 wars against Sweden, Bulgaria and other smaller states. Between 1245 and 1445 the army of Moscow was busily engaged in 163 rebellions and wars against the other Russian principalities.[18] After the seventeenth century, civil wars continued to erupt, not between provinces, but between rulers and the ruled. The seventeenth and eighteenth century peasant wars of Bolotnikov, Razin, Bulavin and Pugachov were succeeded in the nineteenth century by hundreds of small, localised risings, where the peasants rebelled without waiting for a leader. Between 1800 and 1812 there were 165 peasant revolts; between 1812 and 1825 there were 540; between 1825 and 1860 the number rose to over 1,200, and there were more than 30 mass flights to the Caucasus alone. In the late 1850s these rebellions, although crushed with heavy sentences and many deaths, rose to such a pitch that the Tsar was obliged to make some concessions. In 1861 Alexander II emancipated the serfs; but this measure was not only too late but ineffective—for the serf soon realised that only his status had changed; his poverty and his restrictions for the most part remained. During the next three years there were nearly 2,000 revolts. This number rose between 1905 and 1907 to 7,000, involving more than half the country; between 1910 and 1914 the figure was around 13,000.

At the same time bitter wars were being waged by Russia's subject nations, and in the latter part of the nineteenth century industrial war in the form of mass strikes was becoming more and more frequent. In Poland, in spite of heavy repression, there were two great insurrections, in 1830 and 1863; in the latter rising 30,000 Poles lost their lives. In central Asia, Georgia and the Baltic provinces, there were similar desperate rebellions. Wars against Russia's neighbours throughout this time continued. Eight wars were fought against the Poles, the western Slavs, in the sixteenth, seventeenth and eighteenth centuries, and nine wars against Sweden between 1554 and 1809. The Russians fought the Turks nine times in the seventeenth, eighteenth and nineteenth centuries. Persia was Russia's enemy in three wars between 1722 and 1828. Peter the Great waged two wars against China in the seventeenth century. A war with India was fought by Catherine II in 1796 and another campaign was begun by her successor, Paul, in 1801. In 1904 Russia provoked Japan into war by her attempts to take Manchuria while denying Japan any rights in Korea; Finland was attacked in 1941. Every neighbour of Russia has been involved in war with her; every increase in the size of the Russian Empire has been followed by worsening conditions with her new neighbours. The pattern is certainly consistent.

The Russians suffered heavily during the invasions by the French under Napoleon and the Germans under Hitler; but both occupations were short and both wars enabled Russia to increase in size. And she cannot be regarded as a nation that has never invaded, occupied or destroyed another country. The Russians were surrounded by people who, at different times, advanced and occupied parts of their land; but the same can be said of every ethnic group in every part of the world.

Historians and others in the west have shown their goodwill towards Russia by looking for every feature of Russian history that can demonstrate that Russia has always been a European country. But the early rulers of Moscow went out of their way to distance themselves from their peers in Europe. Ivan III was the first Prince of Moscow to call himself 'Sovereign of All Russia', after one of the wars against Lithuania. The Holy Roman Emperor, Frederick III, suggested that Ivan should now call himself King. Ivan's reply is most instructive. The goodwill gesture was rebuffed with the haughty petulance of the newcomer who prefers to remain apart. Instead of King, the title of Tsar was chosen. It is derived from *Caesar* but, as a title shared by no other monarch, it is defiantly non-European. It is one of the Russian words for *King* and was used in Russian texts for the Kings of Judaea and Egypt, the Emperors of Rome and Constantinople, and also for the Mongol princes.

'We, by God's grace', declared Ivan, 'are sovereigns in our land from the beginning, from our first forefathers; and our appointment we hold from God.' The title of King was spurned: 'We have wanted it from no one, and do not want it now.'

This reply would not have been in the least surprising if it had come from Tamburlane or Ghengiz Khan. Ivan's royal rebuke was uttered in 1494; two decades earlier, in 1472, he had married Zoe, the niece of the last Byzantine Emperor, Constantine Paleologus, who had died in battle during the fall of Constantinople in 1453. Ivan could not have married this princess had she not come to Moscow under the auspices of the Pope, who had been made her guardian. The western Christians hoped that this marriage might bring about a healing union between the two halves of their divided Church. Ivan accepted the girl and her Byzantine ideals of complete dictatorship, but ignored any consideration of Christian *rapprochement*. From now on in the Kremlin, decisions were made, as in Byzantium, behind closed doors. The Church, as usual, concurred. But one of the faithful, Prince Patrikeyev who became a monk, had the courage to protest about many features of the highly prosperous marriage between Church and state, and the cruel way the Tsar and the priests treated their own people:

> Where in the traditions of the Gospels, Apostles and Fathers are monks ordered to acquire populous villages and enslave peasants to the brotherhood? We play into the hands of the rich, fawn slavishly, flatter them to be given some little village. We wrong and rob and sell Christians, our brothers. We torture them with scourges like wild beasts.[19]

Unlike the rest of Ivan's illiterate court, Zoe, renamed Sophia, was a woman of some learning, and could speak in several languages. She encouraged Ivan in his territorial expansion and military policy of aggression. As a result he refused to pay tribute to the Mongols but would not fight them even when, in 1480, they advanced to the River Ugra, a hundred miles from Moscow. On this occasion he saved the lives of his subjects as the Mongols suddenly retreated of their own accord. Their leader, Khan Akhmed, was ambushed and killed by a rival Tartar prince, possibly with the encouragement of Ivan himself. Raids and full-scale attacks by the Mongols still occurred, but from now on Moscow no longer paid tribute money to them.

Basil III, Ivan's son by Sophia, was both more devout and more ruthless than his father. His concept of the autocrat was such that his court looked back with regret, finding Basil less genial and accessible than Ivan. His forcible annexations included all those lands still owned by his kinsmen, the other Russian princes. This made no difference to the security of the Russians themselves. Wars of expansion continued relentlessly. Basil's first wife was barren; his second wife was Elena Glinskaya, whose family was originally Mongolian, descendants reputedly of Khan Mamai, who had been vanquished by Dmitri Donskoi at Kulikovo. For twenty-five years Basil had been praying for a son and heir without success. During the night of 25 August 1530, a night of heavy thunder, Elena gave birth to a son, the next ruler of this land of obedient worshippers of God—the autocrat, Ivan IV, soon to be nicknamed *Grozni*, the Threatener, the Terrible.

3

Delight in Killing

The first three years of Ivan's life were happy. His father had divorced his first wife after twenty years because she had failed to produce a child; five years had gone by with his second wife equally barren. Perhaps the all-powerful Tsar was powerless to make a woman fertile. But all worries if not doubts on that score were put to rest when Elena at last produced a male child. Eighteen months later she gave birth to a second son, Yury.

When Ivan was only three his father died. Intrigues and plots now began, which made such an impression on the young boy that fear of treason became rooted in his mind and continued to haunt him even when the reasons for such fear no longer existed. His mother became Regent and ruled with the help of her lover, Prince Ivan Obolenski. By her suspicion and jealousy she made many enemies for her son, removing from the capital, imprisoning or killing all possible claimants to the throne. She aroused the disgust of the court from the start by her choice of lover, an unimpressive figure, and by the way he was given precedence over her other advisers. Even Michael Glinsky, her uncle and guardian, was ignored and within a year thrown into a dungeon where he soon died. Her character is best illustrated by the shameless way she tricked her brother-in-law, Andrei. She harried him with spies and soldiers into open yet reluctant opposition in Novgorod, and enticed him to Moscow with promises of pardon. He was at once imprisoned and violently murdered. Thirty of his followers were hung on gallows placed at intervals on the Novgorod highroad leading out of Moscow.

Many Russians—those who believed in the authority of the Old Testament—had disliked their sovereign's marriage to another woman, while the first was still alive. Basil's long wait of twenty years is proof of his reluctance to break the Church's ruling. Happily untroubled by censorship and fear of imprisonment, Mark, the Patriarch of Jerusalem, felt free to express his opinion. When he received news of Basil's decision to marry again, he made this frightening prophecy: 'If you do this wicked thing, you will have an evil son. Your estate will become prey to terrors and tears. Rivers of blood will flow; the heads of the mighty will fall; your cities will be devoured by flames.'[1]

His forecast had already become true. After five years of Elena's regency, she met the death she had invited—at the hand of a poisoner. Ivan, now eight years old, was left to the mercy of the strongest nobles in the Kremlin. Disputes broke out between the Shuisky and the Belsky families for supremacy. Prince Basil Shuisky finally took control and imprisoned Obolenski without delay, leaving the wretched man to die of starvation. The Shuiskies, a large and powerful family descended from Alexander Nevski, now felt themselves at liberty to treat the Kremlin as their home, and, except for ceremonial occasions, ignored the young Tsar and his brother. Ivan never forgot and never allowed others to forget the misery and humiliation of these years. This is how he himself described the way he was treated, in a letter written when he was thirty-four to Prince Kurbsky:

> On the death of our mother, Elena, we became orphans in the fullest sense. Our subjects had achieved their desire, to have the country without a ruler. They ceased to regard us; being their own masters, they strove only for wealth or glory for themselves, and quarrelled among one another. They seized my mother's treasury; they trampled on her goods. As for my brother Yury and myself, they fed us as though we were foreigners or the most wretched servants. We lacked food and clothing; our will counted for nothing and no one was found to provide for us as children. Once we were playing with Prince Ivan Shuisky (the brother of Basil Shuisky) and he put his elbows on our father's bed, with his leg up on a chair. The children of the nobles took away our father's gold and silver plate and wrote the names of their parents upon it. In all things my will was not my own; everything was contrary to my will. Many a time I did eat late, not in accordance with my will. How can I enumerate the countless sufferings I endured in my boyhood?[2]

The death of Ivan's mother when Ivan was eight was a blow he felt for the rest of his life. From now on he often retreated into extreme self-pity. Soon after Elena's death, his nurse whom he also loved, was taken from him, and three years later the one noble who did befriend him, Vorontsov, was beaten up in his presence, after being falsely accused of plotting. He was rescued only by the intervention of the Metropolitan, the only man anyone respected. He was then banished to a distant province. Murder, imprisonment and torture coloured Ivan's days. One night he was suddenly woken up when one of the Belsky family burst into his room pursued by those who were about to kill him.

Ivan soon learnt that pity, kindness and courtesy were qualities to be despised in a Russian tsar; cruelty, arrogance and terror were more fitting. Such an atmosphere, such privations would seriously affect the character of the most placid child. Ivan had inherited from both his parents an alertness and sensitivity far above the average, and from his grandmother Sophia, the Greek wife of Ivan III, a strain of insanity. Danger lurked on Russia's southern border, and cruelty to man and beast ruled unchecked in the Kremlin. In 1538, when Ivan was eight, the Kazan Tartars made a successful raid into the eastern provinces. Men were killed and captured; others were blinded; arms, legs, ears and noses were hacked off; nuns were raped.

When he was only five, Ivan amused himself catching flies and tearing their wings off. He would take the oil used for the lamps placed in front of the palace icons, pour it onto ants' nests and set fire to them. He also enjoyed fighting with the boyars' children; these games must have been quite savage, as during one of them he broke another child's leg. When he was eleven he raped one of the servant girls, leaving her neck, chest and thighs covered in bruises. Watching men being tortured in the Kremlin encouraged him to maltreat animals. Dogs, cats and bears suffered at his hands. One of his pastimes consisted in taking dogs up to the top of St Saviour's Tower, the Trinity Tower or the Nicholas Tower, well over two hundred feet, and dropping them onto the terrace below. Then he and other children would rush down and watch them dying.

Another sport involved human agony and panic. He and his young friends would ride out of the Kremlin at full speed, causing men, women and children to flee in terror—those, of course, who were not knocked down or struck by flying hooves. There was no redress; no complaints could be made. Even the Chronicle admits that he tortured animals and 'attempted to kill and rob all sorts of people, women as well as men, while galloping and running everywhere'.

One of Ivan the Terrible's pastimes which involved no distress to his compatriots was reading. He avidly read all the books that were available to him—not exactly a wide selection. He read histories of Byzantium, of the early Christian saints, stories of the Khans of the Golden Horde and the chronicles of Kievan Russia—tales of power and conquest. When he was only fourteen he put his strength to the test. On his orders, the royal kennel-keepers seized Prince Andrei Shuisky and threw him to the dogs. He was bitten to death. Before carrying out this sentence, Ivan had promised his court that only one of them would be punished for the general state of disorder in the Kremlin. Anyone who believed a promise given by a Grand Prince of Moscow would have been absurdly naive. Following the death of Andrei Shuisky, thirty boyars, or knights, were strung up on gallows and left to rot. One of his court, Afanazy Buturlin, was impertinent enough to open his mouth one day and utter some criticism of Ivan's general conduct. He was seized at Ivan's command and his tongue was cut out.

One looks in vain for some reaction from the nobility. Why did they not kill the hateful young man before he could give them any further shocks? Death was a common occurrence all round them. There can be only one answer. The teachings of Byzantium, the Mongols and the Christian Church, which all stated that the monarch was divine, must have had a paralysing effect. There was no physical problem; poison could have been easily used; a sudden stab with a dagger would have rid them of this constant threat to their existence. They killed each other, but never their overlord. In his presence they seemed fixed like rabbits caught in a blazing light.

For most of the time the people of Moscow tolerated the government, or misgovernment of the Kremlin, whoever was for the moment in command. Life for Ivan and his nobles was made possible only by the simple-minded service and self-sacrifice of the ordinary Russian. These two qualities have always been 'the basis of the social and political organisation of the country, triumphantly forced on the docile mind of a robust and patient race', as described by K. Waliszewski, in his biography of Ivan. This is 'the secret of its triumph and its glories. The whole of Russia's greatness reposes on this foundation.'[3] Ivan's surest ally was the Church. Here, sadly, there was no Mongol influence, no spirit of toleration, to lighten the heavy burden the Church placed upon every citizen. Withdrawal from membership of the Church was classed as a form of political desertion and could be punished as such. This compulsory allegiance was demanded until the passing of the Toleration Act of 1905.

The Church in medieval Russia sympathised with the people and at the same time preached the virtues of unquestioning obedience. 'The Church exacted much—too much' (Waliszewski). All forms of secular art were condemmed. Back in the fifth century, the Church of Rome had excommunicated all actors and finally closed all theatres in the sixth. Even in England, actors were not allowed to be buried in consecrated ground until the end of the eighteenth century. In medieval Russia all forms of amusement, such as dancing and games of all kinds, were forbidden. The only place where the sexes mixed was the bath house.

Life for the majority of women was that of a beast of burden, often whipped. The penalty for a wife who sought to end her husband's maltreatment or cruelty by poisoning him was to be buried alive, with her head above ground to prolong the agony. In cases where the Church felt it could show some clemency, the accused were forced to become nuns, to wear chains and live in solitary confinement.[4]*

Moscow's young sovereign now let it be known in Vienna and Warsaw that he would like to marry a princess, a member of a European royal house. Not surprisingly, in view of the past decade of misrule in Russia since the death of Basil III, no one stepped forward. Three years later, at the age of sixteen, Ivan gave up the idea of a royal bride and decided instead to marry one of his subjects, a member of a family amongst whom ambition would play a stronger role than caution. After a special service in the Cathedral of the Assumption in Moscow, to which all the nobility had been summoned by the Metropolitan, the company assembled in the largest reception hall of the Kremlin, and heard their monarch make this surprisingly candid speech:

> Putting my trust in the grace of God and of His Immaculate Mother, in the grace and intercession of the great miracle-workers, Peter, Alexei, Jonah and Sergei, and of all Russian miracle-workers, and with thy blessing, O Father, I have decided to marry. I had at first intended to seek marriage in a foreign court, in the house of some King or Tsar; but I have now forgone that intention because I was orphaned and left a small child after the death of my father and mother. And if I take a wife in a foreign country, and afterwards we do not get on well together, it will be difficult for her. Therefore I wish to marry within my own country the one whom God will bless to be my wife, with thy blessing, Q Father.[5]

Here was an announcement that the nobility could welcome. Their experience of foreign brides—Zoe Paleologus and Elena Glinskaya—had not been favourable. Pleasure was turned into excitement when it was announced that, as his father had done, he would choose his bride after an assembly of virgins of rank in the Kremlin. Now the humblest, or most ambitious noble might become related to the sovereign. With less reason, similar approval was also given to a further statement that before his marriage, Ivan intended to promote himself to the rank of Tsar on all occasions—not just for ceremonial functions when foreign ambassadors were present, the formality begun by his grandfather,

* 'Emotionally and sexually in their relationship with males, women in Russia are the most direly unhappy and unsatisfied in the modern, developed world; that is, if the Soviet press and media are to be believed.' Olga Franklin, *The Guardian*, 2 August 1979.

Ivan III: 'Before my marriage', he declared, 'I wish, with thy blessing, O Father Metropolitan, to seek the ancestral rank, such as that of our ancestors, the Tsars and Grand Princes and our kinsman, Vladimir Monomakh. I wish to be invested with that rank.'

In 1547 Ivan was crowned as the Tsar of All the Russias with the crown known as the Cap of Vladimir Monomakh. By popular belief, without a shred of evidence, this fur-lined cap, surmounted by a cross, was given to Monomakh by the Byzantine Emperor, Constantine IX, and, it was supposed, had arrived with a piece of wood believed to be a fragment of the cross on which Jesus was crucified. The regalia used, the people were told, had been handed down from Monomakh, but again there is no evidence for this. Ivan now chose his bride, Anastasia, the daughter of Roman Yurievich Zakharin-Koshkin, a family of Prussian origin, who had moved to Muscovy in the previous century. We do not know how he came to make this choice, but it was one which disappointed the nobility. His grandfather had married a princess, the niece of an Emperor; his father, a member of a distinguished boyar family; as Tsar of All Russia, not merely Grand Prince of Muscovy, Ivan it was hoped, would marry someone of higher nobility than Anastasia. However, she won their gratitude as she was able to exercise some restraint on him. In February 1547, the young Tsar and his bride were married in the Cathedral of the Saviour in Moscow. Festivities in the palace continued until the first day in Lent, when the royal couple gave proof of their piety by journeying forty miles through the snow to the monastery of St Sergei and the Trinity, named after the Metropolitan who had been canonised for his work among the poor in the reign of Dmitri Donskoi. There, in prayer and contemplation, they remained for a whole week.

Ivan, aged only seventeen, was content to leave the work of government in the hands of his uncles, Yury and Michael Glinsky. With discontent growing on all sides, life in Moscow was made yet more precarious by two serious fires in April of this eventful year. In May the citizens of Pskov were courageous or foolhardy enough to mount a petition against the Glinsky family. Seventy men were chosen to present their official complaint, and Ivan met them outside the capital in the village of Ostrovka. He lost his temper, shouted at them and then gave them a foretaste of his cruelty. Hot wine was poured over the heads of these frightened men; some were then subjected to the terror of having their hair and beards singed. They were all ordered to take their clothes off and lie on the ground, which was still covered with snow.

Their lives were saved by the sudden arrival of messengers riding into the village, telling Ivan that yet another fire had broken out in Moscow. The humble petitioners were forgotten and Ivan rode away to the capital.

Fanned by a gale this new fire spread rapidly through the town, killing at least 1,700 people. The blaze leapt across the Kremlin walls and destroyed the timber houses of the Metropolitan and some belonging to boyars, some wooden churches, and the state offices, including the armoury and treasury. Explosions rocked the town as gunpowder in the arsenal caught fire. The survivors demanded revenge against those whom they now reviled as being responsible—the hated Glinsky family, whose old mother was rumoured to be a witch. In this crisis Ivan showed himself doubly to be a coward. Seeing the extent of the fire, he fled to the safety of his palace on the Sparrow Hills, four miles to the west of the city, leaving Yury Glinsky in the Kremlin to restore control when the fire had burnt itself out. He then ordered an inquiry to be held to determine the origin of the fire, choosing those nobles who were enemies of the Glinsky family. Entrusting *them* to find the culprits did nothing to pacify the mob. The situation began to get right out of control. The houses of the Glinsky family were attacked and pillaged, and the most enraged vented their anger on the Glinskys' servants. 'Their slaves perished without number', we are told by the Chronicle, 'and many junior nobles who were reckoned slaves of the family also perished.' They now demanded the death of the head of the family, Prince Yury Glinsky, who at once sought refuge in the Cathedral of the Assumption. Ivan made no attempt to save him. The mob broke in and strangled him. Their blood-lust aroused, the Muscovites marched out of the city to Ivan's palace and demanded Yury Glinsky's brother and Anna, his mother. Ivan retreated to the innermost rooms of the palace and ordered his troops to talk to the leaders, then seize them and behead them in front of the crowd. After this, the cowed demonstrators returned to their devastated city. But this was not the end of the tragedy. During the riot in Moscow many of the citizens had been killed by Ivan's soldiers. The leaders, or men who had been given this label when arrested, were then strung up on huge gallows in Red Square. Having crushed the spirit of his long-suffering subjects in this brutal manner, Ivan then paid the Church to give his savagery its blessing, by giving the Metropolitan a large sum of money for his agreement to pray for the souls of the victims every year.

The continuing decline in personal liberty, accentuated by Ivan's grandfather, Ivan III, was now lowering the morale of the country to such a degree of backwardness and stagnation that even the most inert ruler would have felt obliged to take drastic steps. Ivan III, not surprisingly, died unmourned by his subjects; the Chronicles pass over his death in silence. Even his conquest of the Ukraine, the old provinces of Kievan Russia, seizing it from Lithuania, produced no euphoria, no elation. His reign was one of cultural depression and barrenness, with his subjects starved of the benefits of western arts and civilisation.[6] His grandson was now becoming aware of the increasing problems created by this inward-looking policy. Yet he continued to aggravate these problems by his own intense fears. He feared all criticism, and deputations from the towns no longer dared to approach him with their complaints. He was the first Russian ruler to prohibit travel abroad, being fully aware of the desire of his people to escape.[7]

In the year after the great fire of Moscow, Ivan Peresvyetov, a Lithuanian officer who had served in the Hungarian, Polish and Czech armies, wrote a commentary on the state of Muscovy, comparing it with Turkey and Europe. He attributed the backwardness of the Russians and the inefficiency of the government to the long-standing misrule of the aristocracy—the boyars. He also suggested that the 'men of the court', the junior nobles, who had pledged themselves to long periods of military and government service, be given greater responsibility. He recommended the compilation of a new legal code and, if necessary, a policy of terror to counter the opposition of the boyars for, he claimed, 'without such terror it is impossible to introduce justice in the realm'. Ivan was only too eager to apply this dose, dispensing it so indiscriminately to the poor as well as the rich, that the concept of justice was completely forgotten. Fully aware of Russia's vulnerability, especially on her eastern border, Peresvyetov advocated the conquest of the Kazan Tartars.[8] The next few years were to show the extent of the impact of this report on Ivan.

Before the end of this year of conflagration, 1547, Peresvyetov's forebodings of attack became fact. The Tartars of Kazan made numerous raids on Russian territory, to the north-east and to the south of Moscow. In mid-winter, Ivan led his army out of his capital to capture Kazan. While his men were crossing the Volga, the ice cracked under the weight of his heavy cannon; men and precious weapons sank from view. This was, without doubt, a clear sign of God's displeasure. At the height of the great fire in Moscow, two of the oldest monasteries and most of the churches went up in flames; the hallowed belfry put up by Ivan III also tumbled to the ground. Perhaps these calamities were signs of God's wrath—or were they caused by witchcraft? But now, in this holy war against the infidel Tartars, God was surely telling Ivan to stop fighting. Leaving a small force to deter further raids, he raced back to Moscow to fast and pray. Two years later he attacked again, this time leading an assault of 60,000 men right into Kazan itself. But the citadel held out against the Russians, and on the second day of the battle heavy rain silenced their guns. Ivan once more retreated. He had not yet found favour with the Almighty.

Both the Christian attackers and the Muslim defenders must have been equally confused. In the summer of the following year, 1550, he made the first democratic gesture in the history of Muscovy, calling together a general assembly of all classes. By now the people of Moscow were well aware that they were ruled by no ordinary monarch; receiving this summons, they must have expected further surprises. Ivan did not disappoint them. After much prayer and fasting, he appeared before this assembly of nobles and common people in front of the Kremlin. Turning first to Makary, the Metropolitan, he began his address:

Holy Father, I know thy loving zeal for the welfare of the fatherland. Be thou my champion in the blessed work upon which we are resolved. Early in life God deprived me of father and mother, and the boyars, without care for me, wished to rule the land themselves. In my name they stole power and honour, and grew rich by misrule; they oppressed the people and no one opposed them. In my pitiful childhood I seemed both deaf and dumb. I did not hearken to the wailing of the poor, nor did my lips utter anything. It is impossible to describe and the tongue of man cannot exaggerate, the sinful folly of my youthful days. When God took away my father, the boyars, my guardians and pastors, pretending goodwill toward me, in actual truth sought power for themselves, and in darkness of council seized and killed my father's brothers. Upon the death of my mother, the boyars usurped the Tsardom. On account of my sins, my orphanhood and youth, many people were destroyed in civil strife. I grew up in neglect, without instruction, hardened to the insidious ways of the boyars; and from that time until now, how much I have sinned before God, and what chastisements He has sent upon us!

I did not understand that God was sending great punishments upon me, and I did not repent—but continued to visit Christian people with all manner of violence. God punished me for my sins by famine and flood, but still I did not repent. At last God sent the great fires; fear entered my soul, and trembling entered my bones. I was moved and repented of my wrongdoing. I asked forgiveness of the clergy, and in turn granted forgiveness to the boyars and princes.[9]

You, you evil rebels, unjust stewards, you did what you liked in Russia. What answer will you give us now to our charge? How many tears, how much bloodshed have you caused? I am innocent of that blood, but you will receive judgement at the bar of Heaven for your misdeeds. And you, the people, given to me by God, I pray you to have faith in Him and love towards me. Be magnanimous! It is impossible to redress the wrong which is past. Only in the future can I save you from oppression and robbery. Forget what will not be repeated! Let us put away hate and enmity, and live together in Christian love. Henceforward I will be your Judge and Defender.

Showing admirable timing, he concluded his speech by announcing a major reform. Turning to Alexei Adashev, a young administrative clerk, whom he had made one of his advisers, he declared:

Alexei, I took you from the poor, one of the common people, having heard of your good deeds, and now I am seeking of you something more for the good of my soul, that you will assuage my sorrow and protect the people whom God has given into my keeping. I appoint you to gather the petitions of the poor and the afflicted.[10]

The creation of a new Office of Petitions was the first of Ivan's *prikazi* (commands), the government offices on which all subsequent ministries were modelled until the reign of Peter the Great, one hundred and fifty years later. One of these departments was the Slave Office. During Ivan's reign many new departments were established; by the end of the century there were thirty ministries. This was a rational reform, but the efficiency of the offices was impaired by unnecessary overlapping.

Ivan's National Assembly now began its work. The institution of this parliament was Ivan's most progressive act, and for the next hundred years this democratic body, called together at irregular intervals, but often at moments of crisis, was the most promising feature of the national scene. The exact composition of the assemblies is not known. For ten years, from 1613 to 1622 it was almost an annual event. During this period peasant representation was at its strongest. After the Assembly of 1653, it met twice more in limited form in 1682 and 1698. In the National Assembly of 1649 there were 40 boyars, 14 senior members of the clergy, 153 members of the gentry, and 94 merchants. Only in the last of these full assemblies, in 1649 and 1653, were the gentry and the merchants so preponderant.

One of the main purposes of Ivan's first Assembly was to gather from the members their complaints against the laws of the country. These were based on a code drawn up by Ivan III in 1497, which did nothing to improve the lot of the average Russian and led to much confusion.

The Tsar's huntsman in battle with a bear, from a painting by A. Vasnetsov (*Novosti Press Agency*)

A flogging, from a seventeenth-century print of the Palmkvist Album in the Moscow State Historical Museum (*Novosti Press Agency*)

Ivan the Terrible showing his jewels to Sir Jerome Horsey, the English Ambassador, from a painting by A. Litovchenko (*Novosti Press Agency*)

As a result of these complaints, Ivan, helped by his chief secretary, Adashev, and the Metropolitan, produced the following year a new code in which many of the conflicting clauses relating to the different provinces were ruled out. Much of the authority that had previously been the princes' and the nobles' was thus concentrated in Ivan's hands. The selection of judges was made more efficient, and in this too Ivan increased his power.

Another important reform at this time established a system whereby 'district elders' could be elected locally to deal with robbery and murder, and other crimes. They were given a free hand to judge and execute offenders. Tax assessors were also organised on a local basis.

Ivan had another purpose in calling together this National Assembly. It was his first blow against the nobles, his life-long enemies. In reviling them in his introductory speech, he was not merely playing to the gallery; he was stating his profound hatred of the class which stood in his dictatorial way. The very idea which gave Ivan's reign such ruthless impetus—the sanctity of the autocrat—lay in direct opposition to the principle whereby the princes regarded the tsar as *primus inter pares*—first among equals. This was a conflict as fundamental as the difference between the two languages, Greek and Latin, used to express these principles.

Ivan's hatred of his own aristocracy created a tragic flaw in every town and village in Russia. No country can prosper when the ruling class is divided against itself, when engaged in a continuous civil war, in which both monarch and nobility fear and despise each other. The war did not cease at Ivan's death; he left a legacy of divided authority and mutual contempt. In the barbaric treatment inflicted on many members of Russia's finest families, Ivan created wounds which never healed. No ruler has ever carried out a programme entailing great sacrifices on the part of the common people without first surrounding himself with a body of obedient supporters, dependent upon him for their material well-being. Until now the boyars had been the Grand Prince's chief supporters and executors of his will. But as each Grand Prince had become steadily more autocratic, and as each generation added to the antiquity of his line, so the nobles had become more proud of their own independent position. And this pride Ivan, with his abnormally developed sense of his own supreme importance, could not tolerate.

Russia, after the collapse of the Byzantine Empire, was the senior Christian Orthodox realm—a country chosen by God to lead the world

73

in the only true faith. It must be remembered that until the nineteenth century, religion was not only more widely and deeply felt, but it was also the repository of men's political beliefs, evoking the same fervour that nationalism evokes today. Ivan III felt that the mantle of the last Byzantine Emperor had fallen upon his shoulders as the only powerful Orthodox sovereign. He and his descendants saw themselves as the spiritual head of all Orthodox believers, in Russia, Lithuania, Poland, and in the Turkish Empire. The Byzantine crest, the two-headed eagle, became the royal crest of Russia, and the title of Tsar was adopted, as it reinforced the belief in Russia's spiritual superiority as the inheritor of the one true religion handed down, through Byzantium, from Rome. The completely fallacious legend was also fostered that Rurik, the founder of the dynasty of the Grand Princes of Moscow, was a descendant of the Roman Emperor Augustus. Yet another fabrication was the story that the Apostle, St Andrew, had travelled from Greece up the River Dnieper and had placed a cross on the hill where Kiev now stands. He had, the Russians were told in their early Chronicle, blessed and baptised the local inhabitants and forecast the building of many Christian churches in the land.[11] Ivan was thus blessed from the start with subjects used to subjection and a nobility cravenly impressed by their monarch's aura of divinity.

The first westerner to write about Russia was Sigmund von Herberstein. An account of his two diplomatic missions to Moscow in 1517 and 1526, during the reign of Basil III, on behalf of Maximilian I and Ferdinand I, was published in Vienna in 1549 when Ivan the Terrible was planning his first major reforms. Herberstein's book *Moscovia*, appearing first in Latin, then in German, was a great success and was often republished. There were eighteen editions in its first four decades. His work contained many revealing facts about Ivan's unknown country and the life led by his countrymen:

All in the land call themselves their prince's slaves. The Grand Duke exercises his power over both clergy and laymen, both property and life. None of his councillors has ever dared to gainsay his lord's opinion. One and all agree that their lord's will is the will of God.

It is debatable whether such a people must have such oppressive rulers, or whether the oppressive rulers have made the people stupid. Basil III has been unfortunate in war, yet his people called him successful. When there remained not the half of his troops, they dared to say they had not lost a man. He holds one and all in the same subjection.

If ever they talk to us of Lithuania, they speak mockingly of it, saying for example that when the king or grand duke there dispatches a man upon

Muscovy at the accession of Ivan the Terrible in 1533

an embassy or journey, he replies that his wife is ill or his horse is lame. 'Here this is not so', they say with a smile, 'here it is: you will ride off and obey orders if you want to keep your head upon your body.'

From trustworthy persons I have learned that the girls here rarely remain chaste beyond the age of seven, but have not heard of any credible and reasonable cause. It is not forbidden to merchants to have their pleasure of them, but it is to carry them off. And he who permits himself to carry one off and is caught loses both life and property.

The boyars might be considered nobles in our country. *Boy* in Wendish [the language of the western Slavs in what is now East Germany] means war, so that the boyars might be called warriors. The servants of the wealthy have all been bought among their own or captured people. The peasants are allotted a patch of ground with which they must be content and are a pitiable people, their lives and property the prey of the nobles, and soundly thrashed as well.

A man who sues for the hand of someone's daughter is despised. It is the father who chooses the suitor, saying to him: 'I approve of you and therefore offer my daughter in marriage.' The young man replies: 'I will speak to my friends about it.' If both sides think well of it, negotiations are concluded and the wedding-day named. If the bridegroom wishes to see his bride before the marriage, the father says: 'Ask other people. They will tell you what she is like.' When the bridegroom is committed but the agreement not yet firm, he may not see the bride before the wedding and its consummation.

The wedding guests rarely if ever present money, but other gifts. The bridegroom takes careful note of the source of each present. After the wedding he looks over the presents to see what he intends to keep, sending it to the market for valuation. He returns all the others to where they came from, with a word of thanks. What he has kept he pays for within the year, or cancels the obligation with other gifts. Although they like to conceal it, divorce is commonplace, and bills of divorce are issued.

They do not speak of adultery nor pay regard to it. Their affection for their wives is indifferent, for they take them unseen and must put up with them. No woman who walks in the street is deemed chaste or respectable. The wealthy keep their women so shut up that no one can see or speak to them. They entrust them with nothing beyond spinning and sewing. Women are rarely allowed to go to church, and much less often to visit friends, unless they are grown so old as to be beyond attention and suspicion. Women and their daughters are allowed to assemble in the meadows in summer. There a wheel is commonly rigged up in such a way that one or more who sit upon it are whirled round and round from the bottom to the top. These frolics often bring bad falls. They have no dancing.

Fasts. The fast before Easter they call the great fast and observe them seven weeks long. The later fasts: from the Monday of Trinity week to St Peter's Day. Then comes the fast of Our Lady, lasting from the first day of August until the Assumption. In Advent they fast six whole weeks. The fasting of the monks is much more strict, who may comfort themselves only with a drink, that is common water thickened with gruel or dough. Public confessions and the feast and fast days of the coming week are announced by the priests on Saturday.

The sturdy young lads commonly have some ground within the town where they gather on holidays. As the custom is, one of them gives a whistle, upon which they rush upon each other, striking and punching each other with fists, knees and feet in the face, throat, belly or genitals, so that some are always carried off half dead.

Highwaymen are treated with the severest justice. When captured, their heels are cut off or crushed and they are left lying a day or two until these swell, and it is thus that they are carried about. In their suffering they will answer any questions. When one of them is found guilty, he is hanged. They have no other form of execution unless the culprit is guilty of grave crimes. I have seen men hanging whose feet had fallen off or been eaten by wolves, and seen wolves eating them, so close to the ground are they strung up. Many criminals are taken off to Moscow and other towns. Courts concerned with these matters are held only in winter, the summer being taken up with military business.

The Russians are cunning and deceitful in their trade, making bold to offer their wares at three times their value, and to take the seller's at less than half their worth. They will often delay a month or two.

The Grand Duke leaves his men little rest. He is usually at war . . . Their single tactic is to attack or flee in haste. When they go forth against the enemy, their comfort lies in their numbers. They strive at all costs to outflank him and fall upon him from the rear.[12]

Having reorganised the secular life of Muscovy by his legal and administrative reforms, Ivan now turned his penetrating gaze on the Church. Of all classes, the Russian clergy had been the least disturbed by the Mongol invaders and their own grand princes. Now the people were to see that not even the House of God was to escape the scrutiny of their new master. Only a few months after the new legal code had been drawn up, the bishops and abbots of the realm were summoned to Moscow to give an account of their stewardship. They were first treated to an address by the Tsar, in which he recounted yet again his story of hard luck and the justified displeasure of God. With forceful rhetoric he called upon his flock to join with him in condemnation of his sins: 'Convict me in them', he commanded; 'thunder abroad the Word of God that my soul may live!' [13]

The clergy then listened to an explanation of the principal clauses of the new legal code and were asked to give them their approval. This they did without protest. Now came a less welcome task. Ivan and his two principal advisers, Adashev, the clerk, and Sylvester, a priest, had drafted a lengthy questionnaire covering every ecclesiastical activity.

The two features of Church life that Ivan wished to investigate and eliminate were the great temporal power and the sexual immorality of the monasteries. The astonished clerics also had to answer questions designed to uncover errors that had been made in copying religious texts; evidence of heresy and departure from the authorised ritual were also hunted. The more intelligent priests could not have been justifiably surprised by this inquiry. Since the introduction of Christianity in the tenth century, life in the monasteries had alternated between periods of grim asceticism and hedonistic license; both these forms of conduct were operating at this time. Convents had been conveniently sited close to monasteries; hours of prayer had been forgotten.[14] In addition, the Church had become a vast and prosperous agricultural corporation, built up by grants of land from the government to promote colonisation, and also from good and bad men alike to ensure safe conduct to Heaven. Enormous sums of money were also received from the faithful with this latter aim in view, money which was spent in buying up still more land. More funds came in for the 'repose of souls', in return for which prayers for the departed were offered up, their length and frequency being determined by the amount of money paid. Landowners could purchase the most expensive, most frequently repeated form of mass by donating a village in lieu of cash. Entry fees brought in still more money. These were paid by the novices, buying maintenance for life, and by old men, often on their death-beds. It was considered advisable for salvation, as the great historian Klyuchevsky put it, 'to renounce the world even a moment or two before nature had closed one's eyes to it for ever'. By donations and by business-like purchase, the monasteries now owned nearly a third of Russia.

The information obtained from Ivan's sixty-nine questions led to the announcement that further acquisition of land by the Church was forbidden. This edict proved ineffective; Ivan was a convinced Christian. A practice so firmly rooted required the determined, anti-clerical axe of Peter the Great to bring it to an end. In his efforts to combat the widespread illiteracy of the priests and to avoid further errors in transcription, Ivan announced that church schools were to be started in Moscow and the larger cities, and that in future some religious books would be printed.

Ivan did not allow these secular and ecclesiastical matters to take up too much of his time. He kept up his pressure on Kazan without respite. He conducted relations with the Tartars on two levels, placing a puppet ruler in the city and at the same time building a fortress just inside their territory on the eastern bank of the Volga, as a base for future operations. Building there went ahead rapidly and it soon became a small garrison town. It is strange that the Tartars made no attempt to dislodge the Russians from Svyazhsk, this new forward post, especially as Ivan was now threatened by the Khan of the Crimean Tartars. The Khan had recently taken Astrakhan and planned to capture Kazan. Showing undeniable boldness and a preference for poetic, rather than prosaic ultimatums, he sent Ivan this challenge:

> Thou wast young, but now hast reached the age of reason. Declare thy wish— blood or love. If love, thou wilt send gifts worthy of a prince and 15,000 gold pieces every year. When it may be thy pleasure to fight, I am ready to advance on Moscow, and all thy lands will be under the feet of my horses.

Ivan's only answer was the imprisonment of the Khan's messengers. The threatened attack came a year later, when the Crimean horde, reinforced with Turkish soldiers and several hundred camels, advanced as far as Tula, a hundred miles from Moscow. Ivan had gathered an army of 150,000 (according to contemporary records), probably nearer 100,000, and was on his way to attack Kazan. Sending only his advance guard, Ivan caught the Crimean horde unprepared and put it to flight. The captured prisoners and camels were sent back to Moscow as a foretaste of further successes.

The march to Kazan was now resumed. Ivan's puppet ruler, Shig Ali, had been summoned to Moscow to explain his courageous refusal to become a Christian. He was treated well but kept in the Kremlin. In his place Ivan had sent Prince Mikulinsky as governor. The Tartars accepted him as this only entailed taking in a handful of Russian soldiers. When the Tartars felt strong enough to defend themselves against a determined assault, they closed the gates against the governor and his men, returning one day from Svyazhsk. This was the signal for Ivan to launch his attack. Although Kazan was a military state, its rulers were divided amongst themselves and the people were by no means unanimous in favour of holding out against the Russians. But, stimulated by Ivan's pronouncements that he was waging a holy war against the 'Saracens', the pacifists were overruled and a warm reception was prepared for the invaders. All appeals to surrender were abusively rejected, the Khan declaring: 'All is ready for you here. We invite you to the feast.'

In embarking on this campaign, Russia's first seizure of non-Slav territory since the conquests of Svyatoslav and Vladimir in the tenth century, Ivan had first to overrule the opposition of his boyars. The higher clergy supported him, viewing the defeat of the infidel Tartars and the addition of Kazan to the Christian realm of Russia as being clearly desirable in the eyes of God. But the boyars saw this war in a more mundane light. They were alarmed at the way in which the young Tsar, still only twenty-two, was launching out on a campaign, the size of which was already putting a damaging strain on the country's resources in money and men. They rightly foresaw bigger and bloodier wars to come. In their opinion, the levying, arming and upkeep of this army of around 100,000 men would entail an impoverishment of the population that the results of the campaign could not justify. The subsequent history of Russia shows most clearly the disregard by one individual of the economic state of the country, as so often the ruler has sacrificed the ruled in the execution of great projects and wars of conquest which would, it was hoped, benefit the descendants of the sacrificed. Ivan's invasion and conquest of Kazan had an immediate and lasting beneficial effect, giving security to the whole of eastern Russia, since at this time Kazan was the only powerful military state between Moscow and the north Pacific Ocean. But the Russians were subsequently to suffer again and again for enterprises that yielded no benefit to their descendants.

The assault on Kazan began in late August of 1552. The Tsar was fully confident of success; he learnt the night before that the defenders numbered only 30,000. Ivan's strength was greatly increased by artillery of advanced design and the presence of a Danish mining engineer, whose task was to blow up the mud and timber defences of the town. Standing behind a banner bearing the image of Jesus Christ, Ivan gave the order to advance. Choosing the role of high priest, rather than that of military captain, the young Tsar now thought it a propitious moment to offer up a general prayer to the Almighty and the advance was halted. The Tartars were already aware of the Muscovites' approach, roused by the sound of drums and trumpet blasts. Now they had still more time to prepare their welcome. The Russians resumed their advance and entered the town without opposition, as the defenders had retreated into the citadel. From here they rushed out suddenly, threw themselves on the Russians and drove them out with great slaughter.

On the following day, the Russians suffered a further reverse. A great storm blew down most of the tents and sank many of the boats on the Volga in which lay the food supply, much warm clothing and ammunition. This time Ivan was allowing nothing to deflect him from his goal, and orders were given for further supplies to be sent up and preparations to be made for a siege. Throughout September various points in the town's defences were undermined, one of them being the main water supply. By the end of the month, to prevent further delay, Ivan's generals urged him to begin the final assault. The Tsar agreed—but only after his men had all confessed their sins and partaken of Holy Communion.

When the Russians heard an explosion of their mines, the signal for them to go forward, Ivan was in safety in his field chapel. He saw no reason why he should risk his life. His troops fought their way through the crumbled walls and into the citadel. The Tartars sold their lives dearly and were slain to a man; only the women and children were spared. After the carnage was over, Ivan congratulated his soldiers, calling them 'Macedonians, worthy descendants of those who served the Grand Prince Dmitri Donskoi when he defeated the great Khan Mamai'.

Leaving 5,000 men in the town, and inviting those Tartars who had escaped slaughter by hiding in the surrounding forests, to return and continue their trades, Ivan began a leisurely and triumphal return to his capital. On his way a messenger brought him the joyous news that his Tsarina Anastasia had given birth to a son. Entering Moscow he was given a hero's welcome. To commemorate the great victory, this high noon of Ivan's reign and of medieval Russia, a great cathedral was planned, the weirdly wonderful, fantastic Cathedral of the Intercession of the Blessed Virgin. It may be that both Ivan himself and the Metropolitan Makary had a hand in the general design, an extraordinary mixed-up assembly of conflicting styles, Greek, Roman, Byzantine, Arab, Gothic and Tartar, with elements of the temples of Babylon and Assyria. Several architects were brought from Italy; only three of them are named in the Kremlin archives, Julian Aristo, Philip Manzio and Marcellini.[14] In 1896 and 1957 manuscripts were discovered which mention a Russian architect who was also engaged in creating this fine muddle, Posnik Yakovlev, nicknamed Barma, or the incomprehensible.[15] These architects completed their work in six years.

In 1588, four years after the death of Ivan the Terrible, a small chapel was built next to the cathedral over the grave of a 'Fool in Christ'— Basil, who had courageously denounced Ivan as an evil man in the streets of Moscow. These Fools were fanatical itinerant preachers who were considered mad but holy. Ivan, far from sane and never holy, may have helped as a pall bearer at Basil's funeral. After Ivan's funeral,

Basil was canonised, and the whole splendid building was named the Cathedral of Basil the Blessed. Shakespeare would have relished this rich mixture of ironic symbolism and significant paradox.

Around the central octagonal tower stand four large and four smaller octagonal towers. Each tower and dome is of different height and surface texture; each is coloured differently. They all combine to make a masterpiece of riotous asymmetry. The central tower is crowned by a brightly coloured tent-shaped roof. In addition to the marvellous mixture of exotic styles, there are reminders of the traditional wooden churches of old Russia. During recent restoration work many frescoes painted during the reign of Ivan the Terrible were discovered. Contrasts abound in the cathedral, especially in the bold colours used in the central gallery, with its flower patterns in turquoise and bright crimson. One great composer who loved the cathedral was Modeste Moussorgsky: 'St Basil's puts me in such a romantic mood that it seemed to me that a boyar in a long caftan and a tall hat would pass by at any minute.'

Ivan placed this house of God so that it looked onto the *Lobnoye Mesto*, the Place of Execution, a circular platform on which countless men suffered diabolical torment before they died. *Lobnoye Mesto* means literally the forehead place, or the place of skulls; it is also the Russian term for Calvary. Ivan and his son, the heir to the throne, sat together on this platform on some occasions and watched men dying in agony. In the *byliny*, the popular verse legends, this spot is particularly abominated. This is the place 'where terrible executions are carried out, where eyes are put out from their sockets, and tongues are torn out from their roots'. [16] The most recent twist in the story is the decision of the atheistic Communist government to make St Basil's, the only important cultural achievement of Ivan's reign (apart from another cathedral at the St Sergei and the Trinity Monastery), just a branch of their State Museum. This embarrassing example of divine inspiration is the most spectacular, original and impressive building in the vast Red Square. In the official Moscow Short Guide (1977), in English, there are fifty photographs; not one is of St Basil's.[17] This great Asiatic cathedral, with its twisted, criss-cross, ridged and spiky domes, is a fine memorial of a monarch in whose brain fantasy and fact struggled for supremacy.

4

The Russian Sickle

For a few months, towards the end of 1552, Ivan's sun shone brightly. He was young; his beloved wife had produced an heir to the throne; and his army had returned home victorious. He was not content with the capture of the Khan of Kazan, Edigei; a public confession and conversion would demonstrate to all his subjects the superiority of the Christian God over the despised Muslims. After four months spent in the Kremlin, the Khan appeared before the Muscovites. A hole was made in the ice of the River Moskva, and watched by Ivan, the Metropolitan and the Court he was solemnly immersed and baptised as a Christian. He was asked if any violence had been used to bring about this dramatic change. This was denied and the proceedings were brought to a close with his statement that: 'I hate Mahomet. I love Jesus.'

The Russians were not allowed to rejoice over their great victory for long, for the hand of God struck at Novgorod and Pskov towards the end of 1552. Within a year an ulcerous plague had slain perhaps half a million people in these cities and the surrounding areas. And in the following year Ivan himself was suddenly laid low with a fever which brought him near to death. From now on his days were no longer cloudless. He was already intensely jealous of his position and only too ready to destroy any man who might lessen his power. Now he became abnormally jealous—and abnormally afraid of the wrath and power of God. He was obviously being punished for his sins. From what he thought was his deathbed, he witnessed for the first time an act of real disobedience. He summoned all the Court to his bedside to swear allegiance to his infant son, Dmitry. Only seven boyars and a few palace officials turned up. Neither Adashev nor Sylvester, his advisers, came. As deaths from natural and unnatural causes were such common, everyday events at this time, the boyars had good reason, tinged with optimism, that this highly dangerous sovereign would also be eliminated. The boyars had begun to transfer their allegiance to Prince Vladimir, Ivan's cousin and the son of Andrei, whom Ivan's mother had persecuted and killed. Vladimir was the most likely successor by virtue of rank, prestige and ability. Ivan's brother Yury had neither the desire nor the capacity to rule; his son, Dmitry, was still a baby. The boyars had no wish to return to a period of regency, in which the Tsar's wife and her family would hold the reins. At the battle for Kazan, Prince Vladimir had been the real hero, and he had been given a great ovation when the army came back to Moscow.

But Ivan was not dying. Vladimir and his supporters now came to the royal bedchamber and swore allegiance. The fiery fever, as it was then known, still raged; but Ivan was sufficiently conscious to take note of the latecomers. His nobles had been rash enough to talk amongst themselves and express their dislike of his wife's ambitious family within earshot of the Tsar; they had thought that it was only a matter of hours before he expired. His recovery was as rapid as his collapse, and he surprised the Court by his mildness. Outwardly all was well; inwardly he sank into greater feelings of distrust. After his recovery, he resolved to make a pilgrimage to the northern monastery of St Cyril, and there give thanks to God. Against the advice of his advisers, who wished him first to restore order in the newly won region of Kazan, where harsh measures had led the Tartars to rebel, Ivan set out with his wife, son and brother on this pilgrimage. Sylvester and Adashev tried in vain to persuade him to stay in Moscow. They saw an opportunity of completing the task begun by the capture of Kazan. If an army were sent now to Astrakhan at the mouth of the Volga, the whole river would be theirs, and this could be achieved before the Crimean Tartars could launch a major attack. But Ivan would not listen; the royal party made its way, mostly by boat, through desolate country to this monastery of hallowed memory where his mother had successfully prayed to God for a son. But before they reached their destination, the precious heir to the throne, for reasons unknown, grew weak and died. What Ivan and Anastasia thought, with their profound belief in the unquestionable justice of all acts of God, can easily be imagined. With that fear of a God of Wrath, handed down from Byzantium and the Old Testament, and the ancient Greek belief in the ruthlessness of offended Deity, Ivan plunged still further into prayer and supplication.

On his return to Moscow, he sent his army to punish the rebellious Tartars of Kazan and to press forward to Astrakhan. The citizens of this town were given a hideously frightening warning of what might be in store for them. After the conquest of Kazan many of the inhabitants killed by the Russians were stripped naked, and their bodies were piled up in a heap. Then, we learn from Heinrich von Staden:

> The ankles or feet of the corpses were tied together, and afterwards a long log was taken and stuck between their legs. Then were they thrown into the Volga, twenty, thirty, forty or fifty on a log. The logs with the bodies floated downstream. The Khan of Astrakhan learned of this. He became terrified and fled to the Khan of Crimea, leaving Astrakhan undefended.[1]

The garrison fled before the Russians arrived; the Volga, the great trade route to the Caspian Sea was now entirely Russian. This great and easy victory was preceded by the birth of another heir, named Ivan after his father. After all, the fortunes of the young Tsar, now aged twenty-six, might still prove just as bright as they had promised to be four years earlier. After the capture of Astrakhan, the Russian horsemen rode still further south, as far as the Caucasus Mountains, and the Orthodox Christian prince of the eastern Georgian province of Kakhetia asked for Russian protection. But not until the beginning of the nineteenth century did Russia feel strong enough to extend her border beyond the River Terek. Ivan ordered a city to be built on this river, but he abandoned the project, wisely reluctant to antagonise the Turks of the Ottoman Empire.

After the conquest of Astrakhan a tragi-comedy was staged in the Red Square before a large crowd of Ivan's already bewildered subjects. An envoy from the Shah of Iran had brought with him, as a gift to the Tsar, a very large elephant. Its trainer claimed that it had been taught to bow in the presence of the Tsar of All Russia. People were invited to the Red Square to see this animal and watch it do homage to their lord. After some hours of admiration and general merry-making, the boyars came out of the Kremlin and Ivan took his seat on a huge throne in the middle of the square. The noble animal was brought forward and commanded to bow before the sovereign. In rehearsal all had been well, but now the elephant refused to obey. The merry occasion was then made a ridiculous tragedy by Ivan's hysterical reaction. This magnificent creature, the first the Russians had ever seen, was angrily sentenced to death. 'Cut it to pieces!' was the royal command, which was there and then carried out by his newly formed regiment of musketeers. If they had used their muskets, death would have been swift; but Ivan's orders had to be obeyed to the letter. The Shah's enormous present was attacked and killed by axes and lances.

There would now be no more Tartar raids from the east; but from the south, from the Crimea, Russia was still vulnerable. Raids into her southern provinces were a frequent occurrence. Sometimes the Tartars numbered as many as 200,000. They captured men, women and children, and sold them to Asia Minor and north Africa as slaves. On one of these round-ups, as many as 130,000 Russians were taken, if the figures given by contemporary records can be regarded as accurate. Boys and girls whose parents had been killed or captured were rounded up and carried away in nets. A Lithuanian on his way to the Crimea from Kiev saw a line of Tartars returning from one of these forays: 'Returning from an expedition to Russia, the Tartar bands were bringing back thousands of children of both sexes, in nets tied to their saddles. The children were weeping and wailing. Their hands and feet were bound with leather thongs. Just before they came to Perekop, the Tartar commander gave a sign, at which the horsemen stopped and killed all those children who were sick. They threw the children's bodies into a cess-pit, mutilated and sometimes defiled before their slaughter.' After one clash with Russian troops, the Tartars withdrew leaving 25,000 prisoners, of whom 15,000 were children.[2]

Ignoring Adashev, Sylvester and the rest of his advisers, Ivan withdrew his army from his devastated southern provinces, leaving the peasants there wide open to further deportations by the Tartars. He now embarked on the second major war of his reign—this time to the west. The princes of Moscow had never shown the slightest desire to co-operate with the other Russian princes on an equal footing; they had never shown the slightest desire to establish friendly relations with neighbouring countries. States which were obviously more powerful were left alone; those who were weaker were regarded as potential areas of plunder. Foreigners were treated exactly as the Russians themselves were treated, as inferior creatures, potentially dangerous but possibly worth cultivating if they could provide something which could increase the power of the army. Russia's western neighbours, Poland, Lithuania and Sweden, were not once approached diplomatically by the Russians in any attempt to converse and collaborate in a peaceful atmosphere. They were always treated as potential enemies, and they were justifiably on their guard against further Russian expansion. In their desire to show good will and understanding of Ivan's wars against the west, historians, both Russian and western, have forgotten to show good will towards, and understanding of those countries at the receiving end of Ivan's, and later Peter's, wars. Bernard Pares, for example, says that Ivan 'was one of the earliest and most far-sighted of Russian statesmen; in the hereditary struggle with western enemies, he desired to develop his one free outlet to the west (through Archangel), by which alone he could make sure of obtaining those military and technical experts or materials which he needed to face his enemies on more equal terms.'[3] This, surely, is wisdom after the event. A struggle—war after war after war—may be 'hereditary', but that in itself does not justify it. It merely means that a certain policy, in this case one of suspicion, threat and encroachment, is found to be successful and is carried out generation after generation. In Pares's context, 'hereditary' is used to imply inevitability, as if this was a war Ivan had to wage.

There was nothing inevitable about Ivan's wars against Poland and Lithuania. Neither country could be accused of rigid militarism or aggressiveness. Lithuania, as already mentioned in Herberstein's observations, was looked down upon by the Russians on account of their disobedience towards their sovereign; Poland's undoing lay in their relaxed, democratic attitude to monarchy, each king becoming less and less free to maintain control. On the death of Sigismund Augustus, the last of the Jagieilo dynasty, in 1573, the gentry chose Henry of Valois, later Henry III of France, to be their sovereign. A year later he escaped to France, as he could not accept the many restrictions placed upon him. Shortly before this, in 1569, Lithuania and Poland were united under one king and government. The Orthodox believers were persecuted for their religion, which gave the Russians an additional, holy motive for expansion, but in Russian territory no one was allowed to adhere to Roman Catholicism.

The harmony that existed between Lithuania and Poland, which enabled them to unite their two countries, was of course greatly assisted by their shared religion. But there was nothing inevitable about it, and there was nothing inevitable about the complete non-cooperation and bitter hostility between these two countries and Russia, between the western and the eastern Slavs. Racially they had much in common as the majority in all three countries were Slavs. All were Christian; what is more, the Poles and the Russians both speak a similar tongue, and in Lithuania, the officials at this time were mainly Polish and the gentry soon became of Polish disposition in education and culture. There was no natural barrier keeping these Slavs apart; Russia had much to gain from importing Polish and Lithuanian experts and technology. She chose to make no attempt to negotiate in the normal way, as between two states on an equal footing. While Russian historians have been listened to by western historians, Polish and Lithuanian historians have been ignored.

The same one-sided view has been taken when considering Russia's attempts to establish seaports, especially those with warm water. Scant attention has been paid by western historians to those people who happened to be living in coastal areas around the Baltic and the Black Sea, which the Russians wished to annex. During World War I, to keep Russia in the conflict, western statesmen promised to give her Constantinople at the end of the war, thereby surrendering this magnificent warm-water port which Russia had attacked in the days of Kievan Russia, and had been actively striving for during the greater part of the nineteenth century. Fortunately the new masters in the Kremlin, once they had assumed control in 1917, repudiated every agreement the Tsar had concluded with the bourgeois west. The second grandson of Catherine the Great was christened Constantine as it was hoped that one day he would become the first Russian governor of Constantinople.

Here lies the reason why no serious attempt was made to establish friendly relations with the western Slavs. Right from the start of Russian history, there has been a triple strand of aggressive foreign policy. There is the original, basic element of acquisition, the employment of the army to take over the produce and the manpower of weaker neighbours. Next came the ethnic excuse for expansion, the desire to bring all neighbouring Slavs under one centralised control. Then came the religious or ideological impulse, the divine mission to bring all members of the Orthodox Christian faith under one banner. For these reasons, the Poles, the western Slavs, and the Finns, whose forbears in the days of Kievan Russia occupied northern Russia, and the Yugoslavs, the southern Slavs, have never felt convinced that one day their land would not be attacked and brought under the direct control of Moscow.

When the Christian government of Russia collapsed in 1917, the new administration had an equally useful lever, Communism, with which to prise open or knock down other people's doors. That is why the name on the door, Russia, has been taken down to make way for the less frightening, less chauvinistic title of the Union of Soviet Socialist Republics. This was a club which every country could join.

The size of the Russian army under Ivan the Terrible gives a reliable indication of his uncompromising intentions. Each year his boyars had to muster 65,000 recruits to be ready for action by the end of March. In one of his campaigns in Lithuania his forces numbered 300,000. The gentry owned land in Russia only on condition: they had to fight whenever called upon and they had to supply horses for an enormous division of cavalry. Added to these forces was a large contingent of

A retrospective portrait by V. M. Vasnetsov (1848–1926) of Ivan the Terrible
(*Novosti Press Agency*)

A sculpture of Ivan IV, reconstructed after an examination of his skeleton by the Soviet anthropologist, M. Gerasimov (*Novosti Press Agency*)

Tartars. There was insufficient money available in Russia, even if Ivan had chosen to live in peace with his western neighbours; only the most senior officers, or generals, were paid yearly. Other officers might receive money once in four years; the rest were paid nothing. They lived off the land, so it was obviously less damaging to the already miserable state of the economy if they lived off somebody else's land. Conditions of land tenure stated exactly the number of recruits the owner had to find. Enrolment began at the age of fifteen.[4]

Other rulers faced with such poverty would have decided that they could not afford crippling wars of conquest. A western visitor to Russia, Antony Jenkinson, reported on conditions seen around the country at this time:

> There are a great number of poor people among them which die daily for lack of sustenance, which is a pitiful case to behold. A great many are forced in the winter to dry straw and stamp it to make bread thereof. In the summer they make good shift with grass, herbs and roots; barks of trees are good meat with them at all times. There is no people in the world, as I suppose, that live so miserably; and the most part of them that have sufficient for themselves are so unmerciful that they care not how many they see die of famine in the streets.

Jenkinson also noticed how often the peasants found consolation in drink which, in Tartar fashion, was produced and sold as a nationalised industry:

> One common rule is amongst them, if the woman (the wife) be not beaten with the whip once a week, she will not be good. They are great talkers and liars, flatterers and dissemblers. The women be very obedient to their husbands, and go not often abroad [away from the house]. I heard of men and women that drank away their children and all their goods at the Emperor's taverns.[5]

Jenkinson was the first westerner to journey to Ivan's new possession of Kazan and Astrakhan. He found the land around the lower Volga a desert, after the recent slaughter. Famine and disease had reduced the population still further; 100,000 had died in the last couple of years. The miserable survivors might have been converted to the Christian faith, wrote Jenkinson, 'if the Russians themselves had been good Christians, but how should they show compassion to other nations when they are not merciful unto their own?'

Many Tartar children, he found, could be bought for the price of a loaf of bread. It was this vast, poor, hungry and mainly unpaid army that Ivan was sending to the frontiers of Poland and Lithuania, two

countries which offered richer plunder than was to be found among the
Crimean Tartars. The soldiers had to plunder to live, and it was of
course more enjoyable to plunder another population rather than their
own. Another observer, Richard Chancellor, the first Englishman in
Russia, was dismayed when he found that none of the soldiers, except
foreign mercenaries, received any pay, and that farms and land in
general reverted to the state if the owner had no sons. The old and
disabled were also penalised; a man could be turned out of his house or
cottage if 'he was stricken in age or maimed; and he may not once
repine thereat and cannot say as we, the common people of England
say, if we have anything, that it is God's and our own'. Chancellor
reported that men accused of anything were beaten until they confessed
guilt, and that debtors became slaves:

> The poor are innumerable and live most miserably. I was told that it was a
> great deal merrier living in prison, but for the great beating. [In prison]
> they have meat and drink without any labour and get the charity of well
> disposed people; but being at liberty they get nothing. The Tsar never goes
> to the field himself with under two hundred thousand men; all his men are
> horsemen, all archers. Their armour is a coat of mail with a skull on their
> heads. They are a kind of people most sparing in diet and most patient in
> extremity of cold, above all others. A soldier's drink is cold water from the
> river, mingled with oatmeal, and this is all his good cheer, and he thinketh
> himself well and daintily fed therewith; the hard ground is his feather bed
> and some block or stone his pillow; and as for his horse, he is, as it were, a
> chamberfellow with his master, faring both alike. How justly may this
> barbarous and rude Russ condemn the daintiness and niceness of our
> Captains, who, living in a soil and air much more temperate, yet commonly
> use furred boots and cloaks? As often as the Russians are to skirmish with
> the enemy, they go forth without any order at all, but lying for the most
> part in ambush, do suddenly set upon their enemy.[6]

From 1556 until 1583, the year before Ivan's death, Russia was
almost continually at war. Invading Livonia and Estonia, the two
provinces that to their cost lay defenceless between Russia and the
Baltic, Ivan's troops met with resistance from the people themselves,
incensed by their brutality, as well as from Poland, Lithuania and
Sweden. The people here were not Slavs; they spoke, and still speak
their own language, Estonian, being members of the Finno–Ugrian
race, which spread as far east as the Urals, and as far south as Hungary
and Transylvania, in Roumania. At this time the area was a power
vacuum, ruled by the once powerful but now effete German Knights of
the Sword, descendants of the Germans defeated by Alexander Nevski

three hundred years before. Lithuania and Sweden naturally had plans for this strategically desirable area themselves, and have been criticised for this as if, for some unstated reason, such an acquisition was morally wrong, while the same area could be taken by Russia with perfect rectitude. The only reason for this illogical double standard, which some westerners were to apply to subsequent territorial gains by Russia, is a misplaced sympathy for the underdog. Because of Russia's poverty, her chronic backwardness and her lengthy frontier, she has been exonerated when a richer or smaller country has been eaten into or demolished. Sympathy for the weak is commendable, but the Russian army never has been weak. If the armies of her neighbours had not been weaker than her own, she would not have been able to expand to her present size.

The difficulty of this problem lies in the hard fact that Russia is a land-locked country. The Baltic and the Black Sea have the only coastlines which could give her direct contact with western Europe, in the sixteenth century leading the world in cultural and commercial progress. The Estonians and the Crimean Tartars were thus doomed to extinction as independent states as they lay between Russia and the sea. For this reason few tears have been shed for either state. What is undeniable is Russia's need of direct maritime contact with the west; what must be deplored is the cost in human lives, both Russian and non-Russian, that these conquests entailed.

Ivan's first battle was against Sweden in 1556. His troops advanced and seized Viborg (now just south of the Russo–Finnish border), and the King of Sweden, Gustavus, distracted by Danish rivalry for supremacy in the Baltic, sued for peace. In the following year, 1558, Ivan advanced against the Knights of the Sword and the Lithuanians, and captured the Estonian port of Narva. The campaign continued with Poland joining the war in alliance with Lithuania in 1562. All the early Russian victories were annulled by costly defeats, and at last a truce was signed in 1582. In 1575 Sweden re-entered the war, recouped its losses and imposed peace on Ivan in 1583. During these twenty-seven years of war, Ivan was seldom near the battle areas. He spent most of the time raising fresh armies and fighting the enemy he imagined lay at home—the boyars, those who could have helped the country to lift itself out of the vicious circle of poverty, heavy taxation and depopulation caused by flight, hunger and disease.

During this long and debilitating war, Ivan's soldiers fought with great fortitude and patience. Richard Chancellor, who returned to

England in 1556 with Russia's first ambassador to this country, made this revealing comment about them:

> If they knew their strength, no man were able to make match with them, nor they that dwell near them should have any rest of them. But I think it is not God's will; for I may compare them to a young horse that knoweth not his strength, whom a little child ruleth and guideth with a bridle, for all his great strength, for if he did know it neither child nor man could rule him.[7]

Ivan's ambassador, Osip Nepea, made a poor impression; his mission was not a success as Ivan had chosen a man like himself, deeply suspicious and morose. The English complained that 'he is not as conformable to reason as we thought. He thinks every man will beguile him. As the Russians do not always speak truth themselves, they think that other people are like them.'

The peasant was the chief sufferer as a result of the war with Lithuania; the whole system of agriculture in Russia was made unsound by Ivan's demands, not only on the peasant himself when taken away for service in the army, but also on his master, the landlord, who was frequently away on military service. No real co-operation could be maintained; interest in one's own estate and those who worked on it was constantly impaired. Many of the gentry were very poor, having been given land to cultivate with only one or two labourers. There were so many of these poor gentry that they were given a name, the *odnodvortsy*, men with a court of one. More and more were thus falling into debts which they could not repay, forcing them to move down the social scale into the serf or slave class. Each estate was forced to rely more and more on its own artisans, rather than those of the nearest town; trading was made a form of state service, and many townsmen who had survived by working as both tillers and artisans, were impoverished by Ivan's insistence that every single subject should be registered under one form of employment only.[8]

Life for the ordinary Russian was just as hazardous and unjust as it had been in the days of Ivan's father, Basil III. During that reign a conversation took place in the Semeonov Monastery near Moscow which explains why Russia has for so long been a country of conflict and despair. One of the ablest of the boyars, Ivan Nikitich Bersen Beklemeshev, was ordered out of the Kremlin by Basil, having disagreed with his master in a council meeting. The boyar took refuge in the monastery and there discussed the state of the country with Maxim, a

Greek monk who had been invited to Russia by the Tsar to translate some religious texts. Bersen said to Maxim:

> Our Grand Princes are worse than the Turkish sultans who rule the land of Greece today. In your homeland, justice is harsh, but it is justice of a sort, whereas here in Russia there is greater cruelty and there is no justice. The power of the Grand Prince is boundless. Even if the Grand Prince is a madman or a complete idiot, you have to submit to his will! Ours will always be an unhappy land, for the Princes will always be the masters— and the people will always be the martyrs.

The monk asked if the Metropolitan could curtail this power:

> No, most often the Metropolitan is in league with the stronger side. One crow does not peck out the eyes of another. There is nothing to hope for from him.[9]

There was nothing to hope for from the Tsar, who demonstrated the truth of these statements by executing Bersen publicly in the Red Square outside the Kremlin. Maxim, who also criticised the Church for departures from the original Christian doctrines and finding superstitions which he was asked to investigate, was sent to prison for twenty years.

Why did Ivan the Terrible persist in the Lithuanian campaign for so long with its intolerable strain on the economy? The fact that it went on for twenty-seven years has been glossed over by Russian and western historians. Reasons can be found only in the conflicts raging in his own mind and in his own obsessive, megalomaniac concept of himself as God's minister on earth. If his army had been progressively more successful, his persistence would have had an obvious explanation. In the event, Poland and Sweden deprived him of all his conquests. Other generals in other countries accepted defeat as one of the inevitable hazards of war. Defeat seems to have acted on Ivan's unbounded arrogance and paranoia as a stimulus, an incitement to further sacrifice.

Ivan was convinced that God was directing him in his battles against Lithuania, Poland and Sweden. It must have been difficult for him to fit his desire for a seaport and contact with western Europe into the context of direct communication from the Almighty; what could be more readily acceptable as divine instructions were the attempts he made to capture those towns and regions that had once been occupied by Russians during the previous six centuries. These eastern Slavs were Christians, members of the one true Orthodox Church; they should be rescued from the clutches of the inferior Roman Catholic Church. This logical but dangerous doctrine was piously endorsed by the Church in Moscow. During the reign of Ivan's father, Basil III, one of his monks, Philotheus, wrote him a letter in which this heady propaganda was triumphantly spelled out:

> The Church of Rome fell on account of its heresy; the gates of the second Rome, Constantinople, were hewn down by the axes of the infidel Turks; but the Church of Moscow, the new Rome, shines brighter than the sun over the whole universe. Thou art the ecumenical Sovereign, thou shouldst hold the reins of government in awe of God. All the empires of the Orthodox Christian faith have come into your Kingdom. Thou art the only Tsar of the Christians in the whole world. All the Christian kingdoms have been gathered into thy Tsardom. After this we await the Kingdom of which there shall be no end. Two Romes have fallen, but the third still stands, and a fourth there will not be.[10]

The damage caused by this kind of messianic poison has been long-lasting; and it has affected not only the Tsarist rulers in the Kremlin.

In the previous reign, that of Ivan III, the primate of the Russian Church had declared that 'Moscow is the new Constantinople', and both Church and state made it quite clear that ordinary mortals were not entitled to disagree with this or any other official dogma. Opposition was a criminal offence; merely having a different opinion was a sign of possible treachery. Joseph of Volokolamsk, Ivan III's leading hard-line suppressor of heretics, left no room for any doubt in the mind of any Russian wishing to preserve his own skin: 'The origin of all passions is in opinion; opinion is the second fall of man.' This blanket condemnation of other people's opinions would not be so offensive if it had come from an illiterate thug; Joseph was an intellectual. His library at Volokolamsk by the time of Ivan the Terrible contained 1,150 volumes, a large quantity for any collection at that time. At his insistence, the leaders of a new sect, the Judaisers, comparable to Protestants, were arrested, denounced and burnt to death.

Fired by this religious zeal, Ivan continued to prosecute the war in Lithuania. As it was a holy crusade, it would one day be victorious. Ever since the days of Svyatoslav, six centuries earlier, Russia's neighbours feared the Russians, a perfectly understandable reaction. Ivan's troops, reinforced by his Tartar contingent, now showed the Lithuanians just how accurate these fears were. The invaders behaved most savagely. When a town was captured, the defenders were marched through the streets and beaten with iron rods. Others were tortured and then thrown into the fields, where they were eaten by animals. There was 'such wailing, screams and cries for help', in the words of one contemporary account: 'Who can find the heart to relate all the cruelty of the blood-thirsty Tartar tyrant?' Jerome Horsey who spent eighteen intermittent years in Muscovy has described the way the people were treated in those areas taken by the Russians:

> Lamentable outcries and cruel slaughter, drowning and burning, ravishing of women and maids, stripping them naked without mercy or regard of the frozen weather, tying and binding them by three and by four at their horses' tails, dragging them, some alive, some dead, all bloodying the ways and streets full of carcases of the aged men and women and infants. Infinite numbers were thus sent and dragged into Russia.[11]

Although Ivan's soldiers were victorious for the first six years of the campaign, all was not well in the Kremlin. Sylvester and Adashev did their best to persuade him to put an end to the war but with no success. Hoping to frighten him, Sylvester even threatened him with the wrath of God if he did not withdraw his army from the west. If he did this, he was told, he could then employ his warriors in a crusade against the dangerous Tartars of the Crimea. All advice was ignored. When Ivan discussed the war with them, they vigorously urged their case. 'If I try to object', Ivan maintained, in a letter to Prince Kurbsky, 'they shout at me that my soul is lost.' Ivan sought to restrain Sylvester by reminding him of Aaron, the priest and friend of Moses who was not allowed 'to engage in the government of men'. The courageous monk was then warned by Ivan that 'a kingdom ruled by a priest always comes to ruin'. Irritated by their opposition, the Tsar resorted to insult, calling Adashev a dog which he himself had lifted from a dunghill. Relations between Ivan and these two gifted men deteriorated when they criticised his wife's family, who were trying to extend their influence in the Krem-lin, taking posts outside their capability.

In the early winter, in October 1559, Ivan and Anastasia left the capital on another pilgrimage, this time to the monastery of Mozhaisk, sixty-five miles south-west of Moscow. Receiving news of a defeat in the Lithuanian campaign, Ivan decided to hurry back to the capital, but Anastasia felt unwell. In the eight years after the birth of her first child, Anna, she had borne five other children and all but two had died in infancy. Anna and Dmitry had died after a year; Evdokia after two years, and Maria after three. Only Ivan and Feodor remained; the former was now aged five, the latter two. These frequent births and deaths may have weakened Anastasia; what she was suffering from is unknown. Perhaps the records giving this information were among the court archives burnt when Moscow was racked by fire in 1626. Her condition became worse at Mozhaisk; the medicine she should have taken was either inadequate or unavailable, and Adashev was blamed for this. She recovered enough strength to make the return journey to Moscow. Some months later there was a heated argument with Adashev, perhaps over a matter concerning her family. This emotional quarrel gave her an apoplectic seizure, and she was carried to her bed.[12] It may have triggered off another attack of the disease that brought her down in the winter. This time she was seriously ill. Lying in bed she saw clouds of smoke billowing over the Kremlin, and could perhaps hear the crackle of flames.

Moscow was once again suffering from a disastrous fire, a constant hazard in a vast town of closely packed wooden houses, especially in the dry summer. The blaze reached houses near the Kremlin, and tongues of flame reached up as high as the windows of the *terem*, the women's quarters where Anastasia lived and where she now lay dying. As the conflagration spread, she would have heard the roar of the flames and seen the red glow of destruction from her bed. Ivan took her outside the city to safety in the village of Kolomenskoye, but she still thought she was surrounded by flames. Her agony increased until she died a few days later.

Anastasia had been gentle and devout with a quiet rather than a strong personality, a decided asset in the Kremlin where tsarinas were sometimes loathed or looked down on by the senior boyars if they came from abroad or from a lower class of the nobility. Sophia, the grandmother of Ivan the Terrible, was called the Byzantine Whore by those who hated her arrogance and lack of respect towards the Court. But no one disliked Anastasia, although the senior nobility were disappointed that Ivan, unlike his grandfather or father, had not married a princess or a senior member of the aristocracy. Many Russians had died in this latest fire, and many had died in trying to put it out, but the death of Anastasia meant much to the people of Moscow. At her funeral the coffin was followed by an immense crowd, and by Ivan himself in tears.

This death was a calamity of the first order—for Ivan since she was the one stabilising, restraining force in his life—and for Russia since nothing now stood between the people and the autocrat. Jerome Horsey, who spent many years in Russia in the latter part of Ivan's reign, and who spoke the language fluently, wrote that Anastasia 'ruled him with admirable affability and wisdom'. Until now his life had been marked by genuine, if spasmodic piety; his campaigns, in the east and the west, had been victorious, and his reforms had led his subjects to hope for some improvement in their daily lives. But now Ivan was completely alone— alone with the conflicting passions of religious fanaticism and debauched sensuality. These passions, as they became intensified, provided the motives for his unrestrained cruelty. By torture and multiple slaughter, both the religious maniac and the perverted sadist in Ivan found temporary satisfaction.

5

Increasing Terror

Early in Ivan's reign, Richard Chancellor was impressed by the size of Moscow and the quantity of villages. The capital, he reckoned, was larger than London, and 'the country betwixt Yaroslav and Moscow is very well replenished with small villages, which are so well filled with people that it is a wonder to see them'. Thirty-five years later, in 1588, another English visitor, Giles Fletcher, was appalled by what he saw. This same area of Russia to the north and east of the capital was 'vacant and desolate, without any inhabitant. The like is in all other parts of the realm.' The enemy who caused such devastation was the Tsar himself. In 1571 there was a catastrophic invasion of southern Russia by the Crimean Tartars who reached Moscow. But this disaster would not have occurred on such a scale if Ivan and his army had been there to defend his people. He was four hundred miles away fighting the Lithuanians and Poles, in the quarter-of-a-century-long blood-letting which brought in the end no territorial reward for his country. After the death of Anastasia, the rest of Ivan's life was a tragedy of declining mental and bodily health—and of increasing panic and terror.

If he had died now he might have been remembered as one of Russia's most dynamic and impressive rulers. One act of wisdom was his selection of Adashev and Sylvester as his closest advisers. Adashev drew up the new legal Code of 1551 and was the leading supporter of Ivan's policy of friendship with England. (See Chapter 8.) The sudden promotion of these two commoners to positions of such influence led naturally to intense jealousy among the senior boyars, and Ivan now showed definite weakness in listening to them. They suggested that the Tsar could rule without these upstarts, and that they might have used sorcery to maintain their influence for so long.

In the spring of 1560, several months before the death of Anastasia, Ivan sent Adashev who had no military training to the front in Lithuania, where he was given a senior command, and then to take over as governor of one of the newly captured towns, Fellin. That same summer he was stripped of his command and sent to a prison at Dorpat in Livonia. After two months in prison, this brilliant man died of fever. Before life became any more unpleasant in the Kremlin, the monk Sylvester retired that same spring to the monastery of Kirillov Belozersky, realising that his advice was useless. But this was not good enough, or bad enough, for Ivan. He exiled him to the grim, northern monastery of Solovyetsk on an island in the White Sea. It is not recorded how many years, or months, elapsed before he died here. Of all the boyars and court officials, these were the only men to whose good advice he listened. Sylvester constantly stressed the advantages that could be gained by friendly diplomacy and the serious disadvantages of brute force. Adashev demonstrated the virtues of love and kindness by giving food to the poor and looking after lepers in his own house, even washing them himself, as he has told us in a book on conduct, the *Domostroy* or household management. These two advisers were now rewarded for their desertion seven years earlier when most people thought the Tsar was on his deathbed.

The court was plunged into deep mourning for Anastasia. Ivan gave large sums of money to monasteries where prayers were to be recited for the repose of her soul. One thousand roubles were given to the Troitsa monastery, and another payment was made to the distant monastery of Mount Athos in Greece for repeated masses. While the bells of Moscow's churches tolled in honour of the Tsarina, Ivan himself began to crumble. There were incitements to anger all around him. Everyone was inadequate or untrustworthy; his brother Yury was useless as a companion, being mentally deficient, and his second son, Feodor, was showing a similar tendency. He refused to see either of his sons, and sent them both away from the Kremlin. Fits of anger gave way to periods of silence. Smashing furniture and mementoes, he shouted and bemoaned his fate in front of his court, sometimes falling to the floor and banging his head on the ground.

After seven days of abject misery, he announced to his court that he was going to marry again and that there would be a great feast in the Kremlin to celebrate the good news. The royal bride, they were told, was to be Catherine, the sister of his enemy, Sigismund Augustus, King of Poland. It could have given no one any surprise when this proposal of marriage was firmly declined. Unable to resist the temptation to introduce some humour into this absurd charade, Sigismund deigned to send Ivan a substitute for Catherine, a large white mare. Ivan's reply was that he had dug a large hole in the Kremlin grounds which was specially reserved for Sigismund's head. At the Kremlin banquet marking the end of court mourning, drink flowed without restraint and, while the older boyars were shocked, Ivan urged his Court to drink their fill and put on masks. To a conscientious Christian of the Orthodox faith, any alteration of the human face, such as cutting off the beard, or covering it with a mask, was an act of blasphemy. Prince Michael Repnin refused to put one on and voiced his disapproval at this flagrant abandonment of decorum, especially repugnant coming so soon after the Tsarina's death. He had to wait only a few days before reaping the reward of his disobedience. He might have thought that he was safe while attending a service in the Cathedral of the Assumption but, since the days of Basil II, no man could count on a church or a monastery for sanctuary. During the intoning of the Gospel, Prince Michael was stabbed to death. On the same day, another senior boyar, Prince Yury Kashin was killed on Ivan's orders as he was about to enter a church in Moscow.

No reason was given for this latest killing. But, Ivan tells us in a letter to Prince Kurbsky, it was part of the war he was now waging on anyone who had supported Adashev and Sylvester. It was, in fact, a war he was waging on everyone of any ability and character. No one, not even the sycophants around him, could be trusted. Ivan singled out his two former advisers as being the chief culprits in his misfortunes. They were responsible for Anastasia's death, he maintained. Perhaps, he told a party of Lithuanian envoys, they poisoned her. At all events, Adashev failed to provide the necessary medicine:

> How I recall the merciless journey to the ruling city from Mozhaisk with our ailing Tsaritsa Anastasia. As for prayers and journeys to desert places, on pilgrimage, gifts and vows to the saints for the salvation of our soul, for our bodily health, these things were taken completely from us by your cunning scheming. As for medical skill, for the sake of our health, there was no mention of it at the time . . . For the sake of one little word from her [Anastasia], she ranked as worthless in their eyes [of Adashev and Sylvester], and they cast their anger upon her.[1]

What this word was we do not know. What we do know is that life for everyone became even more precarious. It now became clear that death was not just an ordinary punishment in the eyes of their Tsar; it was for him an obsession. In his study of the criminal mind, E. Lombroso states that 'once the horrible delight of shedding blood has been tasted, the necessity for slaughter can become so imperious that no man can master it' (*L'Uomo Delinquante*, 389). Other despots sent thousands to their deaths; none of them has been called the Terrible. Ivan earned this description by the *nature* of the deaths of his many victims. Not only did he take an active part in the torture and killing of these unfortunate Russians; he encouraged, and sometimes forced, the killers to make each death as hideously painful as possible. Other medieval tyrants, even the Mongols, were satisfied by the death of their enemies. Hitler sent several million Germans to the quick death of a gas chamber; Stalin preferred for a far greater number of Russians the slow death of forced labour; but Ivan the Terrible made special efforts to increase the agony of those about to die. Dying for him was even more interesting than death itself.

Ivan was not satisfied by the deaths of Adashev and Sylvester. Kinship or friendship with the condemned became sufficient cause for arrest, torture and death—as it has continued to be. Without any reason given, Adashev's brother and his twelve-year-old son were seized and killed. A close friend of Adashev, Maria Magdalena, a widow of great piety gifted with the power of healing, was then murdered by Ivan, together with her five sons. Adashev's cousins and brothers-in-law suffered the same fate. After the disastrous fire of 1547 and the riots in Moscow, such acts of savagery had at least been rare; now they became frequent. Ivan and Anastasia had even earned the disapproval of the court for their piety, their strict observance of religious fasts and services. The Englishman Robert Best has written that Ivan 'delight-eth not greatly in hawking, hunting or other pastimes, but in serving God and subduing his enemies'. From now on Ivan spent less time in church and far more time drinking, torturing and killing. Trying pathet-ically to justify his crimes—and he admitted them as such—he wrote in a letter to Prince Kurbsky: 'Had they [Adashev and Sylvester] not parted me from my darling, Cronos would not have had so many victims.'

Giles Fletcher found that watching bear fights with a man delighted the Tsar—'this is his recreation on the holy days'. But the punishment and elimination of his enemies, within and outside Russia, brought him no peace. Violent rages alternated with sudden fits of depression and drunkenness. But as Fletcher reminds us, such conduct was considered normal for Russians: 'To drink drunk is an ordinary matter with them every day of the week.' To defend himself from attack—and to get the blow in first—Ivan carried with him at all times a long staff, made lethal by its iron point.

Russian and western historians have sought to justify some of Ivan's hostility towards the boyars and the people in general, by suggesting

Mounted Muscovite noblemen, showing Tartar influence: quilted clothing, side-arms, saddlery, bridles are of a style that could not be found anywhere in the Europe of Herberstein in whose *Description of Moscow* (1560) this woodcut first appeared (*British Museum*)

that many of the nobles and their supporters were indeed treacherous or quarrelsome, and that they failed to support Ivan in combating the backwardness and conservatism among the nobility and the peasantry. But one looks in vain for any real attempt by Ivan to lift the peasantry out of their primitive state. Giles Fletcher has this to say on the subject:

> Their manner of bringing up, void of all good learning and civil behaviour, is thought by their governors most agreeable to that State, and their manner of government. Which the people would hardly bear, if they were once civilled and brought to more understanding of God, and good policy. This causes the Emperors to keep out all means of making it better.
>
> They are cruel one against another, especially over their inferiors. The whole country is filled with rapine and murder. The number of their vagrant and begging poor is almost infinite. They have no law to restrain whoredom, adultery and like uncleanness of life. As for the truth of his

word, the Russian for the most part maketh small regard for it, so he may gain by a lie and breach of his promise. The Russian neither believeth any thing that another man speaketh, nor speaketh anything himself worthy to be believed. These qualities make them very odious to all their neighbours, specially to the Tartars, that account themselves to be honest and just, in comparison of the Russe. The offence they take at the Russe government, and their manner of behaviour, hath been a great cause to keep the Tartar still Heathenish, and to mislike of the Christian profession.[2]

The nature of Ivan's declaration of war on his north-western neighbours is instructive. The town of Dorpat on the far side of Lake Peipus on Russia's western border, was ordered by Ivan to pay tribute money. A sum of money had been paid, under threat, to Ivan's grandfather, Ivan III, some fifty years earlier. Courageously the citizens of the town objected to this demand and withheld their agreement. The patience of the Tsar of All Russia was exhausted, and his troops crossed the frontier of the whole province. Ivan was confident of victory, placing his trust in God and superior numbers. 'By the all-powerful will of God', he proclaimed, 'since the times of the great ruler, Rurik, the Livonian lands [the country between Pskov and the Baltic] have rightfully formed part of his Tsardom.' In November 1557 he set about the execution of this divine territorial demand by appointing a Tartar, Shig Ali, as commander of an army of 40,000. Three months later, in January 1558, Russian troops began the assault. A year later, the army numbered 130,000 men. In 1560 it had grown to 150,000; by 1580 to 309,000.[3] Livonia was laid waste; all prisoners were killed, and even little children were butchered. The population was subjected to the same treatment inflicted on certain Russians in their own country. In Russia itself punishments included strangling, stabbing, hanging, burying alive, being stripped naked in the open in winter, and being mauled by bears.[4]

At Lenewarden in 1557, Ivan sentenced the aged governor, Marshal Gasperd von Munster, to death, but not before he had both eyes torn out. He was then whipped to death.[5] Commanders of other towns who resisted were stuck on pales, quartered, and hacked to pieces. At Ascheraden, on the Dvina, forty girls were rounded up in a garden and repeatedly raped. Their screams were heard across the river for four hours. One of the most distinguished Livonians, George Wieske, was impaled.[6]

Ivan's inflated idea of his own superiority made it impossible to establish any sensible relationship with the King of Poland. In 1562, Sigismund's sister Catherine, whom Ivan had said he would marry, chose instead John, Duke of Finland, the heir to the throne of Sweden. When Sigismund received Ivan's request for his sister, he indicated that he might agree, but purposely put his price too high: the surrender of Smolensk and Pskov. Ivan took this and the subsequent rejection of his suit as a personal insult, although he had invited it by such presumptuous behaviour. He mobilised an enormous army of over 200,000, half of which were from his new Asiatic territories, and launched a new assault on Livonia, the country between Pskov and the Baltic (in the present century, the area of Estonia and Latvia). Three years before this attack, the German Knights of the Sword had ceded this country to Poland. Resistance was feeble and sporadic; it was in fact useless. The triumphant Muslim Tartars and the Russians enjoyed pillaging countless Roman Catholic churches; the Protestant churches were razed to the ground. Six hundred churches in all were first robbed and then destroyed.[7] Back in Moscow a Fool in Christ, Mikula Svet, who went unclothed in summer and winter, denounced Ivan for his sins, calling him a devourer of Christian flesh.[8]

Huge sums now began to flow into Ivan's treasury. The town of Polotsk was a rich prize which the defenders hung on to for fourteen days. Here the Russians repeated their performance at Kazan, indulging in unrestrained plunder. The importance of this town, once a provincial capital in the Kievan confederacy, more than three hundred years earlier, lay in its direct communication by the western Dvina with the Livonian port of Riga. The Dvina is the ideal water route connecting north-western Russia and the Baltic. Ivan described its banks as worth their weight in silver, its waters worth their weight in gold. As in previous battles, he remained in the rear of his troops as their inspiring genius. He congratulated them on their victory and gave himself a new title, that of Grand Duke of Polotsk. Most of the inhabitants this time were spared, with the exception of one section of the community—those Jews who resisted conversion to Christianity; these men and women were drowned. Another town, Tarvast, was not so fortunate. The governor of Vilno, Nikolai Radziwill, gained a victory over the Russians and recaptured Tarvast. In September 1561, Ivan's army defeated the Lithuanians near Pernau, and then razed the whole town of Tarvast to the ground.

After the conquest of Polotsk in 1563, Ivan agreed to a six months armistice with the King of Poland. The way in which fellow Christians have fought each other for so long in this area gives a clear indication of the bitter hostility between the western, Roman Catholic Slavs and

(*above*) The small state seal of Ivan IV (*Novosti Press Agency*); (*below*) The obverse of the state seal of Ivan IV (*Novosti Press Agency*)

The Chamber of the Throne in the Kremlin, from an etching by the Hon. H. Legge, published in London in 1816 (*BBC Hulton Picture Library*)

One of the salons in the Palace of Terem at the Kremlin (*BBC Hulton Picture Library*)

the eastern Orthodox Slavs, who believed—and still do believe—in their own superiority.

Basil I began the Muscovite conquest of the old Kievan Russian lands with two inconclusive campaigns, in 1406 and 1412. Ivan III began the war again in 1492 supported by the Crimean Tartars, and there was yet another war in 1500. Two campaigns were fought by Basil III, who recaptured Smolensk in 1514. This beautiful town, a prosperous trading centre since the days of Kievan Russia, was Russia's chief loss in the north-west during the Mongol period, being seized by the Lithuanians at the end of the fourteenth century. War was declared again by Helen, the mother of Ivan the Terrible, but neither side gained a clear victory. After Ivan's death, hostilities were resumed in 1604 when the Poles took advantage of the state of collapse into which Russia fell after his catastrophic reign. The Poles took Smolensk and Moscow itself.

The Poles invaded again during the reign of Michael, the first Tsar of the Romanov dynasty; they reached the outskirts of Moscow, and then withdrew, having extracted the surrender of Smolensk. Michael tried to recapture this town in 1632 but failed. His son, Alexis, succeeded in 1654, but, unsatisfied with this victory, the war continued intermittently but ferociously until 1667. Peace was maintained between the two countries until Catherine the Great, with Prussia and Austria, subjected Poland to the shameless partitions of 1772, 1792 and 1795, after which the Poles were denied independence until 1917. The savage campaigns of 1920–1, Stalin's partition of Poland in 1939 with Hitler, and his connivance at the German defeat of the Polish rising in 1944 have served only to intensify the hate engendered by centuries of cruel injustice and count-less atrocities—a hate now stifled, but not extinguished, by the sham camaraderie of compulsory brotherhood.

Ivan's long war with Poland was only one chapter in a long and bloody conflict, but the determination and ferocity of his campaigns encouraged subsequent Tsars to pursue the same game. Poland has always enjoyed a higher standard of living than that of Russia; she has in fact served as Russia's most accessible and convenient major Euro-pean country for plundering. Russia had even more to gain by conquest than by co-operation.

Ivan the Terrible failed to follow up his victory at Polotsk with what could have been the easy defeat of the whole of Livonia. When later he made a determined effort to extend his gains, he was confronted by a brilliant strategist, King Stephen Batory. However, in 1563 the glories of a decade earlier when Kazan was conquered, were recalled once more when Ivan made another triumphal entry into Moscow. He had married again and a son had been born. His second wife was not, like his mother, Elena, of Asiatic descent, but completely Asiatic, being the daughter of Temgruk, a Circassian chief. But now, in Ivan's thirty-third year, disaster became more frequent than success. When only five weeks old, his baby son died. The hand of God struck again with the death of Ivan's brother, Yury. He was mentally backward, but Ivan had felt some affection for him, and had been able to establish some form of attachment to him. According to Kurbsky, Yury was 'born without mind, memory or speech'. Within weeks of his death, the Metropolitan Makary died. After Anastasia, he had exerted the most restraining influence on Ivan. Many considered him to be too indecisive; some thought he was a coward. But it was his misfortune to be the leader of the Church when only one man was free to speak his mind. Several times he tried to resign as Metropolitan; each time Ivan had insisted he should remain. He was the author of two books, *Legends of the Saints* and *The Book of Degrees*, a history of the Russian princes. In 1547, the year of Ivan's coronation, he persuaded the young Tsar to engage the services of several printers from Germany as a result of which religious texts were printed in Moscow, and Russia's first printing house was set up in the capital in 1561. Strict censorship was imposed from the start. In that year two biblical texts were printed, followed in 1564 by another religious treatise, *The Apostle*, and twenty short doctrinal books. The readership of these books was so small that they failed to break down the iron curtain of ignorance that separated Russia from the outside world. The country played no part in the Renaissance or the Reformation, which nurtured the concepts of human dignity and individuality. Ivan's subjects for the most part remained fettered by their own ignorance and the complete absence of any legal opportunity for protest. Complaints were called lamentations; these could result in the plaintiff being condemned to penal servitude. When Makary died, two Russians, Ivan Feodorov and Peter Mstislavets, who had learnt the dangerous art of printing and had been in charge of the Printing House in Moscow, were subjected to such suspicion and hostility from Ivan's officials that to avoid arrest they fled to Lithuania. They were harassed, von Staden tells us, by many officials who were 'ignorant and unskilled in the art of letters'.

Yet another death occurred in the royal family this same year, but this time Ivan was responsible. When his brother died, his widow, Ulyana, chose to retire to a convent and live in complete simplicity, without servants, without the comforts of her former life. For reasons known only to himself, Ivan insisted that she had servants and that her cell should be fully furnished. She refused to live in this manner, thus obstructing the royal will. Ever since his coronation, Ivan had been trying to make it clear to every man and woman that from now on no individual in Russia was entitled to disobey the state, that is to say, the dictator. He did at least show some consistency in his fury when disobeyed: Ulyana was executed.

For no other motive than covetousness, Ivan had Prince Ivan Sheremetiev tortured and killed. Ivan's desire for his wealth was frustrated, however, since he had given everything to the poor. The wretched man was tortured, as Ivan did not believe his denials that he had any money. In this greed for the possessions of his richer subjects, Ivan showed, in a crazed form, the characteristic trait of his forbears, the acquisitive grand princes of Moscow. On the road to Polotsk in January 1563, in the town of Nevel, he murdered Prince Ivan Shakhovskoy, clubbing him to death with a mace. Seeing nothing ahead but the constant threat of arbitrary arrest and torture, men of all walks of life escaped or tried to escape from their unpleasant native land. Those who were caught were returned to the estates they fled from; migration was now the greatest symptom of Russia's sickness. It was a cancer eating its way into the body of a patient already suffering from malnutrition. From the early 1550s whole villages became deserted; mass flights occurred, mainly to the south-east and south, the no man's land between Muscovy and the land of the Crimean Tartars. The Cossacks are, in fact, a whole nation which owed its existence to the tyranny of Russia, as they were all escapers and dissidents, Russians who could no longer tolerate life in Muscovy.

In sole control of this sick society was a man who, in the opinion of Otto Hoetzch, the distinguished German historian and specialist in Russian history, was 'no great statesman and even less of a hero', a man whose government 'came increasingly into conflict with the interests of the people'. When a man is reviled by his contemporaries, we are sometimes tempted to dismiss criticism if it is damning, our optimism coming to the fore and a feeling that the critic is surely not telling the truth. But critics often do reveal or indicate the truth about a man. From youth upwards, Ivan considered himself free to indulge in any excess of sexual conduct, like many another monarch all round the world. During his marriage to Anastasia, sex with other women had not been frequent, and there is no evidence of any serious attachment. But after her death, all restraint was gone. Like an eastern potentate, he kept a harem which would travel around with him. One of the duties of his henchmen was to procure girls from his empire and from newly conquered territories.[9] One of the many members of the aristocracy slain by Ivan was young Prince Dmitri Obolensky-Ovchinin, a nephew of Elena, Ivan's mother. He met his death because of one remark, to Feodor Basmanov, the son of Alexei Basmanov, at this time Ivan's favourite: 'I and my fathers have always served the sovereign usefully, but you serve by vile sodomy.'[10] Another critic of Ivan was Prince Kurbsky, who certainly would have been killed by him if he had not escaped to Lithuania. One of his accusations gives some indication of other practices:

> Even if I am laden with sins, none the less I was born of noble parents, of the family of the Grand Prince of Smolensk, Feodor Rostislavich, and princes of that generation are not accustomed to eat their own bodies and to drink the blood of their brothers—as has long since been the habit of certain other families . . .[11]

Samuel Collins and other visitors to Russia commented on the Samoyeds, the people living in the northern part of Russia, some seven hundred miles from Moscow: 'they eat those whom they conquer in battle . . . and are called man-eaters.'[12] The meaning of *samoyed* in Russian is self eater.

To assess the truth of Kurbsky's accusation, we must put it in the context of what we know of Ivan's predilection for different forms of torture and his sadistic pleasure in watching men and women in the most painful kinds of death.

Ivan was now about to take the most disastrous step of his whole reign, an administrative revolution which caused great handicap. He had already disgraced his country by his barbarically fought war in Livonia. It was conducted with great cruelty and uncertain strategy. In his diplomacy with the Poles, Ivan showed great ineptitude, playing into the hands of their new King, Stephen Batory.[13] In 1558, Ivan made one serious attempt at an alliance with Lithuania, suggesting a joint campaign against the Crimean Tartars, a campaign which would have been beneficial to Lithuania, since her southern border extended as far south as the Black Sea, between the Dnieper and Dniester rivers. This territory had been Lithuanian since 1368, when King Olgerd seized this land from the Tartars. The Lithuanians might have agreed to such an alliance if Ivan had agreed to return Smolensk. This demand was refused and the war between the two countries was resumed. Another obstacle preventing any alliance with the Lithuanians was a justified fear of Russia, now reinforced by Ivan's alarming threats to take over all land once occupied by Russians, however long ago.

A true estimate of Ivan cannot be arrived at by any examination of his extraordinary conduct in isolation. No ruler, however despotic his government, however docile his subjects, is a free agent. He is dominated by his heredity and his environment. Ivan was the descendant of a long line of tough, often completely unscrupulous war-lords, and his large estate was a large, cold and poor piece of land worked by an ignorant and oppressed peasantry. Other countries have had similar problems but they were gradually solved without the misery and suffering that the Russians have undergone. What went wrong?

An answer to this question can be found by looking at another country also at the edge of Europe, England. This country evolved in some respects in the same way as Russia. It is precisely at the stage where England ceased to evolve in the same way that light is shed on one basic cause of Russia's sickness.

The arrival of the Scandinavians in both countries is the starting point for this similar development; and the interval of approximately four hundred years between Hengist's landing in England, around 449, and Rurik's in Russia, around 862, is repeated for the next eight hundred years. Hengist himself may be a mythical character but, as G. M. Trevelyan makes clear in his *History of England*, 'at least he stands as the type of these great, forgotten makers of history, the men who in pursuit of their own hearty lusts for gain and adventure

> sharked up a list of lawless resolutes,
> For food and diet, to some enterprise
> That hath a stomach in it.   *Beowulf*

and with such help unwittingly founded England and all that has come of England in the tide of time.'[14]

The period between the fifth and eleventh centuries in England and between the ninth and fifteenth centuries in Russia are alike stamped by the gradual feudalisation of society. In Russia the land was divided up into the noble's 'white land' and the communally (or individually) held 'black land'; in England the same distinctions existed between the 'book land' and the 'folk land'. Methods of cultivation in both countries were similar, both operating a three-field rotation of crops; and share-holding arrangements were comparable, in the village and the *mir*, the Russian peasant commune. Both countries survived in conditions of great poverty; both countries had to overcome a cold climate and the difficulties of barren or infertile soil. Both countries were open to raids and invasions on all sides. The Angles and the Saxons had no ships to repulse the Viking long-boats; in this they were weaker than the Russians, who were never short of men to fight an invading army, except when engaged in fighting in disproportionately large numbers on another front, as in Ivan the Terrible's Livonian War.

In England the peasants became indebted to the lords through the assistance and protection given to them in the cultivation of their holdings. This process resulted in an increase of serfdom under the Danish kings of England in the eleventh century; in the early Angevin period, under the descendants of Geoffrey Plantagenet, Count of Anjou, during the twelfth century, these semi-independent peasants were grouped together as one class of villeins. The same trend occurred in Russia three hundred years later; after another century, by the middle of the sixteenth century during the reign of Ivan the Terrible, serfdom had become the basic pattern of Russian society. During the next hundred years, the boyars gained legal sanction for the complete control of their serfs. This process was comparable in essence to that of the imposition of villeinage in England between 1150 and 1250.

In addition to the similar social patterns which evolved in the two countries, there are also certain political features common to both. Under William I, William II and Henry I, England became for the first time effectively unified. Four hundred years later, in Russia, unification was achieved by Ivan III, Basil III and Ivan IV, the Terrible. The monarchs in both countries established their power by breaking up or weakening the large, independent estates of the aristocracy; and in both countries the decline of the old nobility was accompanied by the rise of a new privileged class: the knights of the twelfth and thirteenth centuries in England and the 'men of the court', or gentry bound to the sovereign by guarantees of military or civil service, in the sixteenth and seventeenth centuries in Russia. The military obligations of the knights were laid down in the Assize of Arms of 1181; those of the 'men of the court' were decreed by Ivan the Terrible in 1555.

In England in the twelfth century and in Russia in the sixteenth were created those government institutions which formed the basis for the future development of the administrative machine—the Chancery, the Exchequer and system of justiciars in England, and the *prikazi*, or ministries, in Russia. At these times too in both countries, general assemblies were summoned, marking the birth of a parliamentary system.

It is here that the parallel lines diverge. Putting an end to any continuation along similar lines, the monarchy in Russia crushed the spirit of independence in every class and institution. Other forces also contributed to Russia's social stagnation. The English had a foreign dynasty and a foreign episcopate imposed on them in 1066, and this led to an alliance between the barons and the squires against the King. By their victory in the Barons' War in 1264 against Henry III, under the leadership of Simon de Montfort, the upper and middle classes laid the foundations of a truly democratic parliament. The alignment of forces in Russia was completely different. The Russians were ruled all along by a national dynasty, the houses of Rurik and Romanov, backed by the only available form of religion, the national faith of Orthodoxy. Opposition to the Grand Prince, the Tsar or the Metropolitan was immediately branded as treason. There was no middle class with which the upper class could co-operate; and there was no feasible form of Protestantism, which could challenge the dead weight of the Orthodox establishment. The monarchy in Russia eliminated the aristocracy as a power in the land, putting in their place the service gentry, each one of whom was totally dependent on the Tsar. To the tragic impoverishment of their country's future welfare, the 'men of the court' surrendered what power they had as a class by retiring from the government, having gained in 1646 hereditary control over their land and their serfs. By the time Peter the Great came to the throne in 1682, the monarchy found itself in a position of undisputed mastery, the position which Ivan the Terrible insisted on against the opposition of the still independent nobility.[15]

In England the barons and squires were strong enough to create a democracy by weakening the power of the King; in Russia, the monarch and the squires, the service gentry, defeated the barons, the boyars, thus eliminating the only class in Russia during the first thousand years of its history which could educate and civilise the people. The very meaning of the aristocracy is power by the best people. By wholesale slaughter of most of the aristocratic families of medieval Russia, Ivan the Terrible and the other Grand Princes of Russia dealt a blow to the progress and vitality of their country which is still felt today. When a whole class is decimated, especially if it is a class of men and women of ability superior to that of the rest of the nation, the effects of such genocide are bound to be long lasting. One effect of Ivan's hatred of his own aristocracy is that it set a precedent; in fact it has become a habit. With the total annihilation of the aristocracy under Lenin and Stalin, the habit still operates, so it is the aristocracy, the best people, whether titled or not, in the rest of the world who are the next targets for elimination by the heirs of Tsarism. Another reason for this hostility is obvious: the most gifted people in countries outside the borders of Russia are the ones most likely to take active steps to oppose any neutralisation by, or integration into the Soviet commonwealth of nations, the USSR.

Another comparison with England can be made which has a direct bearing on the weakness of the people of all classes in face of the total control imposed upon them by the monarchy in Russia. Resistance was made all the harder by their lack of education and the lack of any literature which could build up the necessary feeling of individualism. This comparison is one which the west gallantly tends to ignore, as it is not complimentary to one party, to Russia. The four-hundred-year gap between England's and Russia's feudal development is small compared with the gap in literary and scientific scholarship. Here one must more than double the time lag.

The Venerable Bede, the father of English historians, was born in 673. He had many disciples and he wrote forty books, his greatest being his *Ecclesiastical History of England* and *De Natura Rerum*, a scientific treatise. The story of *Beowulf* came to England with the Angles in the sixth century; from this original narrative the lengthy poem was composed around 700, and the earliest manuscript in existence today was written three hundred years later. Russia had to wait until the middle of the sixteenth century to read the religious and historical works of Makary, and until the eighteenth century to read the histories of Karamzin, the poems of Derzhavin and the scientific works of Lomonosov, one thousand years after the composition of *Beowulf* and the death of Bede. *The Tale of the Host of Igor* cannot be included here with any certainty, as this supposedly Kievan work may in fact have been written in the eighteenth century. This intellectual tundra was made the more barren by the banning of Latin books and even Latin icons, and the ban placed upon actors, who were put in the same category as witches, as dealers in sorcery.

One further comparison between the Russia of Ivan the Terrible and the west must be made before we look at the final and most damaging war of his reign, the establishment of his *Oprichnina*, his shock troops, his SS or KGB, which bludgeoned his people into an even lower state of confusion and misery. It has been optimistically assumed that the religious faith of the Russians played a similar role in education, welfare and the preservation of morale in times of crisis that it played in the other Christian countries of Europe. If we look below the surface we see that this would be too rosy a picture. In *The Russian Idea*, the great Christian analyst, Nikolai Berdyaev declared that before Tolstoy Russian society was 'indifferent to religion and hostile to Christianity'. In the middle of the nineteenth century, Belinsky wrote to Gogol saying: 'Look round very carefully and you will see that Russians are by nature a profoundly atheistic people.' Nevertheless many visitors to Russia have commented on the piety and devotion of Russian Christians, in their churches and their homes. Giles Fletcher noticed that in the Russia of Ivan the Terrible 'without her cross about her neck, you shall see no Russe woman, be she wife or maid'. But it is more difficult for a visitor to assess the true depth of a foreign country's real understanding of a religion. The outward signs of religious observance, especially if they are part of the ritual of the official state Church, may give a misleading picture of the real strength of that Church. How convincing, or how primitive, were the rituals carried out by the Russian clergy? These are the questions that should be asked. Samuel Collins, physician to the Tsar Alexis for nine years, described the Russian funeral customs in his book *The Present State of Russia*, published in 1671:

> Their burials are strange. The wife of the deceased is obliged to howl most pitifully and hire others to do the like, but little reason have they to do it, considering their severe usage . . . As soon as anyone is dead, they open the windows and set a basin of water for the soul to bathe in, and a bowl of wheat at the head of the corpse, that he may eat, having a long journey to go. After this they put on his feet a pair of black shoes and some kopecks or pieces of money in his mouth, with a certificate in his hand (from the metropolitan of the place) to Saint Nicholas, of his life and conversation.

Samuel Collins also noted that 'it has been thought state policy to forbid all music and jollity among the commons to prevent effeminacy. If a man thinks his wife barren, he will persuade her to turn nun, that he may try another; if she refuses, he will cudgel her into a convent. The beauty of their women they place in their fatness. A lean woman they count unwholesome . . . Hanging has not been in use until lately, for the dull Russ thought if the malefactor were strangled, his soul was forced to sally forth at the postern gate, which made it defiled.'[16]

Observations of this nature reveal the tragic inadequacy of Christian teaching in Russia, a primitiveness which allowed Ivan the Terrible and his descendants to rule unchecked. As Alexander Solzhenitsyn pointed out in *Under the Rubble*, 'the Church, grown utterly decrepit and demoralised by the time of the Revolution, was perhaps one of the chief culprits in Russia's downfall'. An accurate indication of the superficiality of the Church's impact on the Russian mind when Ivan was driving his people to war with their neighbours and to war against each other, during the forthcoming *Oprichnina* regime, is discovered in the nation's use of swear-words. There is no point in using bad language unless your listener is shocked. For this reason the vocabulary of swear-words of any society reveals an instant indication of the subjects considered holy or sacred or tabu in that group. No one uses Muslim oaths in a Christian country. In England, when religion was considered more important than sex, most of our swear-words were biblical. Until the seventeenth century, language that was considered shocking or indecent included such phrases as God's arms, God's limbs, God's body, by God's foot, by God's guts, God's nails, by God's bones, by God's corpse, and God's death. An early corruption of God was Gog or Cock. Swearing by Christ was widespread, Jis, or Gis, being an abbreviation.[17] Ophelia, in Hamlet (Act 4, Scene 4) says: 'By Gis and by Saint Charity!' Zounds is short for God's wounds. Now people are seldom shocked by the bad language in Shakespeare, for few are sufficiently religious.

In medieval Russia, as in the west today, religious swear-words were not used as much as sexual oaths. If religion had the impact on their society that it had on the west, the favourite shock words would have been biblical. Adam Olearius from Leipzig came to Russia in the 1630s, as secretary and counsellor to the embassy of Duke Frederick of Holstein in Moscow. He had this to say in the book he wrote on his return to Germany:

> The Russians are in general a very quarrelsome people who assail each other like dogs, with fierce, harsh words . . . When their indignation flares and they use swear-words, they do not resort to imprecations involving the sacraments, as unfortunately is often the case with us. Instead they use many vile and loathsome words. They have nothing on their tongue more often than 'son of a bitch', 'cur', and 'I fuck your mother' to which they add 'into the grave'. Little children who do not know the name of God have on their lips 'fuck you', and say it as well to their parents as their parents to them.
>
> Recently this foul and shameful swearing was strictly forbidden upon pain of knouting. Certain secretly appointed people were sent to mix with the crowd and, with the help of the *streltsi* [musketeers] and executioners, were to seize swearers and punish them on the spot by beating; but they soon gave it up as a bad job. One should not seek great courtesy and good manners among the Russians. They tell all sorts of shameless fables, and he who can relate the coarsest obscenities and indecencies, accompanied by

the most wanton mimicries is accounted the best companion.

So given are they to the lusts of the flesh that some are addicted to the vile depravity of sodomy not only with boys but also with men and horses. People caught in such obscene acts are not severely punished. Tavern musicians often sing of such loathsome things, while some show them to young people in puppet shows . . . The Russians greatly love tobacco and formerly everyone carried some with him. However it was remarked that people got no good of it. Slaves lost much time in their work, many houses went up in smoke because of carelessness with the flame and sparks, and, before the ikons, worshippers emitted an evil odour. Therefore, in 1634, at the suggestion of the Patriarch, the Grand Prince banned the sale and use of tobacco, along with sale by private taverns of vodka and beer. Offenders were severely punished by slitting of the nostrils and the knout. We saw marks of such punishment on both men and women.[18]

Ivan's attitude to sex, and that of the Church, is clearly indicated by its teaching that even after marriage it was a sinful and defiling act. Before a couple abandoned themselves to such conduct, they were told to make sure that all the icons in the room were covered, and any cross worn on the body was to be removed. It was unthinkable that a Saint, Jesus or God, from the vantage point of an icon, should have to watch a man and woman in the nude enjoying themselves in godless conduct. In the carnival before Lent, when all copulation was banned by the Church, 'they give themselves over', Collins observed, 'to all manner of debauchery and luxury, and in the last week they drink as if they were never to drink more. Some of these going home drunk, if not attended with a sober companion, fall asleep upon the snow (a sad, cold bed) and there they are frozen to death. If any of their acquaintance chance to pass by, though they see them like to perish, yet will they not assist them, to avoid the trouble of examination if they should die in their hands.' Two hundred years later Henry Morley was amazed to see people looking at a wounded man lying on the ground without helping him. According to the law, he was told, 'if anyone interferes and the man dies, he may pay for it with Siberia, or, if he is rich, with an enormous fine'.[19]

It is not surprising that so many men and women of all classes fled south to a warmer land and more enjoyable customs. Sailing down the Volga into the Caspian Sea, a Dutchman, Jean Struys, landed in Circassia, in the seventeenth century. He was delighted to find that women could walk around with their breasts uncovered. These he, found, were like 'two globes, well placed, well shaped and of an incredible firmness; and I can say without exaggeration that nothing is so white or so clean. Their eyes are large, sweet and full of fire, their nose well shaped, their lips vermillion, the mouth small and smiling, their hair of the most beautiful black, sometimes floating and sometimes tied up, frames their faces most agreeably. They have lovely figures, tall and easy and their whole being seems free and relaxed. In spite of these exquisite gifts, they are not afraid of the approach of men, no matter from what country.' Husbands, he noted, were not jealous.[20]

Other Russians fled to Poland and Lithuania. The most distinguished dissident was Prince Andrei Kurbsky, one of Ivan's generals, of royal lineage himself, tracing his descent from Vladimir, Grand Prince of Kiev. He had taken a leading part in the capture of Kazan and Astrakhan, and for his courage had been decorated by the Tsar. He had been in the vanguard of the advance on the Crimea, and had bombarded the Perekop Isthmus with his artillery. His heaviest cannon, the Rhinoceros, can now be seen on display in the Kremlin. He decided not to pursue the attack, when he heard that the Sultan was about to land troops at Ochakov, to the west of the isthmus, which would cut his line of withdrawal. Retreating northwards, Kurbsky set fire to the capital of the Crimean Tartars, Bakhchisarai, and the Khan's beautiful summer palace with its superb fountains. One of the columns in the Grand Palace in the Kremlin incorporates a large block of pink marble, which Kurbsky's men brought back as a trophy. The Khan of the Crimea and the Sultan himself determined that Moscow would be punished for its recent invasions of their land.

In 1564 Kurbsky was commandant of the city of Dorpat, recently seized by the Russians in their war in Livonia. Being an admirer of Adashev and Sylvester, he could never be sure when Ivan was going to subject him to similar punishment. In the spring of this year he lost an important battle near Nevel, north of Vitebsk. His force of 15,000 was defeated by a Polish force of 4,000; he himself was one of the wounded. As this could easily have been seized upon by the Tsar as the sole reason for his arrest, he transferred his allegiance to the King of Poland. After a farewell meeting with his wife and nine-year-old son in Dorpat, he rode during the night of 30 April to Volmar, where he was welcomed with open arms. What happened to his family is not known. Desertion was bad enough in Ivan's judgement. It was, by this time, traditional in Muscovy that deserters and prisoners of war would be instantly killed if they returned to their own country. But now, Prince Kurbsky was adding insolence and many insults to the injury of treason, by urging King Sigismund to intensify the war against Ivan; and he wrote to his discarded master five long letters, explaining his desertion and verbally thrashing him for his cruelty. These letters, and the two that Ivan sent in reply, form one of the most revealing verbal battles in European history. Here we see the head-on collision that is caused by the arrogant and insulting assumption of complete authority by the autocrat, an attitude that was bound to arouse and inflame anyone subjected to his degrading contempt.

This is the conflict that still rages in Russia, the war that the Kremlin wages on its own people, the ceaseless campaign which fills the many prisons, psychiatric hospitals and labour camps, most of them in Siberia, that vast ocean of suffering and despair. In a report by Dr Yuri Orlov, published in September 1979, it is estimated there are five million Russians in forced labour camps.[21]

6

The Kurbsky Letters

In the opinion of J. L. I. Fennell, the translator and editor of Kurbsky's letters and of a brief history of Ivan written by Kurbsky, these documents are 'of capital importance'.[1] They give 'a strangely true and sober picture of the age'; they are written 'by a true Muscovite, with a large amount of factual detail, particularly as regards the lists of Ivan's victims'. They are in this respect comparable to Solzhenitsyn's *Gulag Archipelago*.

Kurbsky's letters and Ivan's replies are especially interesting since we have so few letters of any kind from the Tsar or his court. It is, however, this contrast between the paucity of Russian documents of literary value at this time and the unique quality of this royal correspondence that has led one American historian, Edward L. Keenan, to question its authenticity.[2] It is, in his opinion, too good to be true. The letters, he thinks, were written some sixty to eighty years later. It is only in the last few years that anyone has doubted Kurbsky's and Ivan's authorship; Keenan's book was published in 1971. We are therefore confronted with a text which must carry conviction of its authenticity by its own merits. Each reader can judge for himself whether these letters come from Ivan himself and from his general, or whether they show signs of another hand. If they were not written until the following century, it would be a further indication of the intellectual backwardness of the Russian court at this time. All published correspondence has to be edited; these letters are no exception. However, the original manuscripts, or copies earlier than 1620, cannot be traced.

In essence the argument of both Tsar and general centres on the right of the subject to rebel. Ivan's main complaint is that Kurbsky has 'seized upon such evil thoughts, resisting in all things the Master given you by God'. Both antagonists strengthened their arguments with frequent quotations from the Bible; Ivan compared Kurbsky to Judas; Kurbsky compared Ivan to Saul, who consulted soothsayers. Ivan quoted extensively from Byzantine texts; Kurbsky sent the Tsar a translation of two chapters of Cicero's *Paradoxa Stoicorum* (chapters 2 and 4). These passages contained the following statements:

> You know not, madman, what strength virtue possesses. You simply use the name of virtue; but you do not understand what virtue means. Your lusts torture you; you are in torment day and night; the conscience-pricks of your evil deeds goad you on; wherever you gaze your unjust acts encircle you like furies . . . You are out of your mind and mad . . . That horde of bandits . . . is that a state? See how I despise the weapons of your bandits. Nothing is mine that can be taken away, torn away or lost. If you had rent from me my mind, then I would admit having suffered an offence . . . You, in truth, are not even a citizen now, unless one can be an enemy and a citizen. You have caused a massacre in the forum; you held the temples with armed brigands; you burned the houses of private persons. All the evil men, whose leader you confess yourself to be, whom the laws wish to be punished with exile, are exiles, even if they have not left the land. When the laws ordain that you are an exile, are you not a traitor? By all the general laws you are a traitor.[3]

These charges were made by Cicero against Antonius and Clodius, who exiled him from Rome.

Since many of Kurbsky's accusations can be directed with equal force against Stalin and the communist dictators, his letters have been wisely omitted by the Soviet educational authorities from their standard history text books, and Kurbsky himself is dismissed as an unreliable authority on Ivan's reign.

Kurbsky's first letter to Ivan starts with a bitter attack on his appalling cruelty:

> To the Tsar, exalted above all by God, who appeared formerly most illustrious, particularly in the Orthodox Faith, but who has now, in consequence of our sins, been found to be the contrary of this. If you have understanding, may you understand this with your leprous conscience— such a conscience as cannot be found even among the godless peoples:
>
> Why have you destroyed the strong in Israel, and subjected to various forms of death the generals given to you by God? Why have you spilt their victorious holy blood in the churches of God during services, and stained the thresholds of the churches with the blood of martyrs? And why have you conceived against your well-wishers and against those who lay down their lives for you unheard-of torments and persecution and death, by slanderous invention falsely accusing the Orthodox of treachery and magic and other abuses, and endeavouring with zeal to turn light into darkness, and to call sweetness bitter? . . . Thus have you rewarded us, your poor servants, destroying us by whole families.
>
> Do you think yourself immortal? Or are you carried away by an unheard-of heresy, as one no longer wishing to stand before the impartial judge,

Jesus, begotten of God, who will judge the universe, but especially vain-glorious tormentors? . . . He is my Christ, who sits on the throne of the Cherubim, at the right hand of the Supreme Power on high; he will be the judge between you and me. What evil and persecution have I not suffered from you? And what iniquitous tissues of lies have you not woven against me? I have been driven from the land of God, without guilt, hounded by you . . . You have recompensed me with evil for good and my love with implacable hatred. In front of your army I have marched—and marched again; and no dishonour have I brought on you; but only brilliant victories, with the help of the angel of the Lord, have I won for your glory; and never have I turned the back of your regiments to the foe. I have achieved most glorious conquests to increase your renown.

For many years I have worked with much sweat and patience, and all the time I was separated from my fatherland. I rarely saw my parents, and my wife I have not known . . . I have suffered many wants and illnesses, of which Lord Jesus Christ is witness. I was visited with wounds in various battles, and all my body is already afflicted with sores. But to you all this was nothing; instead you show us your intolerable wrath and bitterest hatred—and, furthermore, burning stoves [on which people were burnt to death] . . .

You will not see my face in this world until the glorious coming of my Christ. Those massacred by you, standing at the throne of our Lord, ask for vengeance against you, while we, who have been banished and driven out by you without justice, cry out day and night to God, however much in your pride you may boast in this temporal, fleeting life, devising vessels of torture against the Christian race, and abusing and trampling on the Angelic Form. [This refers to Ivan's abuse of the monasteries, forcing men and women into monasteries and convents, where they were imprisoned for life. To accept the Angel's Form meant to accept monastic vows.] Your flatterers and comrades of the table urge you on to aphrodisiacal deeds, and, together with their children, act more viciously than the priests of Cronus [the Titan who ate his own children, as he feared they would kill him] . . .

This letter, soaked with my tears I will order to be put into my grave with me, when I come with you before the judgement of my God, Jesus Christ. Written from Volmar, the town of my master, King Augustus Sigismund, from whom I hope to receive much reward and comfort for all my sorrow by his sovereign grace, and still more with God's help.

Kurbsky did not have to wait very long before receiving the Tsar's reply, one of great length, sixteen times as long, finding in the Holy Bible and in his family history ample precedents for his tyrannical rule:

. . . By our Lord Jesus Christ, the conquering banner, the Holy Cross of the only-begotten Word, was given to the first Tsar, Constantine, and to all Orthodox Tsars and upholders of Orthodoxy. And as the words of God

A bedroom in a palace in Moscow. A stove may be seen on the right (*BBC Hulton Picture Library*)

A bedroom in the Kremlin (*BBC Hulton Picture Library*)

(*above*) Interior of the Church of
the Annunciation in the Kremlin.
The stone cellars contain the
library of Ivan the Terrible but
it has not yet been found (*BBC
Hulton Picture Library*);
(*right*) Garment worn by one of
Ivan's Oprichnina, or select
corps (*Novosti Press Agency*)

encircled the whole world like an eagle in flight, so a spark of piety reached the Russian kingdom. The autocracy . . . by the will of God, has its beginning from the great Tsar Vladimir, who enlightened the whole Russian land with holy baptism.

Ivan then named his forbears, Vladimir Monomakh, Alexander Nevski, Dmitri Donskoi, Ivan Kalita, Basil III, 'the acquirer of immemorially hereditary lands', and finally himself as recipients of God's trust. After this long preamble the letter begins:

This is our Christian and humble answer to him who was formerly boyar, adviser and general of our autocratic state, but is now the perjurer of the holy Cross of the Lord and the destroyer of Christianity, to Prince Andrei Mikhailovich Kurbsky.

Why, if you think you have piety, have you cast out your very soul? . . . Why did you betray your soul for the sake of your body? Is it because you were afraid of death at the false instigation of your devilish friends and spies? . . . If you accuse us of warring against Christians, against Germans and Lithuanians, then your accusations are groundless. Even if there were Christians in those lands, we would still wage war according to the customs of our forefathers, as has happened many times before now. In those lands there are no Christians, except for a very few ministers of the Church and secret servants of the Lord.

For the sake of your body you have destroyed your soul, and for the sake of short-lived fame have scorned imperishable glory. Having raged against man, you have risen against God. Consider, wretch, from what heights and into what depths you have descended in body and soul! . . . Why did you despise even the apostle Paul? For he said: 'Let every soul be subject unto the higher powers. For there is no power ordained that is not of God. Whosoever, therefore, resisteth the power, resisteth the ordinance of God.' (Epistle to the Romans, ch 13, v 1 and 2) He who resists power, resists God; and who resists God is called an apostate, which is the worst sin. And these words were said concerning all power, even when power is obtained by blood and strife. But I did not take my kingdom by rape. If you then resist such power, all the more do you resist God. Thus, as the Apostle Paul said (and these words you have also scorned): 'Servants, be obedient to your masters . . .', and 'not only to the good, but also to the froward', (St Paul's first Epistle to Peter, 2, 18) 'not only for wrath, but also for the conscience sake'; for this is the will of God, 'to suffer for well-doing'. And if you are just and pious, why do you not permit yourself to accept suffering from me, your froward (or stubborn) master, and so to inherit the crown of life? . . .

Were you not shamed by your servant, Vaska Shibanov? He preserved his piety, before the Tsar and before all the people, standing at the gates of death; and because of his oath on the Cross he did not renounce you, but, praising you, he did hasten to die for you. But you have not imitated his piety.

Shibanov was interrogated under torture in Moscow and then executed. It is possible that, when Ivan received him, bearing Kurbsky's letter, he was standing on the Red Staircase of the Palace in the Kremlin. Shibanov was commanded to read the letter out loud, whereupon Ivan stuck his iron-pointed staff into his foot, ordering him to continue reading. If this story is true, it is not inconsistent with the many other acts of sheer cruelty that he indulged in. Ivan continued:

Your letter has been received and clearly understood . . . Is this a fitting honour to pay to a master given by God, that you should belch forth poison in a devilish manner?. . . What is it, you dog, that you write, and for what do you grieve, having committed such evil? What will your counsel, stinking worse than shit, resemble? It is unbecoming for rulers either to rage like wild beasts or in silence to abase themselves . . . It is ever befitting for Tsars to be gentle and fierce. If a Tsar does not possess this quality, then he is no Tsar, for the Tsar 'is not a terror to good words, but to the evil'. (St Paul's Epistle to the Romans, ch 13, v 3) . . . You will never find a kingdom which does not fall to ruin when ruled by priests. What are you striving after? To go the way of those Greeks who destroyed their kingdom and became subjects of the Turks?

The strong in Israel we have not destroyed, nor have we slaughtered our generals with various forms of death. We are free to reward our servants, and we are also free to punish them. As for blood in the churches, we have spilt none. And as for victorious and holy blood in our land, it is not evident and we know of none. As for the thresholds of the churches, in as far as our strength and understanding can grasp, and in as far as our subjects show us their willingness to serve, so do the churches of God shine forth, adorned in all manner of ways; such adornments are visible to all foreigners. We do not stain the thresholds with any blood; and at the present time we have no martyrs for the faith . . . Torments and persecutions and various forms of death we have not conceived against anyone . . .

Ivan then describes the way he was treated as a child (see page 62):

What sufferings did I not endure through lack of clothing and through hunger! In all things my will was not my own . . . There was no element of servility to be found in Prince Ivan Shuisky in his attitude to us. Who can endure such arrogance? Many a time did I eat late, not in accordance with my will . . . The boyars fell upon the towns and villages and with the bitterest torment in divers ways did they plunder without mercy the properties of those living there . . . When we reached the fifteenth year of our life, then did we take it upon ourselves to put our kingdom in order, and thanks to the mercy of God, our rule began favourably. [According to the chronicles, this year was the first in his reign in which many were subjected to great cruelty.] Why in your pride do you boast, dog, of your warlike bravery? You are as nought: at home a traitor, in the field bereft of reasoning . . .

Having seen such treachery from our grandees, we took Adashev from the dung heap and placed him together with the grandees, hoping for faithful service from him. What honours and riches did I not heap upon him—and on his family! Afterwards, for the sake of spiritual counsel and the salvation of my soul, I took into my service the priest Sylvester, thinking that he would have care for his soul . . . But he was carried away, like Eli the priest, and began to form friendships as laymen do . . . Whenever we gave any good advice, they did not avail themselves of it; but if they were to give any corrupt advice, then were they acting for the common weal . . . If a Tsar's subjects do not obey him, then never will they cease from internecine strife . . . Hitherto the Russian Masters were questioned by no man; they were free to reward and to punish their subjects, and they did not litigate with them before any judge . . . When the dog-like power of Adashev and you came to an end, then were the Tartar kingdoms rendered submissive to our State in all things, and now more than thirty thousand [Tartar] soldiers set out to aid the Orthodox faith . . .

How scared you were of the Lithuanian army, as though they were bogies to frighten children! Had it not been for your devilish hindrance, then with God's help, would all Germany [meaning Livonia, which had been governed by the German Knights of the Sword] have been under the Orthodox faith . . . We do not destroy you by whole families; but for traitors there is punishment in all places: in that land to which you have gone you will find out about this in greater detail . . . I do not consider myself to be immortal, for death is the debt that all must pay for the sin of Adam. For, even if I wear the purple, none the less I know that, like all men, I am altogether clothed with frailty by nature. I do believe in the last judgement of the Saviour . . . I therefore believe that I as a servant shall receive judgement for my sins . . . I know that Christ our God is the true enemy of vainglorious tormentors. But who is vainglorious? I, who order my servants to carry out my wishes? Or you, who reject my dominion, established at God's behest, and your yoke of servitude? Though consecrated by no one, you assume the dignity of a teacher. Is this pride, for a servant to command his master? Even an ignoramus can understand this! . . . Unjust evil and persecution you have not received from me, and ills and misfortunes we have not brought upon you. Whatever small punishment was inflicted on you, it was for your crime, for you were in agreement with our traitors. Of everything we have not deprived you, and we did not drive you out of the land of God; but you have deprived yourself of all things . . . In all you were better off than your father in our favour, but in bravery you were worse than he; only in treachery have you exceeded him. If such was your condition, why are you dissatisfied? . . .

You did not think me worthy of your full love, for you grieved not with me for our Tsaritsa and our children . . . As for your brilliant victories and most glorious conquests, when did you achieve them? Even if you suffered many wounds, nonetheless you achieved no brilliant victory. And how was it that at our town of Nevel, with fifteen thousand men you were not able to conquer four thousand? Was this a brilliant victory and most glorious conquest? . . . Had you been a warlike man, you would not have recounted your military hardships, but rather would you have striven towards further hardships; but you recount your hardships because you are a deserter . . . You write that you will not show us your face until the Last Judgement of God. You value your face dearly! Who indeed wishes to see such an Ethiopian face? Where will one find a just man who has grey eyes? Your countenance betrays your wicked disposition . . .

I boast of nothing in my pride; indeed I have no need of pride, for I perform my kingly task and consider no man higher than myself. It is you that puff yourself up with pride . . . Against the Christian race we do not devise vessels of torture . . . To the evil are meted out evil punishments, not because we wish it, but of necessity . . . As for the 'priests of Cronus', this you have written in an unseemly manner, barking like a dog or belching forth serpent's venom. The town of Vladimir (or Volmar) in *our* patrimony, the land of Livonia, you call the town of our enemy, King Sigismund—thus do you complete your wicked houndish treachery. You have sought out for yourself a sovereign who by himself rules no one, but who is lower than the lowest servants, for he is ordered by all men. Still less can you find comfort there, for there each one cares for his own . . . You are an adulterer, not in the flesh; but an adulterer in treachery is like an adulterer in the flesh. 'These things thou hast done, and I kept silence; thou thoughtest transgression, that I would be like unto thee; I will reprove thee and set thy sins before thy face. Now consider this, ye that forget God, lest I seize you, and there be none to deliver thee.' (Psalm 50, verses 21, 22)

This strong precept and word, given in the All-Russian ruling Orthodox city of Moscow, the step of our holy threshold, in the year 7072 from the creation of the world (1564) on the fifth day of July.

Ivan the Terrible did not have to wait long before receiving a second letter from his infuriating general, one which must have made him even more ill-tempered.

Short answer of Prince Andrei Kurbsky to the extremely bombastic epistle of the Grand Prince of Moscow. I have received your grandiloquent and big-sounding screed, belched forth in untamable wrath with poisonous words, such as is unbecoming not only to a Tsar, so great and glorified throughout the universe, but even to a simple lowly soldier. All the more so, as it was composed of so many quotations, used with much anger and fierceness, not in measured lines or verses, but beyond measure diffusely and noisily, in whole books and chunks of the Old Testament and epistles! And you write passages about beds, about coats [referring to his childhood] as if they were tales of crazy women. So barbarically do you write that not only learned and skilled men, but also simple people and children would read your letter with astonishment and laughter . . .

It is not befitting for chivalrous men to wrangle like servants, and it is shameful for Christians to belch forth unclean words from their mouths, as

I have many times said before. It is better to put my hope in almighty God, for he is the witness for my soul, for I do not feel myself guilty in anything before you. So let us wait a little; near at hand is the coming of Our Lord God and Saviour, Jesus Christ.

This letter was probably written in 1565. Twelve years later, Ivan retaliated with a second letter to Kurbsky, much shorter this time, but repeating the same message that, as God's agent, he could do what he liked.

. . . I remind you, Prince, with humility, to regard the majesty of God's providence, which awaits my conversion from my sins, still more from my transgressions—I who have committed more lawlessness than Manasseh, apart from apostasy . . . You have desired with the priest Sylvester and with Alexei Adashev and all your families to see all the Russian land under your feet; but God grants power to whom he will. . . .

Why did you separate me from my wife? If only you had not taken from me my young one, then there would have been no 'sacrifices to Cronus'. You will say that I was unable to endure this loss, and that I did not preserve my purity. Well, we are all human. Why did you take the soldier's wife? If only you had not stood up against me with the priest! Then none of this would have happened; all this took place because of your disobedience . . . I was born to rule by the grace of God; I do not remember my father bequeathing the kingdom to me and blessing me—I grew up on the throne . . . I wanted to subdue you to my will; and you, in recompense—how you defiled and outraged the sanctity of the Lord! How many churches and monasteries and holy places have you utterly outraged and defiled!

You have written, recounting your grievances, that we inflicted disgrace upon you, sending you to far-distant towns. But now we, by God's will, in spite of our gray hair, have gone even further than your far-distant towns, and have ridden over all your roads, from and into Lithuania. And where you wished to rest from all your toils, in Volmar, here too, to your place of rest, has God led us; and here we have caught you up; and then you went still further afield . . . Consider what you have done. Mend your ways, that you may think of the salvation of your soul.

Written in our patrimony of the Livonian land, in the town of Volmar, in the year 7086 (1577).

Kurbsky wrote three more letters to Ivan during the next two years; he also wrote a short history of Ivan IV, in which he gives many details of Ivan's killings. Ivan had begun his second letter with a list of the Russian towns which made up his kingdom. This gave Kurbsky the opportunity of rebuking him for his pride in the first of these three letters:

Remaining abroad because of your persecution, I have omitted your grandiose and lengthy title. From the lowly, you, the great Tsar, have no need of this; but in letters from Tsar to Tsar it is customary to read out such titles with excessive verbosity. As for your recounting to me, as to a priest, your confession, I am unworthy to listen to this, even out of the corner of my ear . . . Nevertheless it would indeed be right for all Tsars and Christian peoples to rejoice and be glad if your repentance were true, as was that of Manasseh in the Old Testament. It is said that he repented after much drinking of blood and unrighteousness . . . If only your repentance corresponded with this sacred example! Now you humiliate yourself exceedingly, now you raise yourself up without limit and beyond measure!

Let me, who am able to contain myself, refrain from bickering; for it is exceedingly unbecoming for us warriors to bicker like servants . . . You call us traitors because we were forced by you to kiss the Cross against our will, for it is the custom with you, that should anyone not swear allegiance, he would die the bitterest death. My answer to you is that all wise men are agreed that should anyone swear allegiance or vow against his will, no sin is imputable to him who kisses the Cross, but rather him who forces him to do so. If anyone, because of most fierce persecution, does not flee, then he is, as it were, a murderer of himself, acting against the word of the Lord: 'if they persecute you in this city, flee ye into another.' (Matthew, ch 10, v 23)

You say that I destroyed and fired the churches of God . . . I was fulfilling orders given not by pagan Tsars but by a Christian Tsar. By his order I took the field. But I confess my sin—I was forced by your command to burn down the great town of Vitebsk and in it twenty-four Christian churches . . . As for saying that your Tsaritsa had been bewitched and that you had been separated from her by Sylvester and Adashev and by me, I do not answer for those holy men, for facts cry out, emitting a voice louder than the trumpet, concerning their holiness and virtue. But as for me, even if I am laden with sins, none the less I was born of noble parents, of the family of the Grand Prince of Smolensk, as indeed your Royal Highness knows well from the Russian chronicles; and princes of that generation are not accustomed to eating their own bodies and drinking the blood of their brothers, as has for a long time been the habit of certain others . . .

I guessed your future attitude towards me when you took from me by force my cousin to marry her to your cousin, to marry her into that blood-drinking* family of yours. As for your writing about Kurlyatev, about the Prozorovskys and about the Sitskys . . . and soldiers' wives—this, like tipsy women's tales, needs no answer; according to the wise Solomon, 'it is not fitting to answer a fool'. For all those men, and countless noble men, have already been sacrificed with excruciating ferocity; and in their place remain the vagabonds, whom you strive to appoint as generals. They disappear swiftly from their towns, through fear, not only of a single warrior, but of a leaf blowing in the wind.

*krovopivstvenni. Fennell mistranslates this word as bloodthirsty. The Russian for bloodthirsty is krovozhadni.4

You shut up the kingdom of Russia—in other words, free human nature —as in a fortress of hell. Whoever goes from your land to other countries, you call a traitor; and if he is caught on the frontier, you punish him with various forms of death. And so here, likening themselves to you, they act cruelly. Furthermore, do not presume to write any more to your servants abroad, especially when they know how to answer.

Kurbsky returned to the attack 'a year or two after my last letter', when

I saw what had come to pass—the abhorrent and shameful victory over you and your army, that you had destroyed the glory of the divine memory of the great Russian princes. It is not enough that you were not ashamed . . . of the executions of divers just men to satisfy your lawlessness, such executions as never had been before in Russia . . . I am astonished at this, as are all others who knew you when you lived according to the commandments of the Lord, and had around you chosen men of eminence. But now—into what gulf of folly and madness of corruption have you been dragged . . . And you have been bereft of common sense!

As for your teaching and instructing, they laugh at you here still more and jeer . . . Written in the most glorious city of Polotsk of our sovereign, the illustrious King Stephen, on the third day after the capture of the city (31 August 1579).

Four weeks later Kurbsky wrote his fifth and final letter to the Tsar, having heard more of the turmoil into which Russia had been dragged:

When the corrupted and the cunning corrupted you, you returned to your first state of vomit, when your favourite flatterers had defiled the temple of your body with various forms of uncleanness, and practised their wantonness with pederastic atrocities and other countless and unmentionable wicked deeds . . . Instead of chosen and holy men, who tell you the truth without shame, the devil has brought to your side most foul parasites and maniacs; instead of a brave army, the children of darkness, the bloody *oprichniki*, hundreds and thousands of times worse than hangmen . . . As the blessed David said: 'they shall not stay long before God, who build the throne of iniquity.'

If Tsars or rulers perish who make hard decrees and laws difficult to undergo, how much more must those perish with their houses who not only make decrees which are difficult to obey, but who lay waste their own land and destroy their own subjects by whole families, sparing not even sucking children. Pure maidens are dragged along in wagon loads, mercilessly defiled by one not satisfied with his own five or six wives. [Ivan was living with his sixth wife, Vasilisa Melentyeva.]

Countless other things, as those who come here from your land make known to us, thousands of times more abhorrent and loathsome to God, do I forbear to write.

Recall your first days in which you ruled blessedly!

Destroy not further yourself and your house! Those that swim in Christian blood will disappear with all their house . . . Receive the divine antidote of penitence!

Written in Polotsk, the town of our sovereign, King Stephen, on the 4th day after the victory of Sokol (25 September 1579).

The year before this letter was written, the Danish ambassador in Moscow, Jacob von Ulfeld, reported that the Tsar maintained a harem of 'fifty virgins abducted from Livonia', whom he took with him wherever he went. They were, Kurbsky wrote in his last letter, 'subjected to ravishment unmentionable and dreadful to hear'. Between 1573 and 1578 Kurbsky wrote his *History of the Grand Prince of Moscow*, which gives us the names of many of Ivan's victims, most of them members of the Russian aristocracy. Also described are the hideous ways in which some of these men and women met their deaths. For every boyar mentioned by name there were unnumbered ordinary Russians killed whose names are unrecorded.

Ivan had only one remedy for discontent, disobedience and desertion: the infliction of harsher punishments and more arbitrary executions. Not surprisingly this only accelerated the decline in morale throughout the country, the desire of rich and poor alike to flee and the amount of plots against the tyrant. In 1567, a group of boyars, headed by Ivan Petrovich Chelyadin-Fedorov, made plans to seize the Tsar during one of his visits to the Lithuanian front and hand him over to King Sigismund. Prince Vladimir Andreyevich was chosen by some of the conspirators to be the new monarch. It was Prince Vladimir who would have become Tsar if Ivan had died, as the Count thought he would, in 1553. The plot was discovered and the leaders were killed. Kurbsky gives the details of Ivan's treatment of the rebels:

He put to death his first cousin Vladimir, together with Vladimir's mother, Evfrosinya, Princess Khovansky, a truly holy faster, who shone forth in holy widowhood. Then Ivan ordered to be shot by musket the wife of his cousin, Princess Odoevsky, who was very meek and an adept in kinds of sacred singing, and also two infants, one of whom was about ten years old, the other younger. Many others of their true servants were slain, not only noble men and youths, but also their wives and maidens of distinguished stock and well-born noble families. Ivan put to death Ivan Petrovich Chelyadin-Fedorov, who was already of ripe old age, and his wife Maria, a holy woman, whose only begotten son the Tsar had earlier torn from her bosom and beheaded. The Tsar was so angry with Chelyadin that he not only slew every one of his service noblemen (his personal friends) and subjected them to various kinds of torture, but he burned all his towns and villages, while he travelled with his children of darkness, the *oprichniki;*

and wherever any of them were found, he did not spare them, nor their wives, nor their little children sucking at their mother's breasts. And they say that he even ordered that not a single animal be left alive.

Ivan's policy of *strux*, terror, or *schrechlichkeit*, succeeded in deterring the majority of his countrymen from open rebellion. It has also had another, more surprising effect, making some western historians a little too ready to minimise Ivan's atrocities, unconsciously subscribing to the theory of the divine right of kings to govern abominably. This readiness to genuflect is in fact a tribute to the intensity of the terror that Ivan generated. It is difficult to find another reason for this reluctance to criticise Ivan dispassionately. A good example of this reluctance, this desire to praise Ivan, in spite of all the evidence against him, is clearly shown in the following two remarks in a recent western study of Ivan:

> I have found Ivan far less terrible than the Tsar of legend. This does not mean that the savageries perpetrated in his reign can be denied or extenuated in any way . . . Ivan could be unexpectedly mild and forgiving, even towards individual boyars whose crime was treason. Suspecting Prince Ivan Belsky of planning flight to Lithuania, Ivan ordered him to swear on the Cross that he would not depart from the realm or from his principality. Further, twenty-nine men were required to act as sureties for him and 120 men to be sureties for them. Notwithstanding these extraordinary precautions, Belsky later in the same year pleaded guilty to treason in that he had sent messages to Sigismund Augustus, asking him for a safe conduct to Lithuania. Ivan nevertheless pardoned him. Others enjoyed similar clemency from their unpredictable Tsar.[5]

The reader is entitled to feel not a little confused by this, and remain unconvinced. All tyrants are guilty of occasional clemency.

The distinguished Russian historian Karamzin described Ivan as 'a horrible meteor' and 'a beast, a frantic blood-sucker'.[6] In 1564, when Kurbsky deserted Ivan and fought against him with the Polish army, the Russians may well have hoped that this reverse would induce the Tsar to make their lives a little easier, their poverty a little less severe, their lives a little more secure, their deaths less painful. But this reverse was taken by Ivan as proof that all the boyars were his enemies, therefore enemies of the state, and that his people as a whole must be shaken still harder to convince them of the gulf that separated them, as miserable sinners, from their God-given, God-inspired leader, who could do no wrong. In his two letters to Kurbsky, he repeats over and over again the message that he was authorised by God to kill without mercy, with copious relevant and irrelevant quotations from the Old Testament.

The Bible is quoted so frequently, especially in his verbose first letter, that the reader begins to wish that this ancient collection of Hebrew myth, legend and fact had never been brought to Russia.

In 1564 the Russian people may well have thought that Ivan would now do something to prevent everything from becoming worse. But the worst was yet to come.

7

A State Dismembered

The decisions made by Ivan after Kurbsky's defection were doubly astounding. They confused every citizen in the land and they involved risks to his own safety which demonstrated that he had the profoundest understanding of his subjects' amazing docility. During the second half of 1564, with great secrecy, he planned a new strategy, a counter-attack against his most hated enemies—not the Lithuanians or the Poles, but his own boyars and their countless supporters, his own people. He kept his plans to himself and a few boyars to the very last moment—in fact until after the last moment. It is impossible to describe his mind at this stage, for along with his coldly accurate assessment of his subjects' capacity for passive obedience, he was inflamed by intense fears for his own safety and the conviction that everyone around him was perhaps a traitor. Russia was about to be treated by its own ruler as if it were a foreign country.

In mid-winter the blow fell. In the preceding months some of the junior nobility were ordered to hold themselves in readiness, and to bring their wives and families to Moscow. They were not told on which front they would be fighting. It would have been a reasonable assumption to conclude that nothing of importance would occur during the icy winter, and that they would not have to leave Moscow until the spring. But Ivan had no such predictable plans in mind. In the early hours of 3 December in the Red Square, the curtain went up on the first act of Ivan's new tragedy. Sledges were assembled and loaded with clothing, icons, golden dishes and the royal treasury. Ivan attended a service of Holy Communion in the Uspensky Cathedral, at the end of which the court was asked to say farewell to their sovereign and kiss his hand. Then he and his Circassian wife, Maria, his two sons, Ivan and Feodor, and some of the boyars climbed into sledges and drove away. Everyone was left in ignorance of their destination.

Ivan could not have left Moscow at a worse time of the year. Leaving the Kremlin the royal party first went to Kolomenskoe, a manor now in the southern part of the city. Before they could leave here the freezing cold gave way to a sudden thaw and days of rain, making roads unusable and iced-up rivers uncrossable. It was a fortnight before Ivan could set out on his mysterious pilgrimage. The cold weather returned and progress was slow. Three weeks later he arrived at his destination, the monastery of Alexandrovsk, a small collection of stone buildings tucked away in the dark forests seventy miles north of the capital. The cortège arrived here on Christmas day. The New Year began and still there was no news of the Tsar in Moscow.

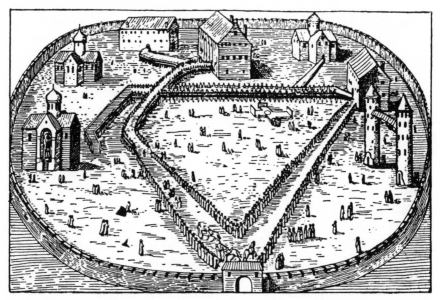

Alexandrovsk from a contemporary drawing. It was at this village, 65 miles north of Moscow, that Ivan set up his police headquarters which he ran on pseudo-monastic lines (*from Y. Ulfeld's Engravings, Frankfurt, 1627*)

Ivan was carrying out an unprecedented manoeuvre, one which dramatically illustrates the quality which separates the Russians from the other nations of the world—their obedience. Ivan was putting himself in a position of extraordinary weakness that would in any other country be considered a tactical blunder of the first order. He was lowering his guard and even turning his back on his enemies, challenging them to strike. In any other country this new move would be a crazy gamble doomed to complete failure. In Moscow the people behaved like a sheep without a shepherd. The shops closed and trading ceased. On 3 January 1565, a whole month after Ivan had disappeared, news at last arrived in Moscow. Messengers from Alexandrovsk brought two letters from the sovereign. They were brief, blunt and frightening.

In Ivan's letter to the Metropolitan violent accusations were hurled against the archbishops, bishops, archimandrites and abbots, boyars, lower boyars, and government officials, everyone in any position of authority. They were all untrustworthy; even the Metropolitan was blamed for interceding on behalf of men condemned by the Tsar. Because of this widespread disobedience Ivan had decided to go: 'Not wishing to endure your treachery any longer, we, with great sorrow in our heart, have quitted the Tsardom—and have gone wherever God may lead us.'[1]

No message from the Tsar could have been more surprising and disturbing, especially to a nation trained to worship their leader. It was so surprising that it strained credulity. What did Ivan *really* mean? His second letter, read out to the waiting citizens, assured his subjects of his good will towards them if they remained faithful to him. This did nothing to calm them, for it only unleashed a welter of ominous questions. It seemed as if he was abdicating and at the same time declaring war on his entire government. In his first letter he accused his chosen officials of stealing land and money from the sovereign, branding these miscreants as thieves. They were also siding with criminals by giving them refuge. In making these damning charges, Ivan was encouraging his people to rebel against the government, and at the same time he commanded them to remain loyal and obedient to all his commands.

Bees in a hive, deprived of their queen, would not be more confused. Ivan gambled on his boyars' cowardice—and won. A deputation of bishops, boyars and court officials, headed by Pimen, Archbishop of Novgorod, and the archimandrite of the Chudov monastery in Moscow, set off across the snow to implore Ivan to return. The Metropolitan Afanasy could have gone to Alexandrovsk at the head of the column, but he chose to stay in the capital. According to the records, the Muscovites decided he should remain, but he may well have had his own reasons for not going: the supplicants were handing Ivan a noose for their own necks. The Tsar petulantly consented to return, but only if he was given complete freedom to punish whom he chose, without any criticism or intercession from the Church or the boyars. In this he cannot be accused of duplicity. He demanded a blank cheque and no one demurred. A special service was held in the monastery of Alexandrovsk, and God was thanked for the Tsar's good will.

Yet another month went by before Ivan finally set foot in Moscow once more. On the following day he appeared before the court and the priests of his Church who had assembled to hear his new programme. Just to look at him gave everyone a shock. The thirty-four-year-old man had prematurely aged. He stooped; his eyes no longer looked alert; he was now nearly bald. At Alexandrovsk he had suffered a shattering nervous breakdown.

With his two letters, to the Metropolitan and the citizens, Ivan had split the country socially in two, encouraging the people to hate the boyars, not just individually but as a class. Now, before his court in the Kremlin, he wielded his axe again and made another savage split. This time the country was literally sawn in half, divided into two separate parts with separate governments. From now on Russia would consist of two states, one to be named the *Oprichnina*, the other the *Zemshchina*, two new names for parts of the country. *Oprich* meant apart, and *oprichnina* was used to denote part of an estate or dowry set aside for the landowner's widow; the latter word Ivan coined from *zemlya*, or land. He would rule the former state with six thousand members of the lower nobility, while the latter was to be handed over to two princes, Ivan Belsky and Ivan Mstislavsky.

To make matters even more confusing, no one could be certain where the borders between the two halves of the country would lie, since the territory of the *Oprichnina* would be made up of a patchwork of estates north, east and west of the capital. Russia was not just to be sawn in half; she was in fact going to be cut up in pieces. The invading army was Ivan's hand-picked division of mounted cavalry, the *Oprichniki*, who were given money and land, and special privileges. The most important of these was their immunity; no one could claim against them for damages or any crime such as murder, robbery or rape. Included in this army, this state security police force, were former bandits, felons and itinerant monks, known as *yuradivye*, or feeble minded ones.[2] These men were allowed to inflict fines and publicly flog those who would not or could not pay. They rode out into the country on their black horses, wearing their special black uniforms, with black boots and a black cowl, seizing estates of small as well as large land-owners. The insignia of these horsemen was a broom and a dog's head, and this was carried in a quiver attached to the saddle, which, like the rest of the harness, was black. Like dogs, they were to nose out all traitors and sweep them off the face of the earth. Nearly half of the entire realm was thus appropriated; those evicted were either settled in the other Russia, the *Zemshchina*, or slain.

Rubbing their noses in their abject defeat, Ivan demanded from the citizens of Moscow sufficient money to 'reimburse the Tsar and Great Sovereign for the expenses he had incurred because of his subjects, who, unworthy of so devoted a ruler, had made it necessary for him to leave the Kremlin and go roving like a beggar'.[3] Russia, that is to say, the *Zemshchina*, had to hand over to the Tsar 100,000 roubles for his allegedly enforced exile from his capital. Extra compensation was also demanded for three horses which had died on the way.

The most fitting description of Russia, of the two Russias of Ivan's new order, was given by Samuel Purchas, in his famous history of medieval voyages in all parts of the world. He started his chapter on the first visitors to Russia from Europe with this chilling summary: 'Tempests and tornadoes have combined in Russia, and there made their Hell-mouth centre, there pitching the tents of destruction, there erecting the thrones of desolation.'[4]

Every visitor to Russia drew the same picture of sheer hell on earth. Giles Fletcher, Antony Jenkinson, Jerome Horsey, Tilman Bredenbach, Paul Oderborn and Reinold Heidensten all give details which confirm the general accuracy of Kurbsky's picture of a country driven to the extremes of suffering and pain. Any attempt by Soviet historians or western writers to minimise the sufferings of the Russian people at this time, either to justify Stalin's cruelties (saying that stern measures are sometimes necessary), or to infer that a Russian Tsar cannot be more savage than a capitalist king, shows a disgraceful lack of sympathy for the countless victims of all classes and ages of Ivan the Terrible.

It was not only the boyars who were shamefully tortured and killed. Giles Fletcher came to Russia in 1588 as the English ambassador, and was kept waiting for so long for official audiences that he had time to write a penetrating account of Ivan's treatment of his subjects. This work, *Of the Russe Commonwealth*, was so shocking that the Muscovy Company, the English traders in Russia, persuaded Lord Burleigh to omit certain passages in the first edition, not on grounds of inaccuracy, but fearing the Russians would stop trading with them if they saw what Fletcher had said. The complete work was not published until 1643.

One of the excluded passages describes what happened when the ordinary Russian found himself arrested for any offence:

> The only method of investigation employed is torture, for here one feels obliged to compel the alleged offender to confess his guilt. Without such confession a conviction is impossible. The culprit is whipped with ox nerves or leather lashes as thick as one's finger, which bite into the flesh; or else he

is tied to a spit and roasted. Alternatively, he may have a rib broken and twisted with red-hot tongs, or the flesh beneath his nails may be cut away.

The results of the investigation are handed to the prefect of the district, who places them upon the council table, after which they are read by a tribunal of justices who neither see nor hear the accused. Capital punishment takes the following forms: Hanging, decapitation, bludgeoning, impalement, drowning, freezing under the ice, burning, etc. Often, those who are sentenced in summer are kept in custody until the winter so that they may be frozen to death.[5]

Fletcher notes that many of the class Ivan hated most, the boyars, were kept in a state hardly better than slavery. Those evicted from their estates were sent to distant provinces

> where they might have neither favour, nor authority, not being native or well known there. Some are sent into Siberia, Kazan, or Astrakhan under pretence of service, and there either made away with or else fast clapped up. Some are put into abbeys and forced to take vows because of some pretended crime.[6]

As titles and property could descend through the female line, noble girls were dragged into convents so that their line would come to an end. A foreign conqueror, in fact, could not have treated the Russians more abominably.

Two days after Ivan's return to Moscow, armed with his subjects' pathetic surrender which was the equivalent of a confession of guilt before arrest, he went into the attack. The first distinguished victim was Prince Alexander Gorbaty-Shuisky; his seventeen-year-old son and four other nobles were also painfully done to death. Giving a clear indication of the horrors in store for anyone suspected of treason, Ivan then ordered the most painful possible form of death to be inflicted on Prince Dmitri Shevyrev, being impaled upon a pointed stake. This form of death is slow, as the weight of the body drags the stake through the intestines and the heart. A whole day elapsed before Shevyrev died.

Many other boyars were banished to distant parts of the country; others were allowed to remain or to escape punishment by paying a heavy bail. The following day several thousand Muscovites were evicted from their homes to make room for the new army of the *Oprichniks*. Prince Ivan Kurakin and Prince Dmitri Nemoi were arrested, forcibly shorn and sent to distant monasteries. Other princes killed by the Tsar were Ivan Kashin and Dmitri Kurlyatev (with his wife and children) who were all strangled. Prince Peter Shchenyatev chose to become a monk in the hope of avoiding death but this did not save him. He had

Building of the Oprichnina Office in Moscow in 1565. It was burnt down in 1571 during the destruction of the town by the Crimean Tartars. It was made of wood with a high stone wall and a heavy gateway. The location of the Oprichnina Office was discovered during excavations in 1934 (*Novosti Press Agency*)

The tomb of Ivan IV in Archangelskaya Cathedral, Moscow. On 23 April 1953, a special commission from the Ministry of Culture, under the direction of Professor Smirnov, opened this sarcophagus. Ivan's skeleton was partially covered with torn pieces of a monk's garment. On the breast lay a monk's apron top embroidered with the scene of the crucifixion on Golgotha (*Novosti Press Agency*)

needles driven under his nails and was then burned to death on a hot pan. Two of his cousins were also killed. Prince Ivan Shishkin was slaughtered with his wife and children.

Killings and expropriations continued through the summer of 1565, and in the freezing winter of that year Ivan sent his *Oprichniks* to take over the houses, estates and farms of twelve thousand families. Men, women and children were chucked out of their homes and driven on foot and in carts to find somewhere to live in Russia's newly conquered eastern territories. This monstrous punitive action had an immediate effect on Ivan's Livonian war, as the army was deprived of countless thousand potential recruits. Heinrich von Staden noted the obligation enforced on Ivan's soldiers that on no account were they allowed to become prisoners of war. Civilians were also under the same prohibition: 'If the people of the Grand Prince (the Tsar) surrender a city, a fortress or a castle, and they return to Russia alive, they are all killed, along with their relatives. In the churches of Russ prayers will be said urging their eternal damnation.'[7]

The Russians might have been less savagely treated if their resident conqueror had been more extrovert, like Genghiz Khan or Tamburlane, whose minds were less chaotic and less tortured by remorse. In consequence, they were able to rule with some consistency and bring some enjoyment and gaiety into the lives of their subjects. Ivan, on the contrary, became hag-ridden with remorse for the sins he was committing, and those being committed in his name. His remorse was stoked by his introvert Christian concepts of hell and damnation, and what he conceived to be his duty, to punish wrong-doers on their way to hell by giving them hell before they died. He felt that he was unfit to sleep near the tombs of his ancestors. Not only was the country divided into two, but the capital itself was sliced in half. Families living in the western districts were thrown out of their houses to make way for the *Oprichniks*, and the Tsar himself moved out of the Kremlin, choosing to live in a fortified mansion built between Arbat and Nikitskaya Streets in the western part of the city, thinking he would be safer there. Only six years later, in 1571, this building went up in flames. But fears of assassination drove Ivan out of this refuge and away from Moscow altogether to his northern retreat at Alexandrovsk, the monastery he was now fortifying, where he could make further plans in his war against the boyars and his ministers, and where he could pray to God for forgiveness for his sins. It is difficult to decide on the degree of his sincerity and his piety, since a man in such a psychopathic state can be frantically self-critical one moment and pathetically amoral the next; and consistency has never been a prominent feature of the Russian character.

The extent of Ivan's monomania showed itself in the oath which each *Oprichnik* swore when joining this élite gang. Each man had to promise complete loyalty and obedience to Ivan himself; there were to be no other loyalties of equal importance. Even family ties were to be disregarded, if loyalty to Ivan demanded it. Perhaps Ivan had in mind the harsh words of Jesus Christ, when he told his right-hand men that he had come 'set a man at variance against his father, and a man's foes shall be they of his own household; he that loveth father and mother more than me is not worthy of me, and he that loveth son or daughter more than me is not worthy of me.' (Matthew ch 10, vv 35–7) Even loyalty to his country, or what he conceived to be such a loyalty, was to take second place to loyalty to Ivan personally. These men were given a personal incentive in every arrest they made. When anyone was convicted of a felony, all his goods were seized. Ivan took half, and the remaining half was to be divided equally between the *Oprichnik* and the informer; thus each Russian was encouraged to denounce his neighbour. If everyone was considered a potential enemy of the state, betrayal of a neighbour was one way of demonstrating one's loyalty, and guarding oneself from arrest.

Heinrich von Staden, who served as one of the *Oprichniks* for seven years, reported that

> Anyone of the *Oprichniks* could accuse any *Zemshchina* man of owing him a certain sum of money. And even if the *Oprichnik* had never known or seen the *Zemshchina* man accused by him, the latter would have to make payment forthwith, or else he would be beaten daily in the market-place with clubs and cudgels until he paid. No one here was spared, neither cleric nor layman. The *Oprichnik* used all kinds of machinations, impossible even to describe, to obtain money and goods from the men of the *Zemshchina*. According to their oath, the *Oprichniks* could not exchange a word with those of the *Zemshchina*, nor intermarry with them. And if any *Oprichnik* had a father or a mother in the *Zemshchina*, he was never allowed to visit them. The grand prince [Ivan] left the Kremlin to the *Zemshchina*.[8]

If Ivan had abdicated from the *Zemshchina*, that part of the country could at least be governed with some attempt at efficiency, as one administrative area. But the boyars in both halves of the country had to refer to Ivan on all matters of importance. Some ministries worked solely within their own territories; the finance departments worked in partnership, and the Foreign Office operated as before the split. If Ivan's aim was to confuse everyone, he certainly succeeded. Life in the royal retreat, the new capital at Alexandrovsk, could not have been more grotesque. Torture and worship went hand in hand. The monastery was converted into a fortress, with a surrounding moat, steep ramparts, palisades and guard posts, and finally a stone wall. Outposts were set up on the approach roads two miles from the monastery itself. Approaching this wolf's lair could be very dangerous. Innocent men, according to von Staden, 'whether they were princes or boyars or their servants, were seized by the guards, bound, and immediately killed. Some were stripped naked in front of Ivan and rolled around in the snow until they died. The same thing happened to those who wanted to leave the camp for Moscow and were caught by the guards.'[9]

Ivan selected an inner circle of 300 'brothers', specially trusted *Oprichniks* to act as monks, drinking companions and hatchet men. What must have confused these thugs was the amount of times they had to go through the motions of religious conduct. At four in the morning their abbot, or Tsar, rose from his bed, roused his two sons, Ivan and Feodor, and rang a bell to call the brethren to matins. Attendance was compulsory. Anyone too drunk or lazy to appear in chapel was jailed for eight days. This early service would drone on for two hours. It was no doubt highly distasteful and uncomfortable for the *Oprichniks*, who had not joined the force for religious reasons. Keeping an eye on his faithful monks, Ivan himself prayed with great zeal, sometimes prostrating himself before the altar of God and striking his forehead on the ground, and bruising himself in the process. Another service was chanted at eight, also lasting two hours. After that, the miserable monks were allowed at last to eat some breakfast. This was more to their liking, as it was like a banquet, with wine and large quantities of food. While trying to forget the drawbacks of their existence in the refectory, Ivan spoilt matters by standing at a lectern reading aloud some pious homily. What was left over from the morning repast was taken out and given to the beggars. After that the royal abbot would eat his late breakfast or lunch alone, sometimes with a real monk in attendance, with whom he would indulge in religious argument.

In the afternoon there was interrogation of prisoners, spiced with some torture, which confirmed that someone hated him, or that there was some plot which made him feel that all this effort, this cold, uncomfortable war-time existence, was justified. At eight in the evening, the monks all trooped into chapel again for vespers, and at ten, Ivan went to bed, when three blind men took it in turn to tell stories until his eyes closed. Only two hours later, he would get up again to attend yet another service. When he was not praying or crying to God, or listening to prisoners crying in far greater torment, he would feast and drink and receive foreign envoys. Remorse would follow licence, and prayers would be offered up for his countless victims, 'whose names, O Lord', he declared, 'Thou Thyself knowest'.

It was a performance of sickening hypocrisy and intolerable conceit. Ivan was obsessed at one and the same time by his own guilt and the imagined guilt of his boyars. He daily feared assassination in this world and damnation in the next; yet he strove to forget God by greater enormities of hideous cruelty, and to forget man by more abject and impassioned pleas for God's forgiveness. He felt himself unfairly treated by fate, handicapped from the start by his loveless childhood and subsequently dogged by misfortunes beyond his control. His anger was for ever inflamed by his boyars who failed to see his nearness to God and their consequent inferiority.

Kurbsky and most of the boyars wished to assist their Tsar as responsible ministers; Ivan could only rule with sycophants and men of inferior capability. He was, it seemed, determined to please nobody, not even the genuine monks at Alexandrovsk, who must have admired their Tsar's conscientious attendance at matins and vespers, his monastic timetable and his insistence that his shock-troops listen frequently to the word of God. But even these holy men must have been shocked by the German Lutherans admitted to Alexandrovsk and entertained by the Tsar. Following what was by now the traditional custom of up-rooting whole communities, Ivan had deported most of the inhabitants of Dorpat, in Livonia, and had dumped them in towns lying east of Moscow. But they were allowed to practise their Lutheran religion, and their pastor was permitted to travel to each community and to visit Alexandrovsk for religious discussions. He even asked him to arrange his library there. Four Lutherans joined his private suite as secretaries, and, as a crowning insult to the faithful in Moscow, permission was given to build a Lutheran church there.

The only recreation allowed outside the beleaguered fortress was bear hunting. This obviously made a change from capturing and killing human enemies. In addition there were looting expeditions, when raiding parties set out far and wide to seize what they could for the embellishment of Alexandrovsk. From Tver and Novgorod the booty was magnificent. Huge brass doors from the cathedrals in those towns were mounted at the western and southern entrances of the Cathedral of the Intercession, built in Alexandrovsk by Ivan's father, Basil III, in 1513. These doors are wooden and covered by sheets of brass, decorated with scenes from the Old Testament. Other trophies brought into Alexandrovsk included golden chalices, cups, ladles, icons, candlesticks, gold and silver cutlery and plate from various towns and citizens.[10]

In 1567 Ivan's war entered a new phase of intensity with the discovery of Ivan Petrovich Chelyadin's conspiracy, mentioned on page 134. Ivan successfully intercepted letters from King Sigismund of Poland to Chelyadin and three princes, Belsky, Mstislavsky and Vorotynsky. There is nothing surprising in this or any other attempt to end Ivan's disastrous rule; the havoc and pain caused by the *Oprichniks* made hostility against him all the greater. In 1621, a Muscovite who had consulted many of the families who survived these grim years, wrote a document entitled *The Piskarev Chronicle*. In this report he states that:

> In the land there was hatred for the Tsar among all the people, and they petitioned him and presented a signed petition concerning the *Oprichnina*, saying it ought not to exist. And here evil men who hate what is good came to the fore; they began to tell slanderous tales to the Grand Prince against all those people, and some perished as a result of these words. They began to incline towards Prince Vladimir Andreyevich, of Staritsa, a cousin of Ivan IV. And there was great woe.[11]

The three princes whose letters had been intercepted managed to escape capture, but Chelyadin and five other princes were caught and killed. Karamzin gives an account of Chelyadin's death. Before the court, the rebel, an old man, was dressed in Ivan's robes and ordered to sit on the throne, wearing the royal crown. The Tsar then bowed before him and said: 'Hail, great Tsar of the Russian land! You have received from me the honour you desired. But having power to make you Tsar, I can also cast you from the throne!'

Ivan then plunged a knife into Chelyadin's heart, and called in his *Oprichniks*, who hacked his body to pieces.[12] It is possible that Chelyadin was disposed of in some other manner, but, considering the far more disgusting killings carried out by Ivan, such an end cannot be considered unlikely. Prince Vladimir, the most popular choice as Ivan's successor, was either poisoned with his wife and children, beheaded or stabbed to death.[13]

Samuel Purchas referred to the death of Chelyadin in his comprehensive study of medieval voyages, *Purchas His Pilgrimes*, in which he quotes from the work of Richard Hakluyt, the *Principal Navigations*, which was first published in 1589:

Ivan Piotrovich Chelyadin, a man of principal command, was set on a throne. Ivan bowed to him, with a knife thrusting him to the heart till his bowels fell out. His servants were slain, 300 others in his castle executed; his boyars gathered into one house and blown up with gunpowder; their wives and daughters ravished before his face and then cut to pieces; the husbandmen's wives stripped naked and driven into a wood and killed.[14]

Other casualties are named by Hakluyt in this work:

Chancellor Dubrovtsi sitting at table with his two sons was cut in pieces; his third son quartered alive with four wheels, each drawn a divers way by 15 men. Micyedovishchly, supreme Notary, his wife was taken and imprisoned some weeks with her handmaid and hanged over her husband's door, and so continued a fortnight, he being driven to go in and out by her all the time. Another notary's wife was raped and then sent home and hanged over her husband's table whereat he was forced daily to eat . . . If he met any woman whose husband he liked not, he caused her to stand naked till all his retinue were passed . . . Cutting out tongues, cutting off hands and feet of his complaining subjects, casting hundreds of men into the water under the ice, 700 women at one time, 378 prisoners at another. Five hundred matrons and virgins of noble blood were raped by Tartars in his sight . . . The Archbishop was set on a mare with his feet tied under the belly and made to play on bag pipes through the city. Monks were spoiled and slain. Theodore Sirconi, founder of twelve monasteries, was tortured to show his treasures and then slain . . . Vyazemesky, Ivan's secretary, died after many days' renewed tortures . . . Ivan recreated himself with letting bears loose in throngs of people.[15]

Prince Kurbsky, in his *History of Ivan IV*, gives further details of the Tsar's military operations against the rising tide of malcontents and traitors:

Ivan travelled around and burned the towns and villages of Ivan Petrovich Chelyadin together with those who lived in them. He came across a house which was very high; and he ordered that Ivan Borisovich Kolychev be securely bound in the very top rooms, and that several barrels of powder be placed beneath the house, as well as beneath others standing near it, which were full of people who had been herded together and locked in.

Ivan himself stood at a distance, with his troops drawn up, as though under the walls of an enemy town, waiting for the house to blow up. And when not only the house, but the others near it blew up and were shattered, then he and all his children of darkness, like a madman surrounded by raving men, yelling at the top of their voices like enemies in battle, and like men who have won a glorious victory, galloped at full rein to gaze upon the mangled corpses of the Christians. Then, far away in the open, Ivan Borisovich was found, tied by one arm to a great beam and sitting safe and sound unharmed, and praising the Lord. In the house he had been stretched out and tied by his arms and legs. Now when this was told to Ivan's children of darkness, one of them rushed up to him before the others. He straightway cut off his head with a sabre and brought it like a priceless gift to the Tsar, his equal in savagery. The Tsar immediately had it sewn up in a leather bag and sent to the man's uncle, Archbishop Philip (the Metropolitan), saying: 'Here is the head of your relative! Your spells were of no avail to him!'[16]

The details of the deaths meted out to members of the aristocracy and court officials during these harrowing years leave a lasting scar upon the mind. Atrocities do not lose their sting when the victims die; they sear the mind and sour the memories of wives, mothers and children, relatives and descendants for generations to come. They leave a permanent stain on the country where these crimes occurred, for we are all, as it were, the grandchildren of one family, for that is what a nation is. Out of kindness to their readers, or of kindness to the Russian government when their books were written, or, if the writer was or is living in Russia, out of fear for his own life, details of some of Ivan's crimes have been just touched on or omitted altogether. All contemporary record *can* be ignored or disparaged or even disbelieved. Statements by survivors of German and Russian death camps *may* in future ages be treated with some scorn as exaggerations or distortions. Some accounts of horrific tragedies of this world may be distorted by the feelings of pain and hatred, or exaggerated in some details; but the events which gave birth to these accounts cannot be forgotten. What cannot be disputed is that the records exist.

Soon after the death of Chelyadin, three princes of the Rostovsky family, and three other princes, Shchenyatev, Pronsky and Kurakin were killed. Prince Kurakin was 'stripped naked, and whipped with six whips of wire which cut his back, belly and bowels to death'. Given by Sir Jerome Horsey, this account is followed by his description of the death of Ivan Obrossimov, one of Ivan's Court officials:

The Emperor lived in great danger and fear of treasons, and his making away, which he daily discovered. Ivan Obrossimov was hanged on a gibbet naked by the heels, the skin and flesh of his body from top to toe cut off, and minced with knives into small gibbets by four *pallacniks*, (executioners); the one, wearied of his long carving, thrust his knife somewhat far into his bowels, the sooner to dispatch him, was presently had to another place of execution and that hand cut off; which being not well seared, he died the next day. Many others were knocked in the head, cast into pools and lakes, their flesh and carcasses fed upon by such huge overgrown pikes, carps, and other fishes. I could enumerate many and much more that have felt the severity and cruelty of this emperor's heavy hand of displeasure, but I forbare to trouble the modest eyes and Christian patience of such as should read it.[17]

Soon after Ivan's marriage to his second wife, Maria, he lost interest in her but she remained in the Kremlin as Tsaritsa until her death in 1569 after eight years of marriage. There were no children by her and when she died court mourning was brief. As when Anastasia died, her death gave rise to rumours, suspicions, tales of poison and witchcraft, and these in turn prompted Ivan to seize and execute those men who were accused of plotting her destruction. Ivan's family remained small, consisting only of two sons, the younger of whom, Feodor, was, like Ivan's brother, mentally backward. The heir to the throne, Ivan Ivanovich, was now fourteen years old, soon to join his father in his dissolute sexual activities. One evening in July 1568, when Ivan was in the Kremlin, he sent a party of his leading *Oprichniks* on a raid, which can only be described as a raping expedition. The party was led by Prince Afanasy Vyazemsky, Malyuta Skuratov and Vasili Gryaznoi. The meaning of *gryazni* in Russian is foul or filthy. These men, with more *Oprichniks* in attendance, barged their way into the houses of several merchants and government officials whom they knew had attractive wives. These women were seized and taken back to the Kremlin. They were paraded before the Tsar, who chose several for himself. The others were raped by Ivan's friends. Later that night Ivan and his henchmen rode out to the suburbs of Moscow, and set light to the houses of certain boyars and dispersed their livestock. The Tsar then raced back to the Kremlin, where he sent the women he and his friends had raped back to their houses.

Life for the inhabitants of this unhappy country deteriorated rapidly as one prince or boyar after another disappeared from his estate, to serve in the Livonian War, or in the newly captured Tartar provinces of Kazan and Astrakhan, or to execution in Moscow. Ivan still had the Church to act as protector of the monarchy and consoler of the bereaved and lonely. But in 1568, the third year of Ivan's new dual kingdom, he made matters even worse by attacking the head of the Church, the Metropolitan Philip. He could not have chosen a man more revered and loved by all classes in the country. The people and the boyars looked to him to make some protest to the Tsar about his loathsome *Oprichniks*. He was the only man in Russia who was regarded as immune to the threats and blows of the Sovereign, being protected from attack by his holy office. The chronicles, as given in the histories of Karamzin and Solovyev, give an unusually detailed account of this sordid episode in Russia's history, a crime and a blunder of lasting magnitude.

Because the boyars, as well as the ordinary people of Moscow pinned their hopes on the Metropolitan to defend them, Ivan took this as clear proof that the holy father was in league with the enemy, the despised aristocracy. Not content with a private confrontation, Ivan decided to humiliate his archbishop in public in his own cathedral. He entered the Kremlin Cathedral of the Assumption, the Uspensky, which his grandfather, Ivan III, had built, and, as light was fading, found Philip standing by the icon screen at the entrance to the sanctuary. Ivan was not alone; some *Oprichniks* came with him to make everyone keep their mouths shut:

'Holy Father', said one of them, 'here is the Sovereign! Bless him!'

Instead of meekly obeying this command, Philip, who had kept his eyes away from Ivan, turned round and courageously replied:

'In the most heathen and barbaric lands there is law and justice; there is compassion towards the people—but not in Russia! The lives and property of our citizens go unprotected. Everywhere there is plunder, everywhere there is murder. And these deeds are done in the name of the Tsar!'

Ivan listened to this and other condemnations of equal gravity. Beating his pointed staff on the ground, he cut the archbishop short, shouting:

'Silence! I will speak! Silence, Holy Father! Be quiet, and bless me!'

Philip's reply could not have been more damning:

'Our silence will lie as a sin upon your soul—and bring death!'
'Those close to me', said Ivan, 'have risen against me, and they seek to harm me. But what business is it of yours to interfere in our royal affairs?'
'I am the pastor of the Christian flock,' Philip replied.
'Philip! Do not thwart our power, for you will bring our wrath upon yourself! It would be better if you left your office as Metropolitan.'
'I did not ask, or seek through others, or by bribery try to acquire this office,' replied Philip. 'Why did you take me from my desert retreat?'[18]

The Tsar could take no more of this and left the cathedral to his archbishop. After giving Philip a rigged trial, before a court which Ivan had assembled with himself as judge, he went into the attack. Philip walked out of this trial to show his contempt of the charges and the court itself. Now the Tsar added blasphemy to the crimes he had already committed. He waited until 8 November 1568, when Philip would be celebrating mass in the Uspensky Cathedral. This is a Saints Day, that of St Michael the Archangel, a day when the congregation would be large. While the service was being conducted Alexei Basmanov, a leader of the *Oprichniks*, marched in with a large platoon of his cut-throats. They advanced towards the Metropolitan and the service came to a halt. One of these black-cowled killers read out the sentence of Ivan's court, declaring that Philip was guilty of crimes which necessitated instant punishment. The holy father was then stripped of his robes and told to put on a plain white monk's garment. He was then, before the whole congregation, marched out of the cathedral. For a whole year he was imprisoned in three different monasteries, each one further from the capital, until in December 1569 his miseries were ended when Malyuta Skuratov entered his cell and strangled him.

This act of extreme stupidity and barbarity was swiftly followed by enormities on a far wider scale. Ivan, at the start of his reign, had sacrificed thousands of his men in the capture of Kazan and Astrakhan in order to put an end to Tartar invasions; now he embarked on a full-scale attack, just as devastating and far crueller than an invasion, on his own territory, the second largest city of Russia, the once-flourishing town of Novgorod.

In mid-winter of 1569, the Tsar, with his elder son, now aged fifteen, and a strong force of soldiers, Russians, Tartars and *Oprichniks*, set out from Alexandrovsk for the next battle in his self-inflicted civil war. Doubting their loyalty and suspecting them of transferring their allegiance to the King of Poland—a perfectly justified desire on their part—and insulted by the civic pride of Pskov and Lord Novgorod the Great, as the inhabitants had called their city since the eleventh century, Ivan had already moved to Moscow 500 families from the former town and 150 from the latter. This did not satisfy his monstrous megalomania or lessen his hatred and aggression. Like Stalin, the Ivan the Terrible of the twentieth century, he wanted evidence of a plot before carrying out his own plot. A letter with the forged signature of the Archbishop of Novgorod, appealing to Sigismund for help, was placed in his own Cathedral of St Sophia, and duly 'discovered' by Ivan's agents. The official story is that there was indeed such a letter written by a man who had been punished in Novgorod for some offence, and who was now planning his revenge. It is difficult to believe this, as it is highly unlikely that the incriminating document would be left in Novgorod's cathedral, a building constantly open to the public.

On their way to Novgorod the army revelled in unchecked carnage. All the towns and villages on the approach to the city, for a distance of 175 miles, were first ransacked and then destroyed. There was no resistance. Men, women and children were treated like enemies, like dumb animals. The towns of Tver and Klin and others were subjected to robbery, arson, rape and murder. At Tver, the Metropolitan Philip lay in a dungeon. Skuratov, on Ivan's orders, demanded his blessing on his sovereign before he commenced his chastisement of Novgorod. Philip refused and was then seized and strangled. For five days the *Oprichniks* drew blood in Tver.

For five weeks they killed in Novgorod. On the way the Fool in Christ, Mikula Svet, boldly confronted the Tsar and called him a bloodsucker. He was not punished, but the innocent in Novgorod were slaughtered. Figures of the total slain vary from 27,000 to 60,000. Many of these men and women only left his life after being flogged to death, roasted over slow fires or drowned in the river. Children and babies were not spared.

Ivan's craze for gold was indulged in to the full. The cathedral, churches, monasteries and mansions in and around the town were ransacked and cleared of all moveable wealth. Ivan Timofeyev, author of *The Annals*, written around 1605, gave this description of Ivan's war against his own people:

> Conceiving a plan filled with fury against his slaves, Ivan IV came to hate all the towns of his land . . . He sacked the Cathedral of St Sophia and took the miracle-working ikons and all the treasures, all valuable things; he robbed the Archbishop's palace and all the monasteries, and tortured all the people and many orthodox believers with terrible tortures. And other people—they talk of about sixty thousand men, women and children—were driven into the great river, and they say the river became dammed. And in other towns belonging to Novgorod he also took people away and robbed monasteries and churches.[19]

Merchandise, whole warehouses of wax, flax, tallow, hides, salt, wines, cloth, and silk were all destroyed by fire. Men and women were brought to Ivan and interrogated and then sent to their deaths. Every painful form of death imaginable was carried out under Ivan's supervision. Ribs were pulled out with red-hot pincers; finger-nails were torn off; men were stuck on stakes and left to die. Special pans were heated on which men were scorched to death. Bodies still alive were dragged by sledges down to the River Volkhov and then thrown in, with babies tied to their mother's back. Men in boats pushed bodies still gasping beneath the surface with boathooks. All the cattle and other livestock in and around the town were slaughtered. There was blood on the snow everywhere.

A glimpse into the ghastly tragedies of this war in Novgorod is given in the chronicle of the Monastery of St Cyril. This book alone registers the deaths of 3,470 victims of Ivan's savagery. Names are given with revealing additions: '. . . with his wife and children; . . . with his daughters; . . . with his two sons, and ten men who came to his help; 20 men belonging to the village; 80 belonging to Matveiche; . . . remember, Lord, the souls of thy servants, inhabitants of this town.'[20]

Another account states that 'poorer persons, by famine forced, did eat the bodies of the slain, and were after slain themselves'.[21]

Over and above his desire to inflict maximum pain, Ivan had a further motive for his diabolical cruelty, the desire to deprive each victim of redemption. If everyone in a family was exterminated, even distant relatives, there would be no one left to pray for the souls of the victims, an important feature of Russian belief. By drowning, dismemberment, being eaten by dogs or fish, or by burning, the sufferer was deprived of a Christian funeral and burial. By this method his enemies were condemned to the torments of hell. Thus, the Russians believed, a man or a woman could be damned for eternity. Many have found comfort in Christianity; many have found it a sad religion, darkened by fears of everlasting pain.

After five whole weeks of this crazy hell, the arch-criminal had the wretched survivors rounded up to hear him deliver a nauseatingly sanctimonious homily:

> People of Great Novgorod, remain alive! Pray to God, to his holy Mother, and to all the saints in our blessed realm that the Lord may grant our Christ-loving army that it may conquer all its enemies both seen and unseen. May God judge that traitor, your Archbishop Pimen and his evil advisers and accomplices. These traitors will be called to account for all this blood. You must not grieve over all that has happened. Live honourably in Novgorod! In my place I am leaving as your governor, my boyar and commander, Prince Danilovich Pronsky.[22]

We learn from Sir Jerome Horsey that, returning to Moscow:

> Ivan employs his officers to drive and take out of the towns and villages within 50 miles compass all sorts of people old and young with their families, goods and cattle, to go cleanse and inhabit this great and ruined city of Novgorod, exposing them to a new slaughter; for many died with pestilence of the infected and noisome air and place they came unto.
> This cruelty bred such a general hatred, fear and discontent through his kingdom that there were many practices and devices how to destroy this tyrant.[23]

On his way back in triumph to his capital, Ivan passed through Pskov. He was planning to subject this town to a similar blood-bath, but he limited himself to just one atrocity and the looting of icons, church vestments and some of the monastery bells. The road to the Church of the Assumption in Pskov is still called Bloody Road. Here, in February 1570, the prior of the Pecherski Monastery, Kornilii, a scholar and architect, met Ivan at the gates of his church. Whatever he said to the Tsar so enraged him that he drew his sword and killed him, severing his head. Ivan lifted up the bleeding corpse and carried it to the cathedral. According to one contemporary writer, Ivan 'repented at once' and made a large donation to Kornilii's monastery.[24] In Pskov Ivan visited the cell of a revered hermit, named Salos, on a fast day. To his horror, the monk called his sovereign 'a bloodsucker, the devourer of Christian flesh'. And then he offered Ivan a piece of raw meat. The Tsar replied that he was a Christian, and therefore he would not eat flesh on a fast day. Salos asked him one question: 'How is that, since you drink human blood?' Unable to reply, Ivan rushed out of the room.

Back in Moscow Ivan decided on a grand climax of horror in the Red Square itself. Many of his most trusted advisers had been named as friends of the accused in Novgorod. Confirmation was found, when the Archbishop of Novgorod was interrogated, that Ivan was hated in the Kremlin. The Muscovites themselves would be spared; only 200 selected prisoners were tortured and killed. But the population were forced to watch while these miserable men—members of the nobility and some of Ivan's former companions, leading killers of the *Oprichnina*, who had been incriminated by torture-wrung confessions of the Novgorodians— were all subjected to an excruciating death. Before being dragged out to the Red Square, these men were first burned and mutilated. Before this spectacle began, Ivan ordered Alexei Basmanov, one of the chief *Oprichniks*, to be killed by his son, who was then killed himself. Another close associate, Prince Vyazemsky, died during his interrogation.

In the central square of Moscow, eighteen gallows and various instruments of torture greeted the reluctant spectators, and here after hideous torment, the prisoners found the welcome release of death. This ghastly circus went on for four hours. Only 200 died that day in July 1570, but the minds of the populace were seared for life. Ivan Viskovaty, a counsellor who had served the Tsar throughout his reign, was stripped naked and hung up by his heels. Then, 'notwithstanding all protestations of innocency', his ears, lips, penis and testicles were cut away.[25] Viskovaty's wife was that evening raped by Ivan, and eighty widows of *Oprichniks* were executed and drowned.

The mutilated bodies were not cleared away when the butchery at last came to an end. They were left in the Red Square for days, evil-smelling and rotting in the mid-summer sun. Dogs were allowed to eat their flesh, until finally *Oprichniks*, armed with long knives and axes, arrived to hack the remains into little pieces. No burial was possible. In the countryside, where the *Oprichniks* had left the bodies of men, women and children lying in houses, roads and fields, many of these corpses lay for weeks. The survivors were so terrified of taking any action that could incriminate them that they refrained from burying the victims, fearing that they might be accused of sympathy with traitors.[26]

Two of the most frightful deaths were inflicted on Ivan's treasurer, Nikita Afanasyevich Founikov, and his beautiful wife, the sister of Prince Vyazemsky. Founikov had also been close to the Tsar since the early days. He was one of the last to swear allegiance to the heir to the throne when Ivan nearly died in 1553, but he remained in office. It is possible that he took steps to prevent money derived from Novgorod going to Ivan's interminable war in Livonia. This wretched man was one of the victims on that terrible day. He was stripped and then dipped first in boiling water then in cold, and this went on until he died. His wife died in a convent in a way that sums up the whole unspeakable horror of the man who devised all these deaths, a man who has merited more than any other murderer in history the name of Terrible. She could not say where or if her husband had hidden any valuable possessions. She was taken to a room where she was stripped naked in the presence of her fifteen-year-old daughter. The only instrument of torture was a simple cord stretched tight from one wall to the other. With her legs either side of this cord, she was dragged backwards and forwards from one end to the other. She was then thrown into a convent, where she died after a short time.[27]

Ivan had sown many evil winds; his people now reaped the whirlwind. The very next sentence in the verse from which this metaphor is taken, from the Old Testament Book of Hosea (ch 8, v 7), describes the next disaster in Russia, caused by the excesses of the *Oprichnina*: 'it hath no stalk; the bud shall yield no meal; if so be it yield, the strangers shall swallow it up.' The farmers produced only enough to feed themselves, to avoid the exorbitant demands of the *Oprichniks* and the army. But this supply failed in the autumn of 1570, after an unusually wet summer. By winter famine stalked the land. And with famine came the plague, killing unnumbered thousands. A Dutch merchant reported that 250,000 Russians died, Jenkinson gave an even larger estimate of this latest catastrophe, 300,000. The iniquities of the *Oprichniks* before the plague struck were summed up in two sentences by Heinrich von Staden: 'The country became desolate; the peasant would like to bury himself alive to escape from injustice.'[28]

After the plague came the Tartars from Crimea. Devlet Girei, the Khan, had received news about the famine, the plague, the absence of Ivan's army in Livonia, and the decimation of the ablest men in Russia. He had sworn vengeance for the loss of Kazan and Astrakhan, and now he felt the time had come for retribution. With an army of 120,000 men, he advanced into Russia and reached the gates of Moscow without resistance. Ivan's soldiers posted on the Oka River were bypassed. Without waiting for the attack on Moscow to begin, Ivan fled to Alexandrovsk, and then still further north to Rostov, 130 miles from the capital. His army, positioned on the Oka River, sixty miles south of Moscow, amounted to 50,000 men. If it had not been for the wasteful Livonian war, this force could have been much stronger. Hatred of the Tsar was such that deserters guided the Tartar advance guard over the river at undefended points; the main body, waiting for orders from Ivan which never came, put up only a token resistance and pulled back, leaving the road to Moscow wide open. An enormous amount of prisoners, perhaps amounting to 150,000, mostly women and girls, were taken by the Tartars, and an envoy from the Khan, finding Ivan at Alexandrovsk, north of the capital, delivered his master's challenge to a duel as he would not fight with his army. Demonstrating clearly what a miserable figure Ivan was presenting to his subjects and to the world, the envoy gave him a knife with which he could kill himself. The Tartars set the suburbs of Moscow on fire; the whole town was engulfed and all but the Kremlin was destroyed. The city was packed with Russians who had come into the town for protection, and they and the citizens rushed to the Kremlin to shelter behind its massive stone walls. But all the gates were barred. Men, women and children threw themselves into the Moskva River; here they suffocated and drowned in such quantity that the river itself was blocked with corpses.

The rapid spread of the fire took the Tartars by surprise, and they made their way back to the Crimea with their gigantic army of prisoners. Their number indicates that many of them felt they had nothing to lose, and that a life of slavery in a warmer climate, in another land, could not be worse than their lives of constant danger in their own country. Ivan came back to the Kremlin when the Tartars had gone, and was greeted by a message from Devlet Girei:

I burn and devastate all before me because of Kazan and Astrakhan. I have burnt your city. I wanted your head and crown, but you did not appear and did not march against us, and still you exalt yourself as the Muscovite monarch.[29]

Even after this catastrophe, Ivan was still the master of his kingdom, which demonstrates how easy it has been to rule the Russians. The Khan demanded the surrender of Kazan and Astrakhan, and threatened to march on Moscow again. Ivan replied that he would perhaps give up Astrakhan and would give him a large sum of money in compensation. In the following summer, Devlet attacked once more. This time Ivan stayed in Novgorod, some three hundred miles from Moscow; but he had had time to send an army south under the command of Prince Michael Vorotynsky. Thanks to their courageous fighting and the skilful leadership of this general, Ivan was saved from a second disaster. After a series of engagements only thirty-five miles from Moscow, the Tartars were defeated and they returned to the Crimea.

After Ivan's orgy of carnage in Novgorod and the ignominious destruction of his capital by the Tartars, after the misery and havoc created by the hated *Oprichniks*, the Russians were too frightened to rid themselves of the author of their distress. No one knows what they really thought about their Tsar; perhaps many still believed that he had been sent by an angry God to chastise them.

8

Ivan and Queen Elizabeth

The history of Anglo-Russian relations is from the Russian point of view largely one of frustration. Many a grandiose scheme of expansion might have been successful, at the expense of Turkey, Persia, India and China, but for English opposition. In the seventeenth and eighteenth centuries, Siberia was simply Russia's back garden, and the region beyond, further east, was unknown and unwanted, but in the nineteenth century this unknown area, eastern Siberia, was opened up and the most disquieting of Russia's new neighbours were the ubiquitous English. In the same century, Russian expansion in the Black Sea area was checked by British support of Turkey and Persia. In central Asia expansion was limited by the British in Afghanistan and India; and in the Far East expansion and development was perhaps going to be threatened by the steady westward march of the British in Canada. One important reason why Alaska was sold to the United States of America in 1867 for a mere seven million dollars was to prevent it being taken by the English. In China too, from 1833, English traders were establishing themselves under the protection of their government agent, and were making their country the most favoured nation. In consequence Russia's overland trade with China, through Kyakhta, south of Lake Baikal, began to dwindle. In 1842 the British occupied Hong Kong, only seventy miles from the main Chinese port of Canton. It was at least logical, in the opinion of some of the Tsar's advisers, that this same acquisitive race with their powerful fleet, might occupy the mouth of the River Amur in eastern Siberia, territory too distant to incur serious Chinese opposition. It was an empty area, waiting for settlement and exploitation.

This role of obstruction was played by England when the history of her relations with Russia had only just begun. In 1551 Sebastian Cabot, the son of John Cabot, the Genoese discoverer of England's first colony, Newfoundland, formed in London together with a group of enterprising city merchants, 'the mysterie and companie of the Marchants adventurers for the discoverie of Regions, Dominions, Islands and places unknowen'. The aim of this company was to discover a new route to China.

The Genoese, Venetians, Spaniards and the Dutch had left the English far behind in the race to the east. The Genoese had established a trading post in southern China in 1337, and were conducting a profitable trade in silks and those spices, cinnamon, nutmeg and pepper, which so enlivened the medieval western meal. These mariners had sailed to the Orient by the south-eastern route, round the Cape of Good Hope and through the Indian Ocean. Cabot was determined to find a shorter way; the ships of his new company would discover a north-east passage. His first expedition consisted of just three ships, the *Edward Bonaventura*, the *Bona Esperanza* and the *Bona Confidencia*, with a total crew of 111 men. Under the command of Sir Hugh Willoughby, the captain of the *Bona Esperanza*, they sailed from Deptford on 10 May 1553. It was arranged that in the event of separation, each ship would make for Vardo, known as Wardhouse, an island off the coast of Lapland, and there wait for the others.

Showing a brave spirit of realism, Henry Sidney, the father of Sir Philip Sidney, addressed the merchants of the new company before the expedition began. He forecast that the mariners might meet 'barbarous and cruel people', and that they would find themselves 'amongst the monstrous and terrible beasts of the sea'.[1] Not surprisingly considering the dangerous route they were taking and the smallness of their ships, disaster struck almost immediately. A few days after leaving the Shetlands, the ships were caught in a heavy storm and soon lost sight of each other. The *Esperanza* and the *Confidencia* and their crew of sixty-one men were discovered in the following spring, frozen like statues on the ice off the coast of Russian Lapland. The third ship, the *Bonaventura*, arrived safely at Vardo. The captain, Richard Chancellor, waited for his colleagues for seven days, and then continued his journey alone. After sailing for two months, he sighted land for the first time. They landed on 24 August at the mouth of the northern River Dvina, in the White Sea, not far from the future site of Archangel.

Chancellor had no idea where he was as he had no maps to guide him. The natives he approached first ran away from him and then returned and kissed his feet. He was, he learnt, in Russia. The local fishermen could not trade with the newcomers without permission from their sovereign. Chancellor asked them to take him and his men to the Tsar, but first a messenger had to be sent to Moscow with the news of the strangers, and instructions were requested. Ivan the Terrible, knowing that his attempts to conquer Livonia would be opposed by Lithuania and Sweden, and that his army was inferior in fire power to his neighbours', was excited by this news of the English and gave orders for their instant transportation to Moscow. Chancellor, impatient of delay, started on the 1,500 mile journey south without waiting for the messenger. He and his men finally arrived in Moscow in December, more than three months after their landing. They were kept waiting twelve days (at liberty to walk about the capital, but under observation) before being taken to the Tsar. Chancellor estimated that Moscow was, as quoted in Hakluyt's *Voyages*, 'greater than London with the suburbs, but for beauty and fairness nothing comparable'. At last the day came when the Englishmen were ushered into the presence of the sovereign. Ivan the Terrible was only twenty-three years old, but as Chancellor afterwards reported to Clement Adams, a tutor at the English Court, there was nothing immature in his bearing:

> Being conducted into the chamber of presence, our men began to wonder at the Majestie of the Emperor. His seat was aloft, in a very royal throne, having on his head a diadem, or Crowne of Gold, apparelled with a robe all of goldsmith's work, and in his hand he held a sceptre garnished and beset with precious stones; and beside all other notes and appearances of honour, there was a Majestie in his countenance proportionable with the excellency of his estate. On the one side of him stood his chief secretary, Mikhailov [Ivan Mikhailovich Viskovaty], the other the great commander of silence, both of them arrayed also in cloth of gold. And there sat the Council of one hundred and fifty in number, all in like sort arrayed, and of great estate.
>
> This so honourable assembly, so great a Majestie of the Emperor, and of the place, might well have amazed our men and dashed them out of countenance. But Master Chancellor, nothing dismayed, saluted and did his duty to the Emperor, after the manner of England, and delivered unto him the letters of our King, Edward the Sixth.[2]

Ivan the Terrible glanced at the letter written in various languages, one of which was Greek, which could be translated into Russian. Later that day the English were invited to a royal banquet. On this too, Adams wrote in some detail, showing what a glaring contrast existed between the opulence at Court and the surrounding poverty:

> They find the Emperor sitting upon an high and stately seat, apparelled with a robe of silver, and with another Diadem on his head, and our men being placed over against him, they sit down. The guests were all apparelled with linen without, and with rich skins within. The Emperor, when he takes any bread or knife in his hand, doth first of all cross himself upon his

forehead. Before the coming in of the meat, the Emperor doth first bestow a piece of bread upon every one of his guests, with a loud pronunciation of his title and honour, in this manner: 'The Great Duke of Moscovie, the Chief Emperor of Russia, John Basiliwich, doth give thee bread.'

Whereupon the guests rise up and, by and by, sit down again. This done the Gentleman Usher comes in with a notable company of servants, carrying the dishes, and having made reverence to the Emperor, puts a young swan in a golden platter upon the table. Touching the rest of the dishes, because they were brought in out of order, our men can report no certainty, but this is true, that all the furniture of the dishes and drinking vessels, which were for the use of a hundred guests, was all of pure gold, and the tables were so laden with vessels of gold, that there was no room for some to stand upon them.

We may not forget that there were 140 servitors arrayed in cloth of gold, that in the dinner time changed thrice their habit and apparel, which servitors were in like sort served with bread from the Emperor, as the rest of the guests. Last of all, dinner being ended, and candles brought in, for by this time night was come, the Emperor calleth all his guests and noblemen by their names, in such sort that it seems miraculous.[3]

At this banquet Ivan sat alone. 'There sat none near him by a great way.' It was not only the servants who changed their apparel. Ivan himself changed his crown once before dinner, and twice during the long repast. Chancellor, having watched several military parades in Moscow, greatly admired the armour of the cavalry, 'a coat of mail with a skull on their heads. Some of their coats are covered with velvet or cloth of gold. Their desire is to be sumptuous in the field. The Duke [Ivan the Terrible] is richly attired above all measure. His pavilion is either covered with cloth of gold or silver, and so set with precious stones that it is wonderful to see it. I have seen the Kings Majesties of England and the French King's pavilion, which are fayre, yet not like unto his.'

In his comments about religion in Russia, Chancellor noted that each corpse was provided with a letter requesting St Peter to see that on arrival in heaven he or she were given a place above the Roman Catholics. Visits were made to Novgorod and Yaroslavl, on the Volga northeast of Moscow, and towards the end of February 1554, the Englishmen left Moscow for the north coast. Their epoch-making visit had been a most promising success. Chancellor carried home with him the Tsar's offer of a commercial treaty with England, which gave English merchants 'free marte with all free liberties, through my whole dominions, with all kinds of wares, to come and go at their pleasure'.[4]

In 1555, the *Bonaventura*, a new *Confidencia* and *Esperanza* sailed again to Russia with Chancellor in command. The letter he brought from Mary, his Queen, and Philip of Spain, whom she had married the previous year, began with this impressive list of titles: 'Mary and Philip, King and Queen of England, France, Naples, Jerusalem and Ireland, Princes of Spain and Sicily, Archdukes of Austria, Dukes of Milan and Brabant.' The letter was written in Italian, Greek and Polish. It must have given Ivan an inflated idea of England's real power in Europe. Further details of mutual trade were discussed, and it was agreed that a Russian ambassador would henceforward represent his country's interests in England, while those of the Muscovy Company, as Cabot's venture came to be known since it was a private enterprise, would be looked after by one permanent agent in Moscow and another in Kolmogory, where Chancellor had first landed. This was to be the chief port for English ships.

On the return journey to England a heavy storm nearly brought the whole expedition to an end. The *Esperanza* and the *Confidencia* were lost with all hands near the Norwegian coast. The *Bonaventura* survived but was dashed against the rocks off the north-east coast of Scotland, near Kinnaird's Head. Chancellor and most of the crew were drowned; Osip Nepea, the first Russian ambassador in England, and a few sailors managed to reach the shore. Nepea had brought with him some precious gifts from the Tsar, yards of cloth of gold and sables; these bundles were washed ashore but the local inhabitants, unlike the obedient natives of Kolmogory, purloined the gifts without hesitation. The ambassador was most distressed. But when he finally arrived in London, he was given a reassuring reception by 140 members of the Muscovy Company, with the same number of servants. On his way into the capital a fox hunt was arranged for his amusement.

In welcoming English merchants to Russia, Ivan the Terrible saw the chance of obtaining weapons for his war against Lithuania and Poland. If a real alliance could be made, perhaps troops might follow. He asked Queen Mary to ban all trade with Poland. At the same time the King of Poland wrote to the English imploring them to refuse all trade with Russia, saying: 'Up to now we could conquer him [the Russian] because he was a stranger to education and did not know the arts.' But Mary, and after her, Elizabeth, ignored both requests; all they wanted was the monopoly of Russia's trade with the west. Nepea refused to grant this, surprised by the indecent haste of the English, whereupon the Secretary of the Muscovy Company wrote to his agent in Moscow, as already quoted, that 'we do not find the ambassador now at the last so conformable to reason as we thought. He is very mistrustful and thinks every man will beguile him'.[5]

Undeterred by Russian reluctance to comply, Antony Jenkinson, one of the most brilliant of England's merchant adventurers, sailed to the White Sea to secure this monopoly in 1557, the last year of Mary's unhappy reign. On his arrival in Moscow, Ivan gave him a magnificent dinner which lasted for five hours, and after it presented him with a fine red damask cloak. The Tsar took an immediate liking to Jenkinson, and was impressed by his wit and knowledge. The English, in fact, were beginning to enjoy a position at Court that other foreigners, and the Russians themselves no doubt, wished they shared.

Jenkinson wisely decided that it would not be advisable to hurry the Tsar into giving any further concessions to the English. He had learnt that in Moscow the best results were often obtained, as in other eastern countries, by simulating indifference or a lack of interest in the calendar. Hastening slowly, he spent four pleasant months enjoying banquets, parades and tours in and around Moscow, and then set out in April 1558 for Bokhara, from where he planned to join one of the caravans that left now and again for the distant, romantic land of Cathay, as China was then called. This was an excellent demonstration of good manners.

Taking with him samples of English cloth and accompanied by two other Englishmen, Richard and Robert Johnson, and a Tartar guide, he went by boat down the Moskva and Oka rivers to Nizhni Novgorod on the Volga, and from there was rowed down this 2,400-mile river to Astrakhan, where it flows into the Caspian Sea. Taking a larger vessel, they crossed to the eastern shore and continued their leisurely way on camels. Apart from being attacked by Turkmen bandits, whom they repulsed with firearms, their journey to Bokhara was uneventful. The little party—the first Englishmen to visit central Asia—-arrived there on 23 December, eight months after leaving Moscow. Jenkinson noted that 'the city is very great and the houses for the most part of earth, but there are also many houses, temples and monuments of stone, sumptuously builded and gilt.' He was at a loss for words when it came to describing the bath houses: 'Bath-stoves, so artificially built, that the like thereof is not in the world: the manner whereof is too long to rehearse.'

The Englishmen were generously entertained by the Khan of Bokhara, who 'caused us to shoot in handguns before him, and did himself practise the use thereof'. The Khan, however, did not behave perfectly. 'After all this great entertainment before my departure he showed himself a very Tartar: for he went to the wars owing me money. He owed me for 19 pieces of Kersey' (a type of English cloth). These local wars did not help Jenkinson in his efforts to reach China. He discovered that they had been erupting sporadically for the last three years, and no one could tell him when the next caravan would be leaving. The journey, there and back in normal times, took nine months. But waiting was out of the question; he was advised to leave Bokhara as the city was about to be put to the sword.

Jenkinson and his friends took the next caravan to Astrakhan, and ten days later came the threatened attack. Bokhara was besieged and pillaged by the Khan of Samarkand. Nearly six months elapsed before Jenkinson returned to Moscow, bringing with him an ambassador and his suite from Bokhara, another envoy from the Kingdom of Balkh (now just south of the border of Afghanistan), and four ambassadors from Urgenj, a small Tartar Khanate south of the Aral Sea, the old capital of Khorezim, sacked by Ghenghiz Khan and levelled to the ground by Tamburlane. Also in Jenkinson's party were twenty-five Russians, who had been 'for a long time slaves in Tartaria'. For Ivan the Terrible he brought a useless, but nevertheless original gift, 'a white Cowes tail of Cathay'. In a study of Anglo-Russian relations by the Russian historian, Dr J. Hamel, a Privy Councillor, published in 1846, this present was described in translation as a yak crupper.[6]

The intrepid Jenkinson returned to England for a year, and was then sent by the new Queen, Elizabeth, back to Moscow. After Ivan had made a further test of his reliability by entrusting him with secret negotiations in Persia, he gave him a letter containing proposals for a close alliance with England. He had already given the English in Russia a monopoly of all trade into Russia via the White Sea, and permission to trade with Persia and China through Russia. Now Ivan asked for favours in return. As these messages were mostly verbal and kept most secret, we do not know the full details. We do know that Ivan asked for an alliance between the two countries, of a defensive and offensive nature, so that they might 'be joined as one'. Elizabeth was asked to be 'friend to his friends and enemy to his enemies and so per contra'. He requested 'masters to come unto him which can make ships and sail them', and he wished 'to have out of England all kinds of artillery and things necessary for war'. He asked for:

> master builders, who can construct for us fortresses, bastions and palaces, also surgeons and apothecaries, also master craftsmen who understand how to prospect for and mine gold and silver.

Still more surprising was Ivan's proposal that he and Elizabeth should exchange a mutual promise of shelter, for, he said, it might well be that one of them would be glad of a country to escape to, 'there to have relief from fear and danger'. Ivan by this time was convinced that all his subjects were either hostile to him or simply incapable of understanding his God-like authority over them, and it was quite logical for him to plan his escape from such unworthy and contemptible men. Sir Jerome Horsey reported that 'he lived in great danger and fear of treasons and being done away with'.[7]

Elizabeth waited before replying to such embarrassing requests. She had no intention of allying her country to another with such strings attached. But the commercial details were agreed to. On September 1567, the Muscovy Company was permitted to travel and trade in Russian territory as far as Kazan, Astrakhan, Narva and Dorpat in Livonia, and as far south as Bulgaria. Nothing was said about a political alliance. Only when Elizabeth heard that rival traders, two of them English, were being allowed to use Ivan's recently won Baltic port of Narva, and that the Muscovy Company's merchants were being hampered by restrictions, did she send a new ambassador, Thomas Randolfe, to Moscow with instructions to 're-establish order in the English commerce'.

Ivan's relations with the English had already shown themselves to be out of the ordinary. He had shown these foreigners favours, both commercial and social, which were not commensurate with the material benefits received. His requests for skilled men were granted in small numbers, and goods were exchanged although the amounts involved were also small, not surprisingly, considering the distance between the two countries. The Muscovites were no doubt surprised by their Tsar's unusual affability when entertaining the Englishmen; they were now given more evidence of Ivan's extraordinary interest in that remote country. What did he want?

But it was not only the Russians who were confused. On his arrival in Moscow, Randolfe was treated coldly and kept waiting four months before seeing the Tsar. What transpired at this meeting is unknown. A few days later, he made a midnight visit to the Kremlin, dressed as a Russian. For three hours he was alone with the Tsar, and we have no details of this meeting either. Randolfe had been instructed by Elizabeth to assure Ivan that he could indeed come to England for shelter. As for the suggestion that she might flee to Russia, that, Randolfe indicated, was unlikely. In fact he was instructed to make it clear that the Queen needed no place of shelter as she was in no danger.

At a later date, Ivan disclosed that Randolfe on this occasion talked only of 'boorish affairs of merchandise and would seldom talk with us of our princely affairs'.[8] In spite of this, the English merchants had their monopoly of the White Sea trade confirmed; they were given the right to trade through Russia with Persia and Bokhara, and they were asked to start an iron mine on the River Vychegda, some seven hundred miles north-east of Moscow. But Queen Elizabeth must have found the news from Russia somewhat alarming. Ivan was building, Horsey tells us, 'many goodly barges at Vologda, and [has] brought his richest treasure to be imbarqued in the same, to pass down the Dvina, and so into England by the English ships.' It looked as if the Tsar of Russia might well come to England for shelter. Elizabeth assured him that a house in this country would be put at his disposal. So as not to encourage him too much, she stipulated that he would have to pay for his lodging, not an unreasonable request, considering his great personal wealth.

Three years had gone by since Ivan's proposals for a formal alliance, the negotiations conducted by Jenkinson which resulted in the commercial charter of September 1567. According to J. Hamel, it was to Jenkinson at this time that Ivan first brought up his most surprising proposal: 'Here private negotiations with Queen Elizabeth with reference to a marriage must have commenced.'[9] Sir Jerome Horsey revealed that Ivan consulted Dr Elisaeus Bomel of Westphalia, who had studied medicine at Cambridge, and was now an astrologer,

> to know his likelihood of successes if he should be a suitor for the hand of the Queen. And though he was much disheartened, not only that he had two wives living and that many kings and great princes had been suitors to Her Majesty and could not prevail, yet he magnified himself his person, his wisdom, greatness and riches above all other princes and said he would have a try, and presently put his last wife into a nunnery.[10]

It is a mistake, Hamel tells us, 'to suppose with Karamzin, that Bomel was the first who suggested to the Tsar the idea of marriage with Elizabeth, for he merely urged him to it anew by his astrological mystifications and calculations.'[11] Horsey, who knew Bomel well in Moscow, related that he had deluded the Emperor, making him believe the Queen of England was young, and that it was very favourable for him to marry her.[12].

Ivan, in 1570, was forty years old, prematurely aged; his second wife, Maria, had died the year before. Elizabeth was three years younger. He hated disobedience; she loved independence. As blunt rejection of foreign suitors was bad for business, Elizabeth had found that silence, or ambiguity, was golden. Her merchants in Russia benefited by her decision not to tell Ivan that she had no intention of becoming a

Tsaritsa, or the wife of any foreigner. But the Tsar of All Russia now lost his temper. Diplomatic correspondence between heads of state is usually drained of personal comments, and strong emotional feelings are usually cloaked by dignified understatements. Almost a whole year had passed without any clear statement from Andrei Savin, his ambassador in London, and when this envoy returned without any important message, Ivan sent this angry letter to Elizabeth on 24 October 1570— when a monarch resorts to insulting remarks about a woman's menstruation, it surely indicates that something more important than trade is involved:

> You have set aside our great affairs, and your council doth deal with our ambassador about merchants' affairs, and your merchants did rule all our business. We had thought that you had been ruler over your land and had sought honour to yourself and profit to your country, and therefore we did pretend those weighty affairs between you and us. But now we perceive that there be other men that do rule, and not men but boors and merchants, the which seek not the wealth and honour of our Majesties, but they seek their own profit of merchandise. And you flow in your maidenly state like a maid. Whoever was trusted in our affairs did deceive us; it were not meet that you should credit them. Seeing it is so, we do set aside these affairs and those boorish merchants that have been the occasion that the pretended wealth and honour of our Majesties hath not come pass(?) but do seek their own wealth, they shall see what traffic they shall have here. All those privileges which we have given shall be from this day of none effect. Your boors (*muzhiks*) do as they like with you. I spit on you and your palace.[13]

This letter may have caused some amusement to Elizabeth and Burghley. It certainly made a change from the run-of-the-mill contents of diplomatic bags. But the news about the English merchants in Russia was serious. The only man who could perhaps save them was Antony Jenkinson. Undeterred by reports that Ivan had sworn to cut off his head if he set foot in Russia again, he returned to Moscow, this time as Ambassador. He was kept waiting for six months in Kolmogory, with no bodyguard and no supply of food given to him. Making his own arrangements, he resolutely waited to see what Ivan had in store for him. He could not have come at a worse time; the whole country, he reported, was 'sore visited by the hand of God with the plague'. No one was allowed to travel within Russia or abroad. He also stated in one of his letters (on 8 August 1571) that hunger had driven the Russians to cannibalism. Some 300,000 had died, it was estimated, and perhaps as many had been taken by the Tartars during their advance into the southern part of the country.[14] During the conflagration in Moscow, the house given to the English merchants had been destroyed and four merchants had died. In the beer-cellar of this house thirty people had gathered for safety, the Englishmen and their families, and their friends and strangers who had fled from the surrounding chaos.

Jenkinson's patience was rewarded. Ivan wrote to Elizabeth saying 'And even now have we had tidings that Antony is here . . . When Antony cometh unto us we will gladly hear him.'[15] Once again the Tsar was won over by Jenkinson's tact and persuasiveness, and after several private conversations with him all the Muscovy Company's privileges were restored. His task successfully accomplished, the Ambassador returned home leaving Ivan still unsatisfied. Angry again, he imposed a tax on the English merchants. This was less than half the amount paid by other foreigners, but it was sufficient to make Elizabeth send a new ambassador, Daniel Sylvester. He arrived in Moscow in 1575 and was greeted with the news that Ivan had abdicated in favour of a Tartar prince. He was summoned to the Kremlin, where indeed he found the Tartar, Simeon Bekbulatovich, sitting on the throne. Ivan was one of the courtiers.

He soon learnt that this new ruler did not really rule, and that Ivan was still pulling the strings. Sylvester was handed an ultimatum: all foreign trade would be given to the Germans, of the Hanseatic League, and the Venetians, unless Ivan received 'full and entire satisfaction' from Elizabeth. The ambassador sailed back to London and returned with the Queen's reply. What this was no one knows; in Kolmogory he was killed by a flash of lightning. His house and all his papers were burnt. A thunderbolt also struck the house a moment before and killed a tailor who had just fitted Sylvester with a new jacket of yellow satin.[16] This news was regarded by Ivan as a clear sign from God. What precisely it indicated in his view, we do not know, but he may have felt that God was paying particular attention to the way he was treating the English. No further restrictions were placed on Elizabeth's merchants. In any case, he still wanted something more than English goods and skills.

By this time Elizabeth must have thought that there would be no further embarrassing proposals of marriage. But there were indeed more surprises. In 1582, when the Tsar was married to his seventh wife, Maria Feodorovna Nagoya, he wrote to Elizabeth proposing marriage to one of her relations. He sent for the agent of the Muscovy Company, Sir Jerome Horsey, and gave him two secret messages for the English Queen. The first was a request for military supplies, gunpowder, salt-petre, lead and brimstone, and the second was a request for an English bride. Horsey was given these messages in a wooden vodka bottle, in his own words, 'not worth three pence'. Then, with '400 Hungers ducketts in gold to be sewed in my boots and quilted in some of my worst garments', he rode across Europe on horseback—Ivan had had enough of the time-consuming maritime communications. On his ride through Lithuania he was twice arrested as a spy, but on both occasions he swore that he was fleeing from Russia as fast as he could. When he delivered his messages to the English Queen, she noticed that they smelt of vodka. Ivan's plea for supplies was readily granted. Horsey returned to Russia the following year with thirteen ships full of war materials, as requested, together with sulphur, lead and copper, to the value of £9,000. This cargo contained no bride for the Tsar, but there was on board an English doctor, Robert Jacob. Ivan engaged him as his private physician and learnt from him that Queen Elizabeth had a niece, Lady Mary Hastings, daughter of the Earl of Huntingdon.

Delighted with this news, Ivan selected a new ambassador, Feodor Pissemsky, and told him to interview this royal niece and obtain a portrait of her. One slight difficulty lay in the fact that he was now living with his seventh wife, which meant that he had exceeded the limit of wives laid down by his Church by four. His third wife was Marfa Sobakina, the daughter of a Novgorod merchant. She had an unfortunate name: *sobaka* means dog. This poor girl died after only sixteen days, killed by poison or witchcraft, it was alleged. In the same year, 1571, he married again; his fourth wife was Anna Koltovskaya, the daughter of a boyar from Kolomna. As he was now breaking the law, the wedding was held privately. After only three years, without any offspring, Ivan grew tired of her and sent her, shorn as a nun, to a nunnery. Accused of treachery, her entire family was murdered by Ivan, but she was allowed to live. She died in 1626. In 1575 he married his fifth wife, Anna Vassilchikova. There was no church wedding, and the bride's family were not even invited to the Kremlin. How long she retained her rank as Tsaritsa is not known. But in the same year he married again for the sixth time; his bride was Vassilissa Melentievna. This marriage was doubly shocking in the eyes of his subjects, as it showed still more contempt for the official limit of three wives, and his bride had already been married to another man. She was referred to at Court as 'the woman'.[17] After three years she was also sent to a convent, accused of infidelity; her alleged lover, Prince Ivan Devtelev, was killed. With all these marriages, Ivan's son by Anastasia, Ivan Ivanovich, remained as the only fit heir to the throne. He was now twenty-

four. Four years later, in 1582, the Tsar married yet again, his seventh
and last wife, once more without any church ceremony. His bride was
Maria Nagaya, the daughter of a Court official. Her family were
members of the Nagai Tartars, from the Azov and Caspian Sea area.
In Russian, *nagaya* means naked.

None of these wives, however, diminished Ivan's desire for an English
girl, preferably a member of the royal family. Ivan's ambassador,
Pissemsky, was told to explain to Queen Elizabeth that his seventh
wife had no legal status—this was quite true, since he had more than
doubled the prescribed quota of spouses. He was also told that Maria
could easily be put aside, that is despatched to a nunnery. At the same
time Ivan thought that England should now do a little more for him
than just send supplies. His long war with Poland had ended with a
disadvantageous peace treaty, so Pissemsky was to ask for troops and
several warships for a renewal of the campaign. In this way the English
could show their gratitude for the many favours he had bestowed on
their merchants in Russia.

Pissemsky and his suite arrived in London in September 1582, when
Francois, Duke of Alençon was hoping to persuade Elizabeth to marry
him. By this time the Queen had found that whoever she married,
whether he was English or foreign, there would be objections from the
Protestants, the Catholics, the Puritans, or from some other section of
the community. Avoiding marriage had proved diplomatically a more
fruitful policy than courting it. Marriage to Alençon would bring with
it a much desired alliance with France, but Elizabeth was not in love
with him and he was somewhat ugly. She loved the handsome Earl of
Leicester, but he was already married, and when his wife died, it was
rumoured that he was responsible for her death. If she married an
Englishman, foreign countries would no longer hope for a dynastic
alliance with England. If she married a foreigner, her subjects would
impugn her patriotism; her sister's Spanish husband, the King of Spain,
had not increased her popularity. When Pissemsky announced in London
that his master wished to marry Elizabeth's niece, the same policy of
simulated indecision was put into action by the English government.
Elizabeth had no intention of letting her niece go to Russia; the object
of Ivan's obsession, Lady Mary Hastings, understandably rejected her
unseen but only too well-known suitor. But the comedy of egos was
enacted; the off-stage lover was not humiliated by a blunt refusal.

After five months Elizabeth said she might agree to some form of
military alliance, but only in return for a monopoly of all the external

trade of Russia. After three more months of outward indecision about the proposed marriage, she agreed that a meeting could be arranged between Pissemsky and the 'Empress of Muscovia', as Lady Mary was nicknamed at court. She was also called Lady Mary Huntingdonska. Now the second act of the comedy could begin.

Sir Jerome Horsey was one of the cast and has given a description of this court play. In May 1583, eight months after Pissemsky's arrival in England, he was introduced to Lady Mary in the garden of York House near Whitehall in London, the house of the Lord Chancellor, Sir Thomas Bromley, who had recently succeeded Sir Nicholas Bacon in that office. 'Her Majesty', Horsey recounted, 'caused that lady to be attended on with divers great ladies and maids of honour and young noblemen.' Lady Mary bowed politely and then stood still, saying nothing. Pissemsky 'cast down his countenance, fell prostrate at her feet, rose, ran back from her, his face still toward her, she and the rest admiring his manner. He said by an interpreter it did suffice him to behold the angel he hoped would be his master's spouse.' He then departed to write his report to the Tsar. He was so embarrassed and confused that he even got Lady Mary's name and rank quite wrong, calling her on one occasion Princess Titounski, and on another the Princess of Houtinsk: 'Marie Hantis is tall, thin, fair-skinned, with blue eyes, a straight nose, and long tapering fingers.'[18]

Ivan might have guessed from this restrained description that some details were omitted. His cautious ambassador thought it wise not to mention that Lady Mary was not pretty, nor that she was made less so by the marks of smallpox. And he made no mention of the fact that she hated the idea of marrying his master. After this comic meeting, Queen Elizabeth thought the matter would be closed, and told Pissemsky that she regretted that Lady Mary had not enough beauty to please the Tsar. He must have surprised her by saying 'I think her fair; the rest is God's affair'. He was given a portrait of Lady Mary and, after a review of the fleet in his honour, he set sail for his own country. Elizabeth once again stressed that she hoped Ivan would come to England whenever he wished.

It was around this time that Russians, or men dressed in Russian costume, appeared for the first time in English literature, in *Love's Labour's Lost*, and *The Order of the Helmet* by Francis Bacon. In both plays men disguise themselves as Russians. It is not known when *Love's Labour Lost* was written, but internal evidence suggests that it was probably in 1594. In Act 5 Scene 2, King Ferdinand of Navarre,

Berowne, Longaville and Dumain appear as Russians, 'full of courtship and of state'. The Shakespearian historian, Sir Sidney Lee, considered that the appearance of Pissemsky and his attendant lords at the English Court, and his comic attempt to secure a bride for Ivan the Terrible, gave the author the idea for this scene. Ferdinand and his lords complete their disguise with visors, a necessary feature of a masque, a form of theatre much admired by Queen Elizabeth.

Men in Russian costumes next appeared in *The Order of the Helmet*, a masque staged at Gray's Inn at Christmas 1594. Francis Bacon was born in York House or in the Palace of Whitehall, and spent much of his childhood and youth there, when Sir Nicholas Bacon was Lord Chancellor, and it is quite likely that he was one of the 'young noblemen' who witnessed the meeting in York House garden of Pissemsky and Lady Mary Hastings. In the brief biography of Bacon by his secretary and chaplain, John Rawley, we are told that he was born 'in York House or York Place in the Strand'; York Place was not in the Strand, but was the name of the Royal Palace of Whitehall. In 1594, when Bacon's masque was presented at Gray's Inn, he was Master of the Revels and was living in an apartment at Gray's Inn. He took part in *The Order of the Helmet* under the name of Henry Helme. The Russians in *Love's Labour's Lost* are accompanied by blackamoors, and in *The Order of the Helmet* by 'Negro-Tartars', black slaves of the Tartars, who themselves were now Russian subjects. Yet another link between the Shakespeare play and the masque is found in a reference to the journey from Moscow in both entertainments. In *Love's Labour's Lost* Rosaline suggests that King Ferdinand is pale, having been 'sea-sick, I think, coming from Muscovy'. In the Gray's Inn masque, the Prince of Purpoole says that he cannot carry out certain ceremonies as he feels, after a visit to Russia, somewhat exhausted 'by length of my journey, and my sickness at sea'.[19] Information about further attempts made by the Russians to increase contacts with the West came from the Danish ambassador in Moscow, Axel Guldenstern.

Queen Elizabeth had by this time (1583) been communicating with Ivan and his ministers for twenty-five years, since the beginning of her reign. On 1 June 1561 Sir Nicholas Bacon wrote to Thomas Cotton, Under Clerk of the Hamper in the Court of Chancery, instructing him to 'allow for certain lace mingled with gold and silver, put to several letters patent sent by the Queen's Majesty to the Emperor of Russia, which lace amounteth in yards to the number of eight, after the rate of six shillings and eight pence for every yard'.[20] And on 1 September 1569,

Elizabeth wrote to Ivan saying that 'he would be very well received in England with his noble consort and his dear children. We have thought good in some secret manner to send your highness, for a manifest and certain token of our good will to your highness' estate and surety, this our secret letter, whereunto none are privie beside ourself, but our most secret council.'[21] The Russian language itself interested her and she expressed her admiration of it to Jerome Horsey. 'I could quickly learn it,' she said; 'it is the famoust [most famous] and most copious language in the world.' Lord Essex was with her at the time, and she suggested to him that he should learn it.[22]

The English ambassador who accompanied Pissemsky back to Russia was Sir Jerome Bowes, not the ideal man for this post. He was conceited, fussy and sometimes tactless. He could not help disappointing Ivan when he told him that Lady Mary Hastings was too weak to undertake the long and uncomfortable journey to Russia, but he annoyed the Tsar when he demanded that England's monopoly of trade through the White Sea should be confirmed. This was now the only sea route available, since Ivan had just lost Narva to the Poles. Ivan did not like this arrogant approach, and asked why he should do so much for Elizabeth, 'if she will do nothing for me'. Bowes then said rashly that there were at least a dozen other relations of the Queen whom the Tsar would prefer. Ivan asked for their names. All Bowes could reply was: 'I have no instructions.'

In a later interview the ambassador complained of his food and also some of the Tsar's ministers. In answer to Ivan's enquiry whether Elizabeth could help him win back territory he had recently lost to Poland, Bowes piously said that conquest was repugnant to his mistress, adding that the Low Countries were begging for her protection. During another meeting, Ivan foolishly boasted to Bowes of his subjects' complete obedience, reinforcing this statement with a demonstration. He ordered one of his courtiers to jump through a window, a command instantly obeyed. How high the window was and the fate of the faithful servant is not known. This possibly appalling incident gave Bowes the opportunity to remark that Queen Elizabeth had better uses for the lives of her subjects.

After one conversation with Bowes, Ivan was incensed by his spirited defence of Queen Elizabeth when the Tsar made some discourteous remarks about her. Bowes was ordered out of the palace but was immediately recalled and praised for his courage and devotion. 'Would to God', said Ivan, 'that I had such a faithful servant.'[23] As Ivan adjusted himself to this eccentric and outspoken Englishman, Bowes became more calm and co-operative. Ivan's love affair with England still persisted; after all, he had proposed to only one of Elizabeth's relations. He would, he declared on one occasion, go to England himself, find a kinswoman of the Queen and marry her there. Bowes was able to report to Elizabeth that Ivan had promised to confirm England's complete trading monopoly via the White Sea and that a new ambassador was going to be sent to London. But she was not asked again to find an eighth wife for Ivan the Terrible, as he died in 1584 before any further attempts could be made.

The last act of this Elizabethan comedy was enacted in 1602 when Tsar Boris Godunov took the next logical step in Ivan's campaign to foster Anglo-Russian relations, a step that Ivan might have been planning himself. Nine young men, members of the nobility, were selected to travel abroad to learn how to read and write the language of the country they were in, and to make a serious study of the customs of the people. Five students went to Lübeck, four to England. Another record mentions eighteen students sent to Germany, France and England. Evidently, they all enjoyed themselves. One of the Russians who came to England, Nikifor Olferiev Grigoriev, developed an interest in the religious customs of the people and became a rector of the parish of Woolley in Huntingdonshire in 1618. He married an English girl and died in Hammersmith, London in 1668. His career in the Church of England came to an end for unknown reasons in 1643. In 1621 the Russian ambassador in London set about trying to bring the emigrés back home; he found that two had died, and a third had gone to Ireland and could not be traced. The contrast between life in England and Russia was such that not one of the students, and not one of the others on the Continent, returned to their native land.[24] Since then, successive Russian governments have lived in fear of their citizens leaving the country and never returning, as they cannot govern without depriving them of freedom. A dog that is chained is encouraged to escape.

9

The Final Atrocity

In spite of all the appalling calamities inflicted on the Russians during the disastrous years of Ivan's reign, those subjects who survived still obeyed him. When one is surrounded by death and destruction, all acts of resistance are regarded as suicidal. According to the land registers, between 83 and 97 per cent of all the peasant houses in north-western Russia were deserted. At the end of Ivan's reign the population of Novgorod was only 20 per cent of its total at the start. In Kolomna, sixty miles south-east of Moscow, nearly all the houses, 95 out of 100, stood empty in 1578.[1] In 1588 Giles Fletcher reported that 'many villages and towns of half a mile and a mile long stand all uninhabited, the people being fled all into other places by reason of the extreme usage and exactions done upon them.'[2] Fletcher also pinpointed the disastrous effect this devastation had on the dwindling resources of the country: 'The more they have, the more danger they are in, not only of their goods, but of their lives also. If they have anything, they conceal it all they can, sometimes hiding it under the ground and in woods, as men are wont to do where they are in fear of foreign invasion.'[3]

The extent of this fear was clearly shown in 1566 when Ivan convened his second National Assembly, sixteen years after the first meeting of this new forum. Boyars and members of the junior nobility were deserting him and joining the forces of Poland and Lithuania; those who still remained in his service and the Metropolitan were urging him to make peace with his western neighbours to give the country a respite from war and constant executions. But all the delegates summoned to this Assembly knew their Tsar; they knew the dangers they would incur by opposing their master's obsession with Livonia; they could easily see that, in Ivan's eyes, the boyars' programme amounted to a retreat, and that Ivan hated making a retreat unless it was forced upon him at a heavy cost in Russian lives. The assembly consisted of 374 delegates, senior boyars and Church dignitaries, leading military serving men (owning land in return for military service) government officials, seventy-five merchants and some landowners from the area of the Lithuanian border. In a speech to the assembly Ivan invited his audience to tell him whether they supported his war of conquest in Livonia, or whether they advised acceptance of the compromise solution suggested by King Sigismund of Poland—the division of Livonia between the two countries, based on those areas already held by each side. All the delegates gave Ivan their support, except the Chancellor, Ivan Viskovaty. He favoured the acceptance of Sigismund's plan, as this held out the possibility of the subsequent withdrawal of the Polish army from western Livonia—a programme of division and neutralisation followed effectively by subsequent Russian governments. All the delegates knew that Ivan hated compromises, so they must have been fully prepared for Ivan's rejection of any vote in favour of peace.

Apart from the delegates' fear of incurring their Tsar's displeasure, there was a reasonable chance of eventual success in Livonia, as the Polish and Lithuanian forces were exhausted after this long and depressing succession of temporary gains and losses. But a victorious end to the war could be achieved only by courageous leadership and intelligent statesmanship. In both fields Ivan proved himself a failure. He intensified the Livonians' hostility by his barbaric treatment of captives; his strategy lacked continuity and persistence; and by his offensive contempt for his fellow Slavs, the Poles, he missed the opportunity of becoming their King when the Polish crown itself became a matter for election by the Polish nobility on the death of Sigismund Augustus in 1572.

At this time Ivan's army amounted to some 40,000 to 60,000 men; some 10,000 of these were Tartars. The Livonians, Sir Jerome Horsey tells us, were 'the fairest people in the world, by reason of their generacion contry [?] and climate, cold and dry . . . The country he had so ransacked and showed so much cruelty in conquering it . . . he fleeced and carried away all the riches and principal people, whose cruelty and tyranny used there is most lamentably set forth in Livonian history . . . the goodliest country, flowing with milk and honey, nothing wanting, and the fairest women and best conditioned people to converse with in the world, but much given to pride, luxury and idleness and pleasure.'[4]

If Ivan had accepted Sigismund's terms for an armistice, he would have gained half the country and a small but valuable section of the Baltic coast; by continuing the war he lost everything his army had won. When he rejected the Polish terms, he repeated his demand for the whole of Livonia and added offensively a demand for the surrender of

Prince Andrei Kurbsky, his most outspoken opponent. Sigismund refused to hand him back and the war continued. Fear of Russia drove Lithuania and Poland closer together and the two countries united under King Sigismund in 1569. The King and the Poles were not in favour of this union at the start of his reign, but it soon became clear that the Russian seizure of Livonia would be followed by attacks on Lithuania and finally on Polish territory, using the usual Muscovite excuses of security and reconquest of land held by the Kievan Princes five hundred years earlier. King Sigismund, in his efforts to bring the war to an end, turned down the offer of an alliance with the Ottoman Empire so as not to impair his negotiations with Ivan. But it was to no avail, as the Tsar still thought he could defeat the Poles.

The death of King Sigismund opened up for Ivan the possibility of the greatest victory of his reign: the winning of the Polish crown. Poland was far ahead of its time in having a constitutional monarchy. But the nobles proved the country's undoing by extending their own power at the monarch's expense. This process had been going on since the latter part of the fourteenth century; when Sigismund died, the franchise for the royal election was extended to the whole of the nobility. This democratic right had existed in Poland since the start of the Jagiellonian dynasty in 1377, when Jagiello, Grand Duke of Lithuania, was elected King. As long as the dynasty continued, no attempt was made to look for another monarch. But now, in 1572, the nobility had to find a new leader. These were the candidates: Ernst, the son of the German Emperor, Maximilian II; the King of Sweden, Erik, and his son; Henri, Duke of Anjou, brother of Charles IX of France; and, at the suggestion of some Orthodox Russian nobles in Lithuania, Ivan the Terrible. Ivan's second son, Feodor, would also have been a candidate, but his father would not give his consent as he was incapable of any adult position of authority.

The only candidate whose cause was furthered by an election agent—for it was in this capacity that the French ambassador campaigned—was Henri, Duke of Anjou, the most unlikely choice on account of his youth and lack of intelligence. Ivan was certainly inept in his efforts to win the Polish crown. He might have won it; as few of the Polish nobles wanted Maximilian or any Habsburg prince because of his suppression of the nobles in Bohemia. Ivan's chances of success were not so weak as they may have seemed at first glance. But he made no attempt to win over individual members of the Polish Senate, and he did not bother to send an ambassador to Warsaw to present his case. In addition, his own pronouncements on the matter were hardly persuasive, and his promises rang a trifle hollow:

> If you want us to rule over you, then it is desirable for you to avoid making us angry and to do what we instruct our boyars to propose to you, in order that Christendom might be at peace. If it please God that I should become sovereign [of Poland and Lithuania], I promise that I shall preserve all the rights and liberties [of the nobility] and even grant more as circumstances require. I do not want to speak of my kindness and cruelty. If the Polish and Lithuanian nobles send their sons to serve me, they will see how cruel and how kind I am.
>
> In your country many people say that I am ill-tempered; it is true that I am ill-tempered and given to anger. I take no pride in it; but let them ask me against whom I am ill-tempered. I will answer that it is against those who are malicious towards me; to those who are loyal I will not grudge this chain of mine or my cloak. If it is not desired to take me as your sovereign, then send to me your great ambassadors so that we may reach a firm understanding. I do not insist on keeping Polotsk; all its territories, including those belonging to Muscovy, I will yield, if only Livonia along the Dvina is ceded to me. Then we will conclude an eternal peace with Lithuania.
>
> We are sovereigns of a state who have descended from Augustus Caesar from the beginning of the ages. This is known to all men.[5]

These pronouncements to the Polish envoys did nothing to allay their fears. Two further acts of folly were his contention that the war between the eastern and the western Slavs was Sigismund's responsibility, not his, and his absurd demand to Erik, King of Sweden, that he should surrender Catherine, the wife of John, Duke of Finland, whom Ivan had tried to marry after Anastasia died. Catherine was the sister of Sigismund, so it should have been obvious to Ivan that this demand by itself would impair his chances of election to the Polish throne. Even the Soviet Russian historian, R. Wipper, in his white-washing biography of Ivan written in 1947, admits that 'the big diplomatic campaign of 1553 to 1576'—the Livonian War—'on which Ivan spent so much energy, ended in failure'.

If Ivan had taken as much trouble and spent as much money as the French ambassador in Warsaw, he might have become King of Poland and Lithuania. The consequences for Russia and eastern Europe would have been profound and long-lasting. Centuries of war and millions of lives might have been saved if the two halves of the Slavic world and the Catholic and Orthodox Christians had united under one sovereign. Ivan was now physically and mentally an old man, although only forty years old; under a monarch who was genuinely concerned with the welfare of his subjects and who was not insanely obsessed by his own supreme importance, the whole expanse of Russia could have benefited by this alliance, deriving by peaceful means the full harvest of European civilisation and culture, recently enriched by the Italian Renaissance. No other monarch in Europe has been given such a golden opportunity; no other major European country has had the chance of uniting peacefully with another major power, one which had formerly been her enemy. The experiment might have failed, and the old vices of religious and political animosity might have won the day. But it might have succeeded, with countless advantages in terms of European and world peace.

The Polish nobles were understandably more impressed by the French candidate's docility than Ivan's claims of Roman imperial ancestry: Prince Henri of Anjou was elected King. But before he had been on the throne a year, his brother, Charles IX, died, and Henri made ready to depart. He found the many restrictions imposed upon him by the Senate intolerable. The nobles forbad his abdication, arguing that he could surely rule France from Warsaw. The frustrated, home-sick King had to flee the country like a criminal or a political refugee. In the following year, 1576, Prince Stephen Batory of Transylvania, a Hungarian, was elected as the new King of Poland. He was a man of great energy and courage.

During the years immediately prior to Stephen's election, Ivan did nothing to win friends in Poland or Lithuania. He had shown in 1571 that he was unable to defend his own capital from the Crimean Tartars, and that he preferred to play the coward's part by staying safely a very long distance from his own troops. When his third wife, Marfa Sobachina, died in November of the same year, only sixteen days after the wedding, having been ill all the time, Ivan lashed out at the families of his first two wives. With bewildering confusion, he regarded his wife's death as a sign of God's anger against him and at the same time looked for culprits around him who had brought about her death by witchcraft or slow poison. Relatives of his first two wives were seized and killed; others met their deaths who were unrelated, but nevertheless implicated in some foul plot. One of the leading *Oprichniks*, Gigory Gryaznoi, brother of Vasili, was poisoned and Prince Mikhailo Temgrukovich, Ivan's second wife's brother, was impaled, dying in extreme agony.

Appalled by the imagined treachery at Court, sickened by his own bloody revenge, disgusted by the shame of his failure to defend Moscow, Ivan plunged into the deepest remorse and despair, for hours kneeling and prostrating himself before his icons, praying for forgiveness and guidance. These feelings of shame must have been intensified by the fact that it was the army of the *Zemshchina*, the part of Russia that he had, as it were, divorced and spurned that had saved Moscow from a second attack by the Tartars, under the leadership of Vorotynsky. In the summer of 1572 Ivan visited the shattered city of Novgorod, which had once been the most prosperous provincial town in Russia. In these gloomy surroundings he felt that death might come at any moment and wrote his will and testament. In stark contrast to the claptrap of contemporary Russian historians, who have endeavoured to present Ivan as an almost ideal national hero, the Tsar wrote about himself more candidly, more unsparingly than any other monarch of any country in the world. His testament is unique in the vehemence of its self-castigation.

Foreigners in Russia expressed their surprise that the Russians still seemed to love their sovereign. He was in fact hated by many, as he himself admits in the testament. It is probably more accurate to say that those who had survived the many catastrophes of his reign found it advisable to keep their mouths shut and demonstrate their 'love' or loyalty only when it was demanded of them.

Much of Ivan's confused, manic-depressive personality is revealed in his testament:

> I, the much-sinning and poor slave of God, Ivan, write this confession, being of sound mind . . . My mind has become covered with sores; my body has become weak; my spirit is afflicted; my spiritual and bodily wounds have increased, and there is no physician to heal me. I waited for someone to pity me, but there was no one. I found no comforters; they have repaid me with evil for my kindness, and with hatred for love.
>
> I am defiled of soul and corrupt of body. I was stripped of the raiment of shelter of grace and was left half dead of wounds, still alive but, because of my sordid actions, worse to God than a stinking and abominable corpse which the priest sees but does not heed, and even the Levite passed me by.
>
> From Adam to this day I have surpassed all sinners in unlawfulness, and because of this I am hated by all . . . I was most corrupt of reason and bestial in mind and thought; my very head I had defiled in my desire for improper deeds. I defiled my mouth with discourse on murder, and on fornication, and on all evil doings, with improper speech and vile language, and intemperance in all kinds of improper deeds. I defiled my hands with the touch of improper things and insatiable rapine, and presumption, and inner murder. I defiled my head with gluttony and drunkenness and I defiled my loins with excessive fornication, with improper restraint, and by surrounding everything with evil. I defiled my feet with a most rapid striving after all things evil, with murder and with an insatiable plundering of the wealth of others, and with improper amusements.

Now I offer advice to you my children. I command you to love one another, and may the God of Peace be with you. Hold firmly to the Orthodox Christian faith, suffer for it manfully, even unto death. Accustom yourselves to the art of war as much as possible. If, because of the multitude of my sins which caused God's wrath to spread, I were exiled by the boyars from my possessions and I wander about my lands, do not languish in your sufferings. Place your sorrow upon the Lord and He will sustain you.

You, my son Ivan, protect my son Feodor as yourself; you are the only ones born of your mother . . . Concerning the *Oprichnina*, which I have established, now it is within the power of my children, Ivan and Feodor, to do with it as they see fit, but the pattern has now been made ready for them . . .

Now I commit my soul to my father and intercessor, Antony, Metropolitan of All Russia . . .[6]

The rest of this document is a detailed list of the towns of Russia and its component regions which Ivan Ivanovich would inherit. The remark about the *Oprichnina* is of the greatest importance. Ivan could not have made a more accurately prophetic statement: the pattern was indeed set. To this day Russians live in fear of the ruler's special state security force. When the communists seized the reins of power in 1917, they kept their subjects fettered with the same shackles, calling their *Oprichniks* the OGPU, then the NKVD, the MGB and, today, the KGB. The Russians still call the members of the KGB the *Oprichniks*.[7] Just as Ivan's chief hatchet men, Vyazemsky, Basmanov and Gryaznoi, were eventually sucked down into the bloody whirlpool of the *Oprichnina*, so Stalin's chief executioners, Yagoda, Yezhov and Beria were finally exterminated by their own corrupt system. In the middle of the last century Alexander Herzen, in exile in London, wrote a letter to the Tsar Alexander II:

The trouble with our country is the way it is governed. The censor kills the word before it is formed. And should it break through now and then, there comes the secret instruction, post-haste by messenger troika—and that's the last you ever see of the author. Just imagine, if Jesus Christ himself started to preach a sermon somewhere on Admiralty Square or in the Summer Gardens (in St Petersburg), there would be no need for Judas. The first police officer would take him to the Third Department, and from there he would be transferred to the army, or—even worse—to the Solovetsky Monastery.[8]

In 1572, soon after writing his damning testament, Ivan disbanded, or said he was disbanding, the loathed *Oprichnina*. Whether this band of privileged policemen was in fact dissolved puzzled not only his frightened and bewildered subjects, it has also confused Russian historians to this day. The *Oprichniks* were ordered off the lands they had ex-propriated, and much confusion reigned as members of the *Zemshchina* were re-settled on their estates. Military service was disrupted; the strength of the army in Livonia was seriously affected and land gained in that country was lost. The landowners and farmers returned to their old estates only to find them, for the most part, in a state of ruin as they had been neglected by the *Oprichniks* and the peasants had fled, or had died of hunger or of the plague. But while the individual members of the *Oprichnina* suffered by this surrender of their land, the organisation itself may well have continued. In the opinion of Karamzin, Solovyev and Klyuchevsky, Ivan continued to rule through the *Oprichnina* administration, abolishing only its name. The Soviet Russian historian, S. V. Veselovsky, on the other hand, has decided that it was disbanded.[9] However, it seems as if it is impossible to state categorically that the *Oprichnina* has ever been terminated.

While the Russians were left in some doubt as to the existence or non-existence of the *Oprichnina* after 1572, Ivan declared that it was now a non-subject, one that no one must mention in public. 'Nobody dared to mention it,' we learn from von Staden, 'on pain of the following punishment: the culprit was bared to the waist and whipped with a knout.' Having been thrashed for protesting about the *Oprichnina*, or merely getting in its way, the Russian citizen was thrashed again for allowing the dreaded name to cross his lips. Russian ambassadors and government officials were told to deny that it had ever existed, if questioned by foreigners. Any interest shown by inquisitive outsiders was to be treated as a form of slander against the sovereign state of Russia.

While the official termination or partial disbanding of the *Oprichnina* produced a lightening of the daily burden of fear and misery for the Russians themselves, the Lithuanians and Livonians were to suffer further as a result of Ivan's determination to seize more territory. In 1573 he went to the battle-front to step up this indecisive, debilita-ting, seemingly endless war. Russian troops advanced over most of northern Livonia and treated the population with senseless brutality. As before, the initially successful offensive then came to a halt, when Ivan returned to Moscow to arrange for the quelling of a revolt among the Kazan Tartars. Without their Tsar, the army's morale again flagged. One by one villages and towns were recaptured by the Livonians and the Lithuanian army.

Back in Moscow the years of 1574 and 1575 were marked with a spate of executions, including those of Prince Nikita Odoyevsky, Mikhail

Morozov with his wife and children, and two boyars, Peter Kurakin and Ivan Buturlin. All were accused of treason. Other executions followed, including those of several leading *Oprichniks*. This blood-letting culminated in the killings of Prince Michael Vorotynsky and Prince Boris Tulupov. Vorotynsky was Russia's most distinguished general; the conquest of Kazan in 1552 had been largely due to his courageous leadership and his victory over the Crimean Tartars in 1572 gave him a prestige that Ivan now found intolerable. He had already suffered imprisonment in the monastery of Belo-ozero in northern Russia for four years between these campaigns, and now he too incurred the suspicion and jealousy of the Tsar. The general was hung head downwards from a tree and burnt to death. Ivan himself watched him die and took an active part, stoking the flames.[10]

In the following year, 1575, another general, Prince Boris Tulupov, was arrested and killed. Since 1570 he had led campaigns in Livonia, and in 1573 had been made a member of the Boyars' Council. As his death was hideously painful, and as it was just one of many agonising punishments inflicted by Ivan, it has seldom been mentioned, and Jerome Horsey's description of it has not been included in previous biographies of Ivan. The reader is spared the revolting details, and Ivan himself is spared the opprobrium. Horsey's description is in fact a tribute paid to the victim and others who suffered similar deaths, and it is also a searing indictment of the Tsar himself:

> Prince Boris Tulupov, a great favourite of that time, being discovered to be a traitor against the emperor and confederate with the discontented nobility, was drawn upon a long sharp stake so made as that it was thrust into his fundament through his body, which came out at his neck, upon which he languished in horrible pain for fifteen hours alive, and spake unto his mother, the duchess, brought to behold that woeful sight. And she, a godly matronly woman, upon like displeasure, was given to one hundred gunners, who defiled her to death one after the other. Her body swollen and lying naked in the place, Ivan commanded his huntsmen to bring their hungry hounds to eat and devour her flesh and bones, dragged everywhere; the emperor at that sight saying: 'Such as I favour, I have honoured, and such as be traitors will I have thus done unto.'[11]

The ghastly impact of Ivan's reign, and the many atrocities committed by him, have left lasting scars on the Russian character and on the subsequent occupants of the Kremlin. Ivan demonstrated to his successors that in Russia the ruler can get away with murder over and over again, that the Russians—not all of them, but enough—even admire a tyrant. One of the many proofs of Ivan's continuing hold upon his successors can be seen in the offically approved biographies written by Soviet Russian historians. Ivan himself would have little to complain of.

The regulation history recommended in all Russian schools is the work of R. Wipper, published in Moscow in 1947. From this hagiography we learn much about the progressive and commendable features of Ivan, as statesman and hero, and about his subjects also:

Giles Fletcher failed to understand the profound gifts, the great mental, social and technical talent of the Russian people. Those historians who harp on Ivan's senseless fury in the years 1568 to 1572 should stop to think how unpatriotic and opposed to the state the upper classes, that is a considerable section of the boyars, clergy and the government officials, were at that time. The plot against the life of the Tsar was most closely connected with the plot to surrender to the enemy not only the newly conquered territories (Livonia), but also ancient Russian lands, large tracts of territory, and the most valuable treasures of the Moscow State. The issue was one of internal sedition, of foreign intervention, and of the partition of a great state.

Was not flight to Lithuania, individually and in entire groups, not only by ordinary government servants accused of committing crimes, but of senior commanders and administrators, and this during a war, the most heinous state crime which Ivan was forced to combat? Ivan in fact under-rated the danger which threatened him and failed to pick out the real traitors in his entourage.

No reform [of the *Oprichnina*] either strategical, administrative, or agrarian, took place in 1572. The entire change was nothing more than a change of personnel. The area of the *Oprichnina* expanded and its administration grew. 'Driven like a wedge into the territory of Muscovy, it was to serve, not only as a weapon in the determined struggle against the feudal princes and boyars by reshuffling their estates, but also as a corps for the creation and organisation of means for waging an earnest struggle against foreign enemies.' (P. A. Sadikov)

Ivan was a far-sighted military and technical organiser. He felt entirely in his element in international affairs, and in this he felt superior to all his rivals. I would characterise him as one of the greatest diplomats of all time. He sometimes resorted to biting sarcasm . . . Ivan could easily become a charming conversationalist, a benign peace-maker and a friend of freedom and liberty.

The enhanced attention to Ivan's cruelties, the stern and withering moral verdict on his personality, the proneness to regard him as a man of un-balanced mind, all belong to the age of sentimental enlightenment and high society liberalism.[12]

In the *Short History of the USSR*, published in Moscow in 1965, I. I. Smirnov tells us something we might not have guessed, that during the long Livonian War 'the anti-feudal friendship of the Russian and Baltic peoples' was firmly established. In Paul Duke's recent *History of Russia* we learn that another Soviet Russian historian, R. G. Skrynnikov, considers that 'neither the short-term nor the long-term consequences of the *Oprichnina* should be exaggerated.' In other words, noses should not be poked into this distressing chapter of Ivan's reign. And, of course, neither the short-term nor the long-term consequences of Lenin, or Stalin, or of Soviet Russian historiography, should be exaggerated.

Three years after the actual or ostensible termination of the *Oprichnina*, Ivan sprang another but painless surprise on his court. In 1565, when he split the country in half, he abdicated or went through the motions of abdicating from one section of it, the *Zemshchina*. Now he abdicated from the whole of his realm. Before his court he handed his crown to a Tartar official, Sain Bulat of Kasimov. From now on this puppet Tsar would be called Tsar Simeon, as on his conversion to Christianity he had taken the name of Simeon Bekbulatovich. State documents of the time refer to him as Grand Prince Semeon of All Russia. Ivan the Terrible assumed the name of Ivan Moskovsky, and lived as a boyar in a house in Petrovka Street, not far from the Kremlin. This gesture was yet another demonstration of the tight hold he still possessed over the lives of his subjects, but Simeon was not a ruler in any real sense; he was not particularly intelligent and he commanded no support from any group of boyars. This charade may have been a token of friendship for the many Tartars in his kingdom. But Sir Jerome Horsey and Giles Fletcher saw another motive for this mock abdication. It was, in their view, just a stratagem for getting someone else to clear up the mess and muddle created first by the setting up of the *Oprichnina*, and then by its partial cancellation. He retreated into the background, in other words, 'to take no notice of any debts owing' (Horsey); 'all charters to bishoprics and monasteries cancelled. By this practice he wrung from the bishoprics and monasteries, besides the lands which he annexed to the crown, a huge sum of money' (Fletcher). Russian historians are divided on whether or not any of these charters were cancelled.

In his Letter, written c1605, Ivan Timofeyev makes this critical comment about Ivan's pseudo-abdication: 'Conceiving a plan filled with fury against his slaves, Ivan IV came to hate all the towns of his land . . . He created consternation among all the people, and for a time he set up in his stead, passing over the son of his blood, another faithful Tsar, Semeon Bekbulatovich, from among the Tartars, and he humbled himself servilely and retained for himself a small part of his possessions, but soon he took everything back, thus making sport of God's people.

He killed many loyal magnates of his realm.'[13] At Court, Ivan would bow before the Tartar Tsar, saying: 'Ivan Vasilievich, Prince of Moscow, who has come to do you homage.' When questioned by a foreign diplomat about the new Tsar's real status, Ivan replied: 'Tsar Simeon has my crown, but I have seven more.' After a year this particular charade was abruptly finished; Simeon was made governor of the province of Tver, and Ivan resumed his throne.

Finding that his premonitions about death, and fears of assassination by his boyars were proving, for the time being at any rate, groundless, Ivan now made a final attempt to gain the whole of Livonia and its Baltic coast. Hating compromise, he rejected all the proposals by the Polish King and the Austrian Emperor to call a halt to all military operations in Livonia. He even turned down what other monarchs in his place would have found an attractive alternative plan of conquest. The Austrians invited Ivan to join them in an alliance of Christian states in a concerted attack on the infidel Turks. If they could be driven out of Constantinople, this rich prize could be Ivan's. But such was his obsession with Livonia that this golden opportunity was thrown away. Towards the end of the same year, 1576, Ivan raised the matter himself on the accession of Rudolph, the new Austrian Emperor, hoping that he would help him overthrow the brilliant new King of Poland, Stephen Bathory. But Rudolph rejected Ivan's proposal, as he feared Russian expansion at the Turks' expense. Ivan's forces gained several indecisive victories but suffered too many defeats. These victories proved counterproductive, as they united the Swedish, Lithuanian and Polish commanders and the nobility in a determined effort to drive the Russians back. They had now realised that a Russian occupation of Livonia might encourage Ivan, or a successor, to advance into east Prussia and northern Lithuania. Ivan had another surprise when he learnt that he was not the only monarch intent on conquest. Stephen Batory was now convinced of the necessity of defeating Ivan not only in Livonia but also in his own kingdom, even if this meant the conquest of Muscovy.

Before King Stephen had taken command of the Polish and Lithuanian forces, Ivan could well have marched on Warsaw. But now his strategy was needlessly cautious and erratic. Stephen chose this moment to launch a strong offensive, and in 1580 entered Russian territory. He took Polotsk and advanced as far as Pskov, where the Russians put up a stubborn and successful resistance. Ivan had no share in this defence; his orders to his commanders had degenerated into vague exhortations such as this: 'Carry on as God shall guide you. My hope is centred upon

God's help and your zeal.' Stephen rebuked Ivan for his cowardice and challenged him—as the Khan of the Crimean Tartars had done— to a duel face to face: 'Why did you not come out against us with your troops? Why did you not protect your subjects? Even a poor hen protects her chicks from the hawk with her wings. But you, a double-headed eagle, hide yourself!'[14]

Stephen Batory's military and diplomatic successes during the final years of the Livonian War would have been considerably impaired if Ivan had taken the opportunity offered to him of making an alliance with Denmark. Frederick II, the Danish King, suggested some form of co-operation, as he mistrusted both Sweden and Poland. Ivan failed to appreciate how helpful Denmark could be to Russia, and rejected Frederick's offer of eternal peace and co-operation with arrogance and condescension. But this offer of friendship came in 1576, before Stephen mounted his offensive against Russia. Four years later, with Pskov under siege, with all Russian gains in Livonia threatening to disappear, and with the Poles advancing into Russian territory in the province of Pskov, Ivan now was forced to seek an armistice. He first asked the Austrian Emperor if he would act as mediator. As he refused the invitation, the Tsar looked elsewhere for a monarch who could save him from complete surrender.

Ivan appealed to the Pope, Gregory XIII, to save him, to act as a mediator before the situation deteriorated any further. This was a completely unprecedented step for a grand prince of Muscovy, for a member of the House of Rurik, which had always regarded the Roman Catholic faith with the contempt implied in the very word used for their own Church—Orthodox, or true in doctrine. Any other faith by impication was untrue, misguided—in a word, wrong, to be shunned and treated with contempt. Christian theologians in every century have deplored the disunity that has disgraced the Church and lowered its reputation. Now in 1580 the leader of the largest Orthodox country was respectfully asking the head of the Catholic Church to bring an end to Poland's increasingly dangerous attacks upon her. Ivan could have agreed to negotiations for peace, dealing directly with King Stephen, but this for Ivan would have been even more humiliating than appealing to the Pope. Ivan and his country suffered unnecessary burdens over and over again since he fervently believed his own propaganda; he enslaved himself and his subjects to his own exalted image.

While the tone of Ivan's appeal was respectful, his presentation of the facts of the struggle was hardly truthful. King Stephen, he argued, had started the war and Russia was fighting for Christianity, since Poland was in league with the infidel Turks. Pope Gregory agreed to help, and sent Antonio Possevino, a Jesuit priest, to Warsaw and Moscow to act as mediator. Gregory hoped that Ivan could be persuaded to do something to bridge the gap that existed between the eastern and western Churches, but the immediate task was to bring these two Christian nations together and to stop them tearing each other to pieces. The Russians, in particular, were in the direst need. Tens of thousands of Russian lives had been sacrificed in this long war; Russia's wealth was being tragically dissipated, with no chance now of success in Livonia; her troops were exhausted and were hated not only in the Baltic region but also on Russian soil, where they were based, as they had drained the already meagre resources of the people. The whole gamble had failed, with appalling consequences, as was to be clearly shown during the next hundred years, a period which began with fifteen years of disorder, a period so chaotic that it became known as the Time of Troubles. In the seventeenth century, the slowness of Russia's political, social and military progress demonstrates that the Livonian War and Ivan's savage executions threw back development in these three areas more than a hundred years.

Ivan failed to conquer Livonia with his own enormous army; he failed to gain control of it by using a puppet ruler, Magnus, Prince of Denmark, making him King of Livonia; and he failed to retain thirty-five towns in Livonia, as demanded in the first round of talks with Possevino and the Poles. He refused to consider the Pope's request that a Catholic church might be built in Moscow, although he welcomed Venetian merchants into Russia. 'We have not had Roman churches in the past,' he declared, 'nor will we have them in future.' (The first Roman Catholic church in Russia was built in Moscow in 1698 by General Patrick Gordon, Peter the Great's friend and adviser.) At the peace negotiations, Ivan's envoys finally, after many delays, agreed to the ceding of the whole of Livonia and the important town of Polotsk to Poland. The envoys slipped in a remark, stating that they also ceded Courland, the western province of Livonia adjoining east Prussia, and the port of Riga at the mouth of the Dvina. If they had been allowed to get away with this deceitful trick, surrendering land that was not theirs to give, Russia at some future date could have used this peace treaty as justification for an attack. Possevino was not deceived. He refused to allow this particular 'surrender' to be included in the treaty, and rebuked the Russian envoys: 'You have come here to steal, not to negotiate.' After twelve months of discussions, the treaty was at last signed on 6 January 1582. In the following year Ivan signed a truce with Sweden, surrendering all claim to the port of Reval and the country of Estonia.

King Stephen sent messages of good will to Ivan and proposed the establishment of regular trading activities between the two countries. Ivan failed to respond to this initiative; although only fifty-two, he was an old man nearing his end, surrounded by treachery, or what he saw as treachery, at home and forced to accept defeat abroad. The Pope had hoped Ivan could be persuaded to form an alliance with Poland and Austria to make common cause against the Ottoman Empire, and that he might agree to some kind of union with the Catholic Church. In both projects he failed. Ivan had no wish to involve his exhausted army in yet more war; and he was unable to enter into any negotiation which would involve him in compromise and concessions. He preferred the cold climate of disunity in which both sides remain frozen, each on their own side of the border. 'If we start to talk about religion', he said to Possevino, 'then each being jealous for his own faith, will praise it above the other's. Quarrels will ensue, and we fear that hostility will arise between us. You say that your Roman faith is one with the Greek faith, but we do not hold to the Greeks, but to the one true Christian faith. The Pope is not Christ; the throne on which he is borne is not a cloud, and those who carry him are not angels. Nor is it right for Pope Gregory to liken himself to Christ.' At a later stage in this conversation, Ivan lost his composure: 'Your Roman Pope', he said, 'is not a shepherd at all; he is a wolf.'[15] Even Possevino's request that Russians should be allowed to go to Rome and study Latin was turned down.

Now when all looked dark and bleak, with Ivan's dreams of conquest in Europe in ruins, his subjects presented him with a real victory, the winning of new land in Asia—the vast expanse of Siberia. Here lay a new land for exploitation, rich in minerals and furs; it also proved an ideal prison, cold, forbidding and conveniently far from Moscow.

In 1582 a party of Cossacks arrived in Moscow with 5,000 pelts, of sable, beaver, fox and bear, and also a Siberian Tartar chief. There had been expeditions across the Urals before, but none of them achieved any lasting result. Three were carried out in the eleventh century and two in the twelfth by the men of Novgorod; and in 1499 4,000 men from Moscow reached the River Ob. The last expedition brought back a thousand prisoners. On all these hazardous journeys many men died from the intense cold and from attacks by the natives. On each occasion the Russians had followed the course of the River Pechora, which meant crossing the Urals in the far north, where not only was the climate against them, but the mountains also, as the highest passes are in that area. Since 1499, the land beyond the mountains had remained for the Muscovites an area of mystery and legend.

The leader of this latest voyage of discovery was Yermak Timofeyev, an outlaw on the run from Ivan's soldiers who were ordered to capture him and others who were robbing Russian trading vessels on the Volga and raiding the Nagai Tartars. Yermak's father had joined the Cossacks, Russians who, chased by the law, or of their own choice had come south to escape from the incessant wars and heavy taxes which made life in Muscovy so unbearable. After they had raided the capital of the Nagais, Saraichik, and taken many girls for sale to the harems of the Crimea and the Ottoman Empire, the Khan complained to Ivan the Terrible. Having no desire to add to his troubles by becoming entangled in another war, Ivan gave orders for the arrest of Yermak and his companions, and for the execution of the chief trouble-makers. Their best escape route was to the north-east, up the River Kama. It was here that Yermak came into his own, as this was the land of his childhood. He and his men were entering territory owned by the wealthy family of enterprising pioneers, the Stroganovs, who had been given control over some 14 million acres for colonisation and the development of salt refineries and iron mines.

At the time of Yermak's arrival, the Stroganovs were wondering how they could take advantage of Ivan's recently given permission to extend their control beyond the Urals. The Tartar Khan of that region had already offered to pay an annual tribute of 1,000 roubles in return for a guarantee of peace, but since then a more powerful Tartar horde, led by Kuchum, an old, half-blind chieftain of great courage and resourcefulness, had advanced from the south, killed the Khan and occupied his territory. Kuchum, the son of the Emir of Bokhara, claimed to be a direct descendant of the great Ghenghiz Khan. He refused to pay tribute to the Tsar, sent raiding parties across the mountains, and on one of these raids killed an official sent by Ivan to the Stroganov lands. The Stroganovs lost no time in letting the Tsar know of this latest news, and cleverly asked for permission—something seldom requested—to advance into Siberia to put an end to these incursions. They hoped that this would induce Ivan to send them a large body of soldiers. The Tsar's reply was a new charter, giving the Stroganovs authority to extend their control over the 'Siberian Ukraine', (or border-land). This was just what they wanted; but the immediate problem of finding enough men to fight the Tartars was still unsolved.

Yermak and his men provided the answer. The Stroganovs gave them a few muskets and three hundred of their own men, some of whom were German and Lithuanian prisoners captured during the Livonian War. Yermak's private army now amounted to 840 men. On 1 September 1581, they set off in a fleet of rough-hewn boats on their voyage of discovery across the Urals. Just prior to this, Ivan the Terrible heard that the Stroganovs were mounting an armed expedition and were engaging outlawed robbers for the purpose. As this news coincided with another report of a further disastrous raid by the subject tribes of Pelym, far to the north of Kuchum's territory, the Tsar concluded, wrongly, that these two events were connected, and that the Cossacks were merely stirring up trouble, just as they had done on the Volga. He ordered the whole expedition's immediate withdrawal, threatening disgrace for the Stroganovs and hanging for Yermak if his orders were disobeyed.

As it took more than a month for messengers to cover the six hundred miles between Moscow and the upper Kama, the Stroganovs were in the happy position of being unable to carry out this unpleasant command. By the time it had arrived at its destination, Yermak was well away across the Urals, and the foundations for Russia's greatest dominion were being laid. The Urals, a low range of mountains with only a few peaks over 3,000ft, provided no obstacle to Yermak and his Cossacks. They rowed up two tributaries of the Kama, and then, leaving their boats, crossed the ridge and made their way to the nearest river flowing down to the limitless plain beyond. Here they built new boats. For five days their journey was uninterrupted. They were then attacked by natives shooting arrows from the banks, but a few shots from the muskets dispelled them. Shortly after, they captured one of Kuchum's men. For his benefit a coat of mail was shot by a musket, after which he was released so that he could tell his own people what lay in store for them if they resisted.

A clever stratagem was also used in Yermak's first battle with the Tartars. At a point where the River Tobol narrows, Kuchum had thrown iron chains across it and stationed his army on each bank. Yermak must have been told about this ambush, for he landed his men on either bank, higher up the river, filled several boats with bundles of sticks, clothed in Cossack garments, and, with one man in each to steer, sent them towards the enemy. He timed his main attack when the decoy boats were near the Tartars and drawing their fire. Caught unawares by the Russians on each bank, and horrified by the muskets, the Tartars fled in disorder. After two more battles further down the river, during which for the first time they suffered serious casualties, losing 107 men, they reached Sibir, Kuchum's capital. It was eight weeks since they had left the Stroganovs, and they had travelled about three hundred and fifty miles. They found the town, a cluster of wood and daub houses, completely deserted. They found much to plunder in furs and carpets, and some golden ornaments, but there was little to eat there. Luckily the local natives, the Ostyaks, were opposed to Kuchum, mainly because of his efforts to convert them to Islam, and they brought them food. The Cossacks remained in Sibir for the winter. In December, a party of twenty Russians was surprised and massacred by Makhmetkul, Kuchum's cavalry leader, who with his father had moved south after the defeat of their army. As a reprisal, a party of ten Cossacks captured Makhmetkul in a sudden raid on his camp.

Yermak hoped that the power of the Tartars had now been broken, since Kuchum, over eighty years old and now quite blind, was without his right-hand man. The Cossacks rowed down the River Irtysh, and then down the Ob, one of the three great rivers of Siberia that flow into the Arctic Ocean. The strain of this voyage was now telling on Yermak. His force, already seriously weakened by those killed and wounded, was further depleted by desertion, for many of his men wanted to return to their former, safer life across the Urals. He himself had no intention of turning back until his new domain was firmly established as Russian territory. Before exploring any further, he wrote to the Stroganovs and to the Tsar, giving a full report on his discoveries. In his letter to Ivan, he craved forgiveness for his crimes, and humbly requested the despatch of soldiers and a governor to hold this newest colony of the Russian Empire. To make the letter more impressive, he sent as its bearer his own right-hand man, Ivan Koltzo, who had been condemned to death for piracy on the Volga. It was this delegation's arrival in Moscow in 1582 that made such a great impression. Ivan was more than pleased with the Cossacks. Their past offences were forgiven; money was distributed to each member of the party, and, as a special present for Yermak Ivan gave them one of his own fur cloaks and two suits of finely made armour. He also arranged for the despatch of a military governor, Prince Semeon Bolkhovsky, and 500 soldiers for the new province.[16]

In spite of the long winters and short summers, the Russians pushed forward into Asia with speed. In 1632 Yakutsk, 2,500 miles east of the

Urals, was founded. The year before, the extreme north-east coast of Siberia was reached, the Cossacks finding heaps of mammoth tusks near the River Kolyma, where gold was to be found in the nineteenth century. During the seventeenth and eighteenth centuries, over 20,000 frozen mammoths were found in Siberia. The shores of the Pacific were reached in 1636, only fifty-five years after Yermak had set out from the Kama. The distance from the Urals to the Pacific coast, where the early pioneers caught their first glimpse of the sea at the mouth of the River Amur is nearly 3,000 miles as the crow flies. In view of the almost complete lack of support from their government, the natural reluctance of the Russians to emigrate in large numbers to this cold land, and the frustrating legal restrictions which prevented most of them from moving to any other part of the country, the achievements of the few who opened up this vast, rich dominion are indeed truly heroic. For several weeks in the winter the quicksilver in thermometers freezes, a sign that the temperature has fallen below minus 38.4°C. At Verkoyansk, 400 miles north of Yakutsk, the temperature descends to minus 70°C.

In 1580 the ageing Tsar made one more assault on the Church. Coveting their riches, he once again assembled the leading clerics and subjected them to a stinging harangue. He warned them of the dangers that menaced them and their Church from the powerful forces of Stephen Batory, and expressed great scorn that, in spite of these dangers, the priests contributed nothing to the maintenance of the country's defences, and still lived prosperously. Sir Jerome Horsey, whom Ivan often took into his confidence, quoted part of his long oration:

> The nobility and people cry out with their complaints . . . [that] you do maintain your hierarchy and all the treasure of the land, by trading in all kind of merchandise, having privilege to pay no customs to our crown, nor charge of wars. By terrifying of the noblest, ablest, and best sort of our subjects their dying consciences, have gotten the third part of the towns, and villages of this kingdom into your possessions by your witchery and enchantments and sorcery. You buy and sell the souls of our people. You live a most idle life in all pleasure and delicacy. You commit most horrible sins, extortion, bribery, and excess usury. You abound in all the bloody and crying sins, oppression, gluttony, idleness and sodomy, and worse, if worse, with beasts.
>
> Maybe your prayers avail not neither for me nor my people. We have much to answer before God to suffer you to live, and so many more worthy to die for you. God forgive my partakership with you . . . Often have I been moved for your dissolution to the reparation and re-establishing of thousands of my ancient and poorest nobility, from whose ancestors most

of your revenues came, and to whom it most justly belongs, that have left and spent their honours, lives and livings for your safeties and enrichments, my rich people and subjects impoverished through your rapine and devilish illusions; by the contrary a flourishing commonwealth would be established and sustained, a fair example by that valorous King Henry the Eighth of England. My nobility and subjects are decayed and our treasure exhausted . . .

I command that by such a day you bring us a faithful and true inventory what treasure and yearly revenues all your houses have in their possessions. Necessity will permit no delay or excuse. The king and princes of Poland and Lithuania, the king of Sweden, and the king of Denmark all combine and our rebels confederating with that mighty power prepared by the Krym (Tartars). [17]

This unsparing criticism was followed by several days of discussion with the bishops and priests—a pastime which Ivan greatly enjoyed. The clergy, duly frightened by the royal harangue and flattered by Ivan's interest in points of doctrine and ritual, were then, according to Horsey, obliged to witness the revolting spectacle of seven friars being thrown, one by one, into a bear pit and there being mauled to death. While accepting the essential accuracy of Horsey's account of Ivan's address, some Russian historians suggest that his description of the massacre in the bear pit is based on tales he had heard about the killing of leading churchmen on other occasions.[18] It seems unlikely that Horsey, being well informed about the monarch's speech, would take the trouble to fabricate about what happened after it. So many documents have been destroyed or suppressed in Russia but it has not been possible to censor material brought out of the country by foreign witnesses. During the rest of Ivan's reign, monasteries were not allowed to accept any further bequests of land.[19]

Much of what Ivan said in his speech to the clergy at this Church Council was justified. Monasteries had taken advantage of their special status, as the only establishments in the country for the most part free of harassment and interference by the *Oprichniks*. Some of them, not surprisingly, had harboured prostitutes.[19] The Tsar himself had hardly behaved as a model of righteous living. One of the entertainments in his court involved the stripping of groups of young peasant girls and forcing them to chase poultry while being shot at with arrows. Horsey's description of Ivan's bear pit fits in all too well with the grotesque killings he had devised all his life. There were few forms of entertainment for anyone in Russia in the Middle Ages; Ivan himself enjoyed watching people die, and he liked others to see the show with him.

Horsey prefaced his account with a revealing comment about the nobles' and the Church's hatred of their monarch:

> The chief bishops, priors and abbots assembled and dissembled often times together, much perplexed and divided, seeking and devising with the discontented nobility how to turn head and make a war of resistance, but there wanted such a head or general that had courage sufficient to guide or lead such an army as could encounter his puissant power, they altogether unprovided both of horse and arms . . . The emperor commands his great bears, wild, fierce and hungry, to be brought out of their dark caves and cages, upon St Isiah's Day, in a spacious place, high walled. About seven of those principal rebellious big fat friars were brought forth, one after another, with his cross and beads in his hand, and a boar spear of five foot in length in the other hand for his defence. A wild bear was let loose, made mad with the cry and shouting of the people, runs fiercely at him, catches and crushes his head, body, bowels, legs, and arms, tears his weeds in pieces till he came to his flesh, blood, and bones, and so devours his first friar for his prey. The bear also shot and killed with pieces by the gunners pell-mell. And so another friar and a fresh bear was singly hand to hand brought forth till they were all seven devoured in manner as the first was, saving one friar, bestirred his spear so nimbly, setting the end thereof in the ground, guiding it to the breast of the bear that ran himself through upon it, and yet not escaped devouring after the bear was hurt,both dying in the place. The friar was canonized for a valiant saint by the rest of his living brothers of the Troitsa Monastery.[20]

Ivan threatened to burn seven more friars. The inventories he demanded were all produced and this saved the monasteries from dissolution, but in spite of their grovelling they still had to comply with Ivan's demand for 300,000 marks sterling.[21]

In the year following Ivan's second Church Council, on 14 November 1581, Ivan, now aged fifty-one and ageing rapidly, committed the final atrocity of his reign. He was still using the monastery of Alexandrovsk as his battle headquarters, his retreat where he could beg God to forgive him, his favourite place for eating and drinking, rape and fornication. His son, the heir to the throne, Ivan Ivanovich, was now twenty-seven; he had proved himself to be, in his father's eyes, an ideal successor, not only intelligent, unlike his only other son, but also an uncomplaining accomplice at orgies, torture sessions, and mass killings. Unlike the rest of his court, Ivan Ivanovich had aroused no feelings of jealousy or suspicion. The important town of Pskov at this time was under a heavy siege by the Poles, led by King Stephen. It may be that the Tsarevich, ashamed of his father's and his own absence from the front, demanded that he at least should be allowed to redeem his honour by joining in the battle. This may or may not have been the start of an argument between father and son, during which the Tsar lost his temper.

The Papal envoy, Possevino, was in Moscow early in the following year and was told another cause of this outburst. With Ivan and his son at Alexandrovsk was his son's wife, Evdokia, who was now seven months pregnant. The Tsar entered her apartment and found her not wearing all the garments that the Church prescribed a woman in her condition should be wearing. Because of this, or for some other reason, Ivan lost his temper, knocked her down and kicked her repeatedly. His son heard her screams, rushed into the room and tried to defend her. Ivan struck his son on the temple with his iron-pointed staff and he collapsed to the ground. Boris Godunov was also in the room. He tried to protect the prince, but he was too late. If he had interposed a second earlier he himself would have been killed or badly wounded; if he had not done so, he may well have been killed later for his cowardice. In this room of blood and screams, Ivan held his son in his arms; his daughter-in-law was carried to a bed. The following night, she mis-carried, and three days later on 19 November, the murdered Tsarevich died. Ivan had not only slaughtered his only fit son and heir; he had also kicked to death his grandson. Evdokia also died soon after this catastrophe.

It would have been better for Ivan—and for Russia—if he had died now. He remained alive for another three years, even more unhinged, even more ravaged by self-loathing and despair. In the Kremlin the silence of the night was frequently broken by his moans and cries, as he wandered about from room to room looking for his son. He tore at his hair and beard, and shouted at his courtiers and then begged them for forgiveness. He was shamed by his remaining son, Feodor, whom he called 'a sacristan, not a Tsar's son'. All Feodor took an interest in was bell-ringing. Once again he gave his boyars a chance to choose another Tsar, by formally announcing to his Court that he would spend the rest of his life in solitude as a monk far away from Moscow. This might have been yet one more trap to find yet more traitors. But his ministers, the majority of them, may have been convinced that Ivan was being sincere. The reply they gave, as reported in the chronicles, is revealing: 'Do not leave us! We do not want a Tsar other than him given to us by God.'[22] In other words, they would remain loyal to Ivan and obey him, whatever he did—because he was God on earth. Any attempt to kill him would be, for those who believed in his divinity, as unthinkable as trying to kill God. This insect-like obedience was the result of the centuries-old indoctrination by the Church, reinforced by brute force and the constant fear of punishment.

Ivan had lived his entire life in a vacuum. It may have been this lack of contact with the ordinary world of action and reaction, in which normal people learn what they can and cannot do that drove him into madness. Writing soon after his death, Ivan Timofeyev summed up his reign: Ivan 'devasted his land. He would have gone out of his mind and destroyed all the land had the Lord not put an end to his life.'[23] The end was certainly a long time coming.

Early in 1584 a comet was seen over Russia, brightening the night sky. The people could not be blamed if they took this as a sign that God himself had at last lost his patience with Ivan Grozni. This is how Ivan interpreted this strange sight.[24] This too would have bolstered his faith in his own divinity to find the Almighty communicating with him so dramatically. The tail of this comet, combined perhaps with the Northern Lights, appeared in the shape of a cross. Eager to know more of God's intentions, the Tsar now summoned sixty astrologers from the northern part of his kingdom to deliberate on the subject of his death. A house in Moscow was put at the disposal of this national convention. The main object of the exercise was to calculate the exact date of Ivan's death. Taking note no doubt of his rapidly failing health, the respected astrologers considered that this summons would not involve them in any danger to themselves. For this, they would have consulted their own charts.

Ivan was certainly approaching death. What exactly he was suffering from is, like so many other details of his life, not known for certain. It may have been a kidney ailment, or diffuse cerebral syphilis and syphilis of the aortic valve. His body became swollen and, it was reported by those who had to come near him, he emitted an unendurable smell, indicating internal putrefaction. One part of his body which swelled, we are told by Jerome Horsey, was his testicles, 'with which he had most horribly offended, boasting of a thousand virgins he had deflowered, and thousands of children of his begetting destroyed.'[25]

The astrologers conferred together and discovered the day on which their sovereign would die. They could have played safe and pretended that they had decided on a day several months in the future. But such deception was not resorted to. The fatal day was almost here. So as not to enrage the inflammable tyrant, they decided to withhold this information, but, as Horsey noted, 'he fell in rage and told them they were very likely to be all burned that day'. Labouring under this threat, the astrologers divulged that his last day would be 18 March, within the next week or two.

On 15 March Jerome Horsey was invited to join certain members of the court in Ivan's treasury in the Kremlin. Ivan was carried into the room, sitting in a chair, from which he made a rambling speech about his jewellery, some of which was placed before him. Horsey recounted some of his remarks:

'The loadstone you all know hath great and hidden virtue, without which the seas are not navigable . . . This fair coral and this fair turquoise you see; take in your hand; of his nature are orient colours; put them on my hand and arm. I am poisoned with disease; you see they show their virtue by the change of their pure colour into pall; declares my death. Reach out my staff royal, an unicorn's horn garnished with diamonds, rubies, sapphires, emeralds, and other precious stones that are rich in value—cost seventy thousand marks sterling, of David Gower, from the people of Augsburg. Seek out for some spiders.'

Caused his physician to scrape a circle thereof upon the table; put within it one spider and so one other which died, and some other without that ran alive apace from it.

'It is too late, it will not preserve me. This diamond is the orient's richest and most precious of all other. I never affected it; it restrains fury and luxury and abstinacy [sic] and chastity; the least parcel of it in powder will poison a horse given to drink, much more a man.'

Points at the ruby. 'O! this is most comfortable to the heart, brain, vigor, and memory of man, clarifies congealed and corrupt blood.' Then at the emerald. 'The nature of the rainbow, this precious stone is an enemy to uncleanness. Try it; though man and wife cohabit in lust together, having this stone about them, it will burst at the spending of nature. The sapphire I greatly delight in. It preserves and increaseth courage, joys the heart, pleasing to all the vital senses, precious and very sovereign for the eyes, clears the sight, takes away bloodshot, and strengthens the muscles and strings thereof.' Then takes the onyx in hand. 'All these are God's wonderful gifts, secrets in nature, and yet reveals them to man's use and contemplation, as friends to grace and virtue, and enemies to vice. I feint; carry me away till another time.'[26]

The sixty astrologers by this time must have felt most uneasy. On 17 March Ivan, still in pain, sent a message to his soothsayers telling them that they were going to be burnt to death for their inaccuracy. When 18 March dawned, he was still bearing up; he was, in fact, fit enough to take a warm bath, in which he 'solaced himself and made merry with pleasant songs as he useth to do'. An outburst of rage against the astrologers was calmed by a courtier, who evidently had great respect for their calling. 'Sir', he said, 'be not so wrathful. You know the day is come and ends with the setting of the sun.' After a very long soak in the hot water—Horsey says about four hours—Ivan lay on his bed and began to set up his chessboard for a game with Boris Godunov or one of the other men in the room. Suddenly he cried out and fell backward onto the bed. By the time a doctor and a priest arrived he was, in the words of Horsey, 'stark dead'.

The corpse was shaved and shorn, following Muscovite royal custom, declared a monk by the Metropolitan, then clad in monk's robes and buried alongside his murdered son in the sanctuary of Arkhangelsky Cathedral in the Kremlin. Buried with him was a beautiful goblet of Venetian glass, containing the chrism, the Church's special ointment for healing the sick and purifying the dead.

Immediately after the death of Ivan, Jerome Horsey recounts that he 'offered myself, men, powder and pistols', to attend Boris Godunov, the new Tsar Feodor's right-hand man. He accepted Horsey 'with a cheerful countenance. The Metropolitan, bishops, and other of the nobility flocked into the castle (the Kremlin), holding it for a day of jubilee for their redemption.' God had finally killed the tyrant that had killed so many of his countrymen. The Russians, demoralised and barbarously maltreated, were a nation of the bereaved, the survivors of a holocaust. Ivan's death brought instant relief to the country, having lived through a long, appalling nightmare. The people were soon to experience another nightmare, the Time of Troubles, when disorder and chaos, civil war and invasion, brought further misery to the nation. This would not have happened if Russia had not been so enfeebled by Ivan's capricious administration, his bludgeoning of the aristocracy, his fruitless Livonian War and finally his elimination of the God-given Tsarevich, who would have ruled with the people's pious goodwill.

In spite of all his many faults, Ivan has inspired Russian and western historians to dip their pens into the ink-wells of fantasy and romance. A good example of this romantic attitude to Ivan is found in Ivan Koslov's far from eulogistic study of the terrible Tsar: 'Ivan was the mystic, the visionary, the avenger, the hater, the conqueror. His personality was the mystique that was—and still is to a large extent—Russia itself.' Many Russians would object to such a close connection being made between Ivan the Terrible and the people themselves. A. S. Khomyakov, in his drama of *Yermak*, called Ivan 'a ferocious and wild madman, slavedriver of Christians, crowned enemy of his native land'. Karamzin, in his detailed survey of Russian history recounted many sordid details about Ivan's conduct, but he did not feel free to tell the whole story. 'It is possible', he wrote, 'that the censors will not allow me to speak freely about the cruelties of Tsar Ivan Vasilievich . . . The life of a tyrant is a tragedy for mankind, but his history is always beneficial for sovereigns and people. To inspire aversion to evil is to inspire love towards virtue. May there be no one like him in the future!'[27]

Here Karamzin's prayer was not answered. Ivan's successors were naturally impressed by the way he got away with murder time and time again. They were dealing with the same material, the passionate, argumentative, but docile Slavs, who wanted to believe in the divinity of their Tsar. An observant Swedish diplomat in the seventeenth century found that Tsar Alexei, who ruled from 1645 to 1676, was fascinated by the history of Ivan Grozni:

> The Tsar is so engrossed by the reading of works on the history of Ivan and his wars, that he must want to follow in his footsteps. The Tsar, vain and barbarously cruel, and thus capable of anything, is obliged to find pleasures in tales from the history of Ivan and his tyranny.[28]

Peter the Great used Ivan's methods of administration and copied his rule by terror. He too regarded the army as the central pivot of his foreign policy; he too considered that Russia must continually extend her borders. Livonia was once again the battleground and once more Tartar soldiers were used in large numbers to terrorise and slaughter the population. Ivan killed so many Russians that one is forced to conclude that he despised them. He at least remained in Moscow, when he was not in retreat at Alexandrovsk. Peter the Great loathed Moscow and sacrificed unnumbered thousands of Russians in the construction of a new capital, nearly four hundred miles away. But in carrying out this monstrous act of sacrilege, making Moscow, the focal point of the Russians' patriotic pride, a mere provincial centre, Peter had been taught by Ivan that the Russians will accept being treated like farm-yard animals. Those who protest are simply shot or imprisoned. Ivan the Terrible, declared Peter, 'was my forerunner and model. I have always tried to imitate his bravery and the wisdom of his government.' But it was not only these qualities that he emulated.

Lenin, Stalin and their successors have based their government on Ivan's ruthless methods. Ivan was Stalin's man of iron. And Hitler learnt much from Stalin.[29] Like Ivan, these three twentieth-century tyrants used their country's vulnerability as the reason for their total control over the lives of their subjects. Under Stalin it was strictly forbidden to say a word against Ivan, because Stalin regarded him as his model, his spiritual father, the man who could commit any crime.

Like Ivan, Lenin, Stalin and Hitler created a powerful state security police force which deprived every citizen of security. All four proclaimed that these stern measures were necessary to achieve security from attack by hostile neighbours and from misgovernment by their own aristocracy or their own bourgeoisie. In the process the Germans and the Russians have lived in daily fear of attack by a hostile dictator and the misgovernment of his unruly 'security' men. Ivan, Peter, Stalin and Hitler all worshipped supreme power and despised compromise, toleration and mercy. Russia and Germany have both been tied to inefficient economic systems, criminally wasteful of human lives. Both systems have found labour camps indispensable, providing slave labour and an effective way of silencing their many opponents. Both systems have terrorised the people by midnight arrests and mind-wearying interrogations. Both Nazi Germany and communist Russia have made their people loathed by more civilised peoples subjected to their rule. Both have believed that the end justifies the means; both achieved great national strength; both have caused great national misery.

The reign of Ivan the Terrible was undoubtedly a success in terms of immediate territorial aggrandisement, and as the inspiration of subsequent wars of conquest. But it was also a disaster, culturally, socially and spiritually. Taking a Christian or a humanist standpoint, one cannot be surprised that when diabolical savagery is perpetrated, the effects on the survivors and their descendants can be long-lasting. The screams of Ivan's many victims can still be heard.

Chapter Notes

CHAPTER I   IVAN'S INHERITANCE: THE EASTERN SLAVS ON AN ENDLESS PLAIN

1   Laurens van der Post *A Portrait of All the Russias* (Hogarth Press, 1964)
2   *Essays in Russian History* ed Alan D. Ferguson and Alfred Lewin (Archon Books, 1964). Philip Lozinski *The Name Slav* 21–28
3   George Vernadsky *Ancient Russia* (New Haven, 1951) 50
4   Dmitri Obolensky *The Byzantine Commonwealth* (Weidenfeld & Nicolson, 1971) 182. *De Rossorum Incursione, Homilia I: Fragmenta Historicum Graecorum* (Paris, 1870) 162–7. *The Homilies of Photius* (Cambridge, Massachusetts, 1958) trans C. Mango 82–95
5   *The Russian Primary Chronicle* trans. S. H. Cross and O. P. Sherbowitz-Wetzor (Cambridge, Massachusetts, 1953). S. M. Totne *The Scandinavians in History* (Edward Arnold, 1948) 42
6   Ibid 43
7   H. R. Ellis Davidson *The Viking Road to Byzantium* (George Allen & Unwin, 1976) 63
8   *Historia Nova*, Book IV, 59 (Second half of fifth century) ed J. Buchanan and H. Davis (Trinity University Press, San Antonio, Texas, 1967)
9   Joel Carmichael *A Cultural History of Russia* (Weidenfeld & Nicolson, 1968) 34, 38
10 H. R. Ellis Davidson *The Viking Road to Byzantium* (Allen & Unwin, 1976) 276. Anna Comnena *The Alexiad* trans E. A. S. Dawes (London, 1928) XI, 292
11 H. R. Ellis Davidson *The Viking Road to Byzantium* 110
12 Ibid 112
13 Ibid 135
14 Louis Réau *L'Art Russe des Origines à Pierre le Grand* (Paris, 1921). Werner Keller *Are the Russians Ten Feet Tall* (Thames & Hudson, 1961) 29
15 Ronald Hingley *A Concise History of Russia* (Thames & Hudson, 1972) 15
16 Ellis Davidson *The Viking Road to Byzantium* 152. E. H. Minns *Scythians and Greeks* (Cambridge University Press, 1913) 536
17 Joel Carmichael *A Cultural History of Russia* 28, 29
18 G. P. Fedotov *The Russian Religious Mind vol 1 Kievan Christianity* (Cambridge, Massachusetts, 1966) 380
19 Ellis Davidson 206, 199
20 Dmitri Obolensky *The Byzantine Commonwealth* 366
21 Bernard Pares *A History of Russia* (Cape, 1936) 54
22 Alfred Swan *Russian Music* (John Baker, 1973)
23 James Mavor *An Economic History of Russia* (J. M. Dent, 1914) 18, 19
24 *The Samizdat Register* ed Roy Medvedev (Merlin Press, 1977) 283
25 V. O. Klyuchevsky *Course of Russian History* 1911. *The Russian Primary Chronicle* 206–15

CHAPTER NOTES

CHAPTER 2   IVAN'S INHERITANCE: THE MONGOL HAMMER

1   Stuart Legg *The Heartland* (Secker & Warburg, 1970) 264. *Cambridge History of India* 84
2   Peter Brent *The Mongol Empire* (Weidenfeld & Nicolson, 1976) 117–8
3   Paul Dukes *A History of Russia* (Macmillan, 1974) 27. S. A. Zenkovsky *Medieval Russia's Epics* (New York, 1963) 18
4   Bertold Spuler *History of the Mongols* (Routledge & Kegan Paul, 1972) 74
5   Ibid 82
6   Ibid 52–4
7   Ibid 71
8   N. Waliszewski *Ivan the Terrible* (Archon Books, 1966) 57, 374. Ronald Hingley *The Tsars* (Weidenfeld & Nicolson, 1968) 56–7
9   Bertold Spuler *History of the Mongols* 71–9
10 Ibid 176–7
11 Ronald Hingley *A Concise History of Russia* (Thames & Hudson, 1972) 28
12 Ibid 33
13 Bernard Pares *A History of Russia* (Cape, 1944) 112
14 Herman Andreyev *Samizdat Register* (Merlin Press, 1977) 297
15 Lev Kopelev Ibid 232
16 Herman Andreyev Ibid 294
17 Ibid 294–5
18 Victor Alexandrov *The Kremlin* (Allen & Unwin, 1963) 59
19 Bernard Pares *A History of Russia* 124

CHAPTER 3   DELIGHT IN KILLING

1   Jules Koslov *Ivan the Terrible* (W. H. Allen, 1961) 49
2   J. L. I. Fennell (trans and ed) *The Correspondence between Prince A. M. Kurbsky and Tsar Ivan IV of Russia* (Cambridge, 1955)
3   K. Waliszewski *Ivan the Terrible* (Archon Books, 1966) 108
4   Ibid 113
5   S. M. Solovyev *History of Russia* (Moscow, 1960) Book 3, Vol 6 431
6   J. L. I. Fennell *Ivan the Great of Moscow* (Macmillan, 1961) 354
7   Herman Andreyev *Samizdat Register* (Merlin Press, 1977) 298
8   A. A. Zimin, D. S. Likhachev eds *The Works of I. Peresvetov* (Moscow, 1956). *A Source Book for Russian History* ed George Vernadsky (Yale, 1972)
9   Solovyev Book 3, Vol 6, 435
10 N. M. Karamzin *History of the Russian State* (St Petersburg, 1842) Book 2, Vol 8 col 64–5
11 Sigismund von Herberstein *Description of Moscow* (J. M. Dent, 1969) 87
12 Ibid 43–80
13 Karamzin Book 2, Vol 8 col 68
14 Victor Alexandrov *The Kremlin* (Allen & Unwin, 1963) 88
15 V. Chernov *Moscow, A Short Guide* (Progress Publishers, Moscow, 1977) 48–9
16 N. Kershaw Chadwick *Russian Heroic Poetry* (Cambridge, 1932) 195
17 V. Chernov op. cit.

CHAPTER NOTES

CHAPTER 4   THE RUSSIAN SICKLE

1   Heinrich von Staden *The Land and Government of Muscovy* trans and ed Thomas Esper (Stanford University Press, 1967) 56

2   Victor Alexandrov *The Kremlin* (Allen & Unwin, 1963) 88

3   Bernard Pares *A History of Russia* (Cape, 1944) 135

4   Ibid 147–8

5   Francesca Wilson *Muscovy* (Allen & Unwin, 1970) 39

6   Ibid 28–9

7   Ibid 33

8   Bernard Pares *A History of Russia* 149

9   Victor Alexandrov *The Kremlin* 74–5

10 V. Malinen *Starets Filofei* (Kiev 1901) 50-5

11 Jules Koslov *Ivan the Terrible* (W. H. Allen, 1961) 99

12 Victor Alexandrov *The Kremlin* 90

CHAPTER 5   INCREASING TERROR

1   S. M. Soloviev *Istoriia Rossii* (Moscow, 1962–6) Book 3, Vol 6, 539, J. L. I. Fennell (trans and ed) *The Correspondence between Prince A. M. Kurbsky and Tsar Ivan IV of Russia* (Cambridge, 1955)

2   Giles Fletcher *The English Works of Giles Fletcher* ed Lloyd E. Berry (University of Wisconsin Press, 1964) 297, 304–5

3   Soloviev *Istoriia Rossii* Book 3, Vol 6, 495

4   N. Yevreinov *History of Corporal Punishment in Russia* (St Petersburg, no date)

5   N. Karamzin *History of Russia* Vol 9, 465

6   K. Waliszewski *Ivan the Terrible* 214

7   Edward A. Bond, ed *Russia at the Close of the Sixteenth Century* (Burt Franklin, 1966) 147

8   Ibid 148

9   Jules Koslov *Ivan the Terrible* 26

10 Ian Grey *Ivan the Terrible* 143

11 Jules Koslov *Ivan the Terrible* 103

12 Francesca Wilson *Muscovy Through Foreign Eyes* (Allen & Unwin, 1970) 83. Samuel Collins *The Present State of Russia* (London, 1671)

13 K. Waliszewski *Ivan the Terrible* 215. N. Karamzin *History of Russia* Vol 9

14 G. M. Trevelyan *History of England* (Longmans, 1952) 32

15 The author is indebted to A. Miller for his comparative study of Russia and England in the Slavonic Revue, April 1936, ch 6

16 Francesca Wilson *Muscovy Through Foreign Eyes* 80–1

17 Ashley Montagu *The Anatomy of Swearing* (Rapp and Whiting, 1968)

18 Francesca Wilson *Muscovy Through Foreign Eyes* 73–4

19 Ibid 80

20 Ibid 90

21 *La Libre Belgique* September 1979 *Daily Telegraph* 15 September 1979

CHAPTER 6   THE KURBSKY LETTERS

1   *Prince A. M. Kurbsky's History of Ivan IV* trans and ed J. L. I. Fennell (Cambridge, 1965) viii, ix. *The Correspondence between Prince A. M. Kurbsky and Tsar Ivan IV* trans and ed by J. L. I. Fennell (Cambridge, 1955)
2   Edward L. Keenan *The Kurbski-Grozni Apocrypha* (Harvard, 1971)
3   *The Correspondence* as above 219–227
4   Ibid 213
5   Ian Grey *Ivan the Terrible* (Hodder and Stoughton, 1964) xii, 143. In this book Kurbsky, but not Ivan, is accused of distortion. Contemporary accounts indicate which of the correspondents is the more prone to this weakness. Ian Grey correctly states that the Bible 'had dyed his [Ivan's] mind and become part of his thinking'.
6   N. M. Karamzin *History of the Russian State* 12 Vols (St Petersburg, 1818–29) Vol 5. Historians in Russia have always been afraid of the censor. J. L. Black *Nicholas Karamzin and Russian Society in the Nineteenth Century* (University of Toronto Press, 1975)

CHAPTER 7   A STATE DISMEMBERED

1   Karamzin Book 2, Vol 9 col 43
2   Victor Alexandrov *The Kremlin* 92
3   Ibid 91
4   Samuel Purchas *Purchas His Pilgrimes* (James MacLehose, 1906) Vol 14, 111
5   Victor Alexandrov *The Kremlin* 91
6   Francesca Wilson *Russia Through Foreign Eyes* (Allen & Unwin, 1970) 56
7   Heinrich von Staden *The Land and Government of Muscovy* trans & ed Thomas Esper (Stanford University Press, 1967) 56
8   *A Source Book for Russian History* ed George Vernadsky (Yale, 1972) Vol 1, 147
9   Heinrich von Staden *The Land and Government of Muscovy* 25
10   G. Bocharov, V. Vygolov *Alexandrovskaya Sloboda* (Moscow, 1970) 47
11   *A Source Book for Russian History* vol 1, 141
12   Karamzin Book 3, Vol 9 cols 58, 59
13   Ibid cols 83–4. Solovyev Book 3, Vol 6, 734
14   *Purchas His Pilgrimes* Vol 14, 111
15   Ibid 112
16   *Prince Kurbsky's History of Ivan IV* ed J. L. I. Fennell 217
17   *Russia at the Close of the Sixteenth Century* ed Edward A. Bond (Burt Franklin, 1971) 172
18   Karamzin op. cit. cols 60–63, 86. Solovyev op. cit. 556
19   *Samizdat Register* ed Roy Medvedev (Merlin Press, 1977) 263
20   K. Waliszewski *Ivan the Terrible* 267
21   *Purchas His Pilgrimes* Vol 14, 112
22   Solovyev Book 3, Vol 6, 560
23   *Russia at the Close of the Sixteenth Century* 162
24   *Samizdat Register* 263
25   *Samuel Purchas* Vol 14, 112
26   Jules Koslov *Ivan the Terrible* 183, 205
27   Ibid 152
28   *Samizdat Register* 295
29   Solovyev Book 3, Vol 6, 607

CHAPTER 8   IVAN AND QUEEN ELIZABETH

1   Francesca Wilson *Russia Through Foreign Eyes* 24
2   Richard Hakluyt *The principal navigations, voyages, and discoveries of the English nation* (James MacLehose, 1903) Vol 2, 225
3   Ibid 256
4   J. Hamel *England and Russia* (1st ed 1854, Frank Cass, 1968) 107
5   Francesca Wilson op cit. 34
6   J. Hamel op. cit. 165
7   Francesca Wilson op. cit. 49
8   E. D. Morgan, C. H. Coote, eds *Early Voyages and Travels in Russia and Persia* Hakluyt Society, 1886 Vol 2, 295
9   J. Hamel *England and Russia* (Frank Cass, 1968) 179
10 Francesca Wilson op. cit. 49
11 J. Hamel op. cit. 203
12 Ibid 205
13 Ibid 207
14 E. D. Morgan op. cit. 336
15 Ibid 302
16 *Russia at the Close of the Sixteenth Century* ed E. A. Bond 184
17 Karamzin Book 3, Vol 9 cols 161, 162, note 494
18 N. Casimir, 'John the Terrible and Elizabeth of England' in *The Reliquary* Vol 16 (1875–6) 12–13
19 *Love's Labour's Lost* ed Richard David (Arden Edition, Methuen, 1977) xxvii
20 J. Hamel op. cit. 167
21 Ibid 201–2
22 Ibid 241
23 N. Casimir op. cit. 17. Richard Hakluyt op. cit. 321
24 S. F. Platonov *Boris Godunov* (Academic International Press, 1973) 122. Ian Grey *Boris Godunov* (Hodder and Stoughton, 1973) 124, 154–5. S. Konovalov 'Anglo-Russian Relations', 1620–4, in *Oxford Slavonic Papers* IV (1953) 80–2

CHAPTER 9   THE FINAL ATROCITY

1   Ian Gray *Boris Godunov* (Hodder and Stoughton, 1973) 124
2   E. A. Bond *Russia at the Close of the Sixteenth Century* 35
3   Francesca Wilson *Russia Through Foreign Eyes* 57
4   Lloyd Berry ed *Rude and Barbarous Kingdom* (University of Wisconsin Press, 1968) Sir Jerome Horsey 286–7
5   S. M. Solovyev *History of Russia from Earliest Times* (Moscow, 1960) Book 3, vol 6, 587, 620, 621
6   Robert Craig Howes trans and ed *The Testaments of the Grand Princes of Moscow* (Cornell University Press, 1967) 307
7   Ronald Hingley *The Russian Secret Police* (Hutchinson, 1970) 3
8   *Samizdat Register* ed Roy Medvedev (Merlin Press, 1977) 268
9   S. V. Veselovsky *Voprosy Istorii* (Moscow, 1946, No 1) 86–104
10 Ronald Hingley *A Concise History of Russia* (Thames & Hudson, 1972) 50. Solovyev op. cit. 565. Kurbsky states that Vorotynsky died while being interrogated and tortured
11 Lloyd E. Berry op. cit. 278
12 R. Wipper *Ivan Grozni* (Moscow, 1947) 150, 159, 163–5, 171
13 E. A. Bond op. cit. 145

14 J. Koslov *Ivan the Terrible* 226
15 S. M. Solovyev op. cit. 671–2
16 Philip Longworth *The Cossacks* (Holt, Rinehart and Winston, 1970) 53–60
17 Lloyd E. Berry op. cit. 282–3
18 Ibid 280–4
19 J. Koslov op. cit. 371
20 Lloyd E. Berry op. cit. 283–4
21 Ibid 285
22 N. M. Karamzin *History of the Russian State* (St Petersburg, 1842) Book 3, Vol 9 col 210
23 *Samizdat Register* 262
24 N. M. Karamzin op. cit. col 256
25 Lloyd E. Berry op. cit. 304
26 Ibid 305–6
27 J. L. Black *Nicholas Karamzin and Russian Society in the Nineteenth Century* (University of Toronto Press, 1975) 115
28 A. I. Zoerski *Tsar Aleksei Mihailovich* (Petrograd University, 1917) 269
29 W. Lacquer *Russia and Germany* (Weidenfeld & Nicolson, 1965) chs 4, 8, 13. Ruth Fischer *Stalin and German Communism* (Harvard University Press, 1948) ch 28

The Dynasty of Rurik

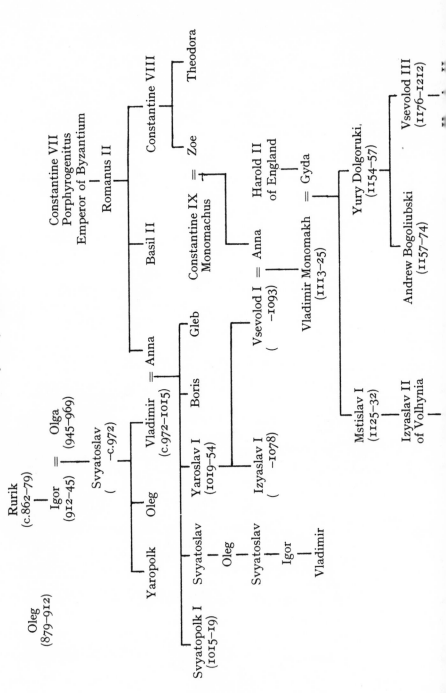

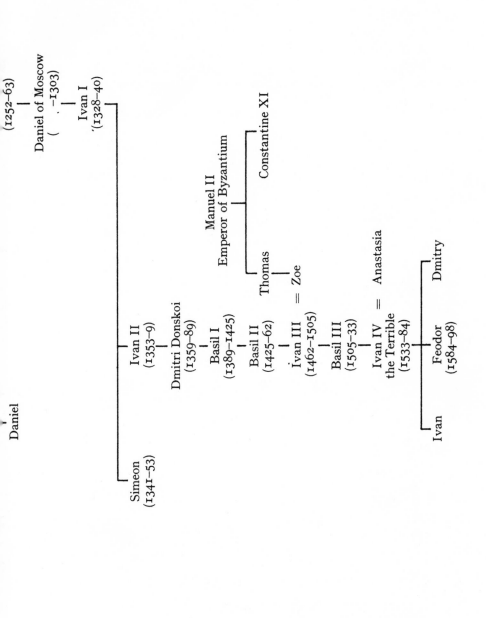

Daniel

Daniel of Moscow
(. –1303)
(1252–63)

Ivan I
'(1328–40)

Simeon
(1341–53)

Ivan II
(1353–9)

Dmitri Donskoi
(1359–89)

Basil I
(1389–1425)

Basil II
(1425–62)

Manuel II
Emperor of Byzantium

Thomas   Constantine XI

= Zoe

Ivan III
(1462–1505)

Basil III
(1505–33)

Ivan IV
the Terrible   = Anastasia
(1533–84)

Ivan   Feodor   Dmitry
(1584–98)

Bibliography

James Billington *The Icon and the Axe* (Weidenfeld & Nicolson 1966)
Joel Carmichael *A Cultural History of Russia* (Weidenfeld & Nicolson 1968)
Robert Conquest *The Nation Killers* (Macmillan 1970)
Dmitri Obolensky *The Byzantine Commonwealth* (Weidenfeld & Nicolson 1971)
Basil Dmytryshyn *A History of Russia* (Prentice Hall 1977)
Roman Dyboski *Outlines of Polish History* (Allen & Unwin 1941)
Alexander Eliot *A Concise History of Greece* (Cassell 1972)
H. R. Ellis Davidson *The Viking Road to Byzantium* (Allen & Unwin 1976)
J. L. I. Fennell *Ivan the Great of Moscow* (London 1963)
Stephen Graham *Boris Godunov* (London 1933)
B. D. Grekov *Kievan Russia* (Moscow 1948)
B. D. Grekov *The Culture of Kiev Rus* (Moscow 1947)
O. Halecki *A History of Poland* (J. M. Dent 1955)
Gavin Hambly *Central Asia* (Weidenfeld & Nicolson 1969)
Ronald Hingley *A Concise History of Russia* (Thames & Hudson 1972)
Ronald Hingley *The Tsars* (Weidenfeld & Nicolson 1968)
Robert Craig Howes, ed *The Testaments of the Grand Princes of Moscow* (Cornell University Press 1967)
Werner Keller *Are the Russians Ten Feet Tall?* (Thames & Hudson 1961)
H. Lloyd-James, ed *The Greeks* (A. C. Watts 1962)·
Philip Longworth *The Cossacks* (Holt, Rinehart and Winston 1970)
Bernard Pares *A History of Russia* (Jonathan Cape 1944)
M. N. Pokrovsky *History of Russia* (Russell and Russell 1966)
I. de Rachewiltz *Papal Envoys to the Great Khan* (Faber 1971)
W. F. Reddaway, ed The Cambridge History of Poland (Cambridge 1950)
Nicholas V. Riasanovsky *A History of Russia* (OUP 1963)
Alexander Solzhenitsyn *Letter to the Soviet Leaders* (Index on Censorship 1974)
I. Timofeyev *Annals* ed V. P. Adrianova-Peretts (Moscow 1951)
S. M. Toyne *The Scandinavians in History* (Edward Arnold 1948)
Laurens van der Post *A Portrait of All the Russias* (Hogarth Press 1967)
George Vernadsky *The Mongols and Russia* (Yale 1953)
George Vernadsky *The Origins of Russia* (OUP 1959)
Speros Vryonis *Byzantium and Europe* (Thames & Hudson 1967)
F. W. Walbank *The Awful Revolution* (Liverpool University Press, 1969)
Reinhard Wittram *Russia and Europe* (Thames & Hudson 1973)

Index